7/12/06
London

12.99

THE EGYPTIANS

D1125796

Of all ancient societies, Egypt perhaps has the widest popular appeal. The huge amounts of archaeological material, from the vast and imposing temples to the small objects of daily life, make us believe that we can approach the society and empathize with it.

This study introduces the reader to the broad span of Egyptian history and cultural development from its origins to the arrival of Islam. It examines the structure of Egyptian society, its changes over time, and the ways in which the economy and religious institutions were used to bind society together. Challenging some of the accepted truths and highlighting the enormous gaps in our knowledge, the author also explains the place of Egypt in the Western European tradition that led to the development of academic Egyptology, and considers how the West has constructed its own version of the Egyptian past.

Robert G. Morkot lectures in Egyptology at the University of Exeter. His areas of interest include relations between Egypt and other ancient societies, notably Nubia, and Egypt in the Western tradition. Among his publications are *The Black Pharaohs, Egypt's Nubian Rulers* (2000) and *The Historical Dictionary of Ancient Egyptian Warfare* (2003).

THE EGYPTIANS

An Introduction

Robert G. Morkot

Routledge
Taylor & Francis Group

LONDON AND NEW YORK

First published 2005
by Routledge
2 Park Square, Milton Park, Abingdon, Oxon OX14 4RN

Simultaneously published in the USA and Canada
by Routledge
270 Madison Ave, New York, NY 10016

Routledge is an imprint of the Taylor & Francis Group

© 2005 Robert G. Morkot

Typeset in Garamond 3 by
Florence Production Ltd, Stoodleigh, Devon
Printed and bound in Great Britain by
TJ International Ltd, Padstow, Cornwall

All rights reserved. No part of this book may
be reprinted or reproduced or utilized in any form or by
any electronic, mechanical, or other means, now known or hereafter
invented, including photocopying and recording, or in any
information storage or retrieval system, without
permission in writing from the publishers.

British Library Cataloguing in Publication Data
A catalogue record for this book is available
from the British Library

Library of Congress Cataloging in Publication Data
A catalog record for this book has been requested

ISBN 0–415–27103–7 (hbk)
ISBN 0–415–27104–5 (pbk)

CONTENTS

ILLUSTRATIONS

FIGURES

ILLUSTRATIONS

TABLE

PREFACE

Writing a 'general' and 'introductory' book on ancient Egypt is a daunting and challenging task. However deep one's specialist knowledge, this is the opportunity to reveal one's ignorance to the world. It is tempting to repeat the 'accepted lies of our discipline', but if you want to argue detailed rejections of them, there is not really the space to do it to the satisfaction of colleagues.

The approach to ancient Egypt that I have adopted in this book is modelled very closely on introductory courses I have taught over a number of years. These go back to ask some very basic questions, such as 'Where is Egypt?' and 'Who were the Egyptians?'. The answers are frequently far from straightforward, and allow us to look at the broader issues of what Egypt means and has meant. So, rather than a stream of 'facts', accepted truths or the opinions of Egyptologists, I have deliberately tried to raise the question of the limits of our evidence. In confronting these issues, I also deal with an issue that is perhaps much less appealing to the general reader, but immensely significant: how has the Egyptian past been reconstructed in terms of its history, culture and society? This in turn raises the issues of imperialism and appropriation which are now widely discussed in ancient history, and increasingly so in Egyptology. But I have tried to avoid this becoming entirely discourse, and present a wide range of 'information' and 'facts' that represent our (academic Egyptology's) current view of ancient Egypt. Inevitably, my own interests and preoccupations will come through, perhaps to the annoyance of colleagues, but I have tried to raise issues that are not always covered in other general introductions.

I have dispensed with the paraphernalia of footnotes in favour of a more straightforward guide to further reading.

ACKNOWLEDGEMENTS

My thanks go to Richard Stoneman for asking me to write this book, and to the readers of the original outline for their valuable and constructive comments, which I have tried to incorporate. My thanks also go to Stephen Quirke and the late Dominic Montserrat, who have presented the range of alternative Egypts in their work, both written and, in Stephen's case, practical, through his pioneering curatorship at the Petrie Museum. The series of volumes *Encounters with Ancient Egypt*, deriving from a conference at the Institute of Archaeology, University College London, devised by Dominic Montserrat and John Tait, presents this range of alternative Egypts and marks a shift in attitude among (some) Egyptologists. Dominic's death has deprived British Egyptology of one of its most challenging and enquiring teachers.

My thanks, as always, to John Vincent and Peter James for support, advice and ideas. Also to my students and classes for being victims of experiments, not always successful, in trying to understand ancient Egypt and what it means to us now.

All illustrations are by the author, unless they are credited otherwise.

1

DEFINING ANCIENT
EGYPT

Unlike 'ancient Greece', which, culturally, embraced a region far
wider than the narrow geographical limits of its modern namesake,
or 'Rome', which was culturally diverse within its broad political
boundaries, Egypt, ancient, medieval, and modern, is closely defined
in geographical terms. Yet 'placing' Egypt in the world is actually
fraught with difficulties: Egypt belongs in different places according
to historical and political episodes, cultural changes, and individual
viewpoints. The question 'Where is Egypt?' can elicit a wide range
of responses, most of them 'correct' in some senses, but all of them
requiring some qualification.

WHERE IS EGYPT?

The most obvious answer, but not necessarily the one most
frequently given, is 'Africa'. To an African-American/British audience, this would be the first, and perhaps only, location, not only
in simple geographical terms, but in broader cultural and percep-
tual ones as well. Others might prefer to limit the reply with 'north'
or 'north-east' Africa, effectively separating Egypt from 'black
Africa'. For European scholarship Egypt's cultural place in 'Africa',
and Africa's cultural impact on Egypt, have been constantly changing. Much early Egyptology viewed Egypt as distinctly African,
but the borders were redefined in the nineteenth century, drawing
a line across Sudan, south of which became the world of ethnology
and anthropology, contrasted with archaeology (large stone-built
monuments) and written records to the north. Some Egyptologists
and anthropologists have argued that there was an African basis to

Egyptian culture and institutions, notably the kingship; others have preferred to treat Egypt as totally separate from Africa. There can be no doubt that the origins of Egyptian civilization lie in Africa. But the name, and perception, of 'Africa' is itself an important issue. Today, we tend to speak about Africa and 'African' peoples and cultures as if somehow they were a homogeneous entity. This in itself is a residue of colonial attitudes that denies the variety and complexity of cultures and peoples in that vast continent. Indeed, the name 'Africa' is a fine example of the specific becoming general. Deriving from the name of a small 'tribal' group of part of Tunisia, the Afri, Africa was the name given to a Roman province, and then became more widely applied first by the Byzantines, and then (as Ifriqiya) by the Arab conquerors, as a general term for north-west Africa. It was adopted by Europeans for the same region, eventually being used for the whole continent. Africa is, quite literally, a colonial name.

In the European academic tradition, in museums and universities, Egypt has been included in the 'Near East' for a range of reasons. The Near East was a term used for the former territories of the Ottoman Empire, and had a utility that the inaccurate modern replacement 'Middle East' lacks. Middle East now seems to be used as a confused blanket term for the Islamic world (itself confused with the 'Arab world'). The ancient Near East can, legitimately, be treated as a central interacting block of states, from (modern) Iran in the east to Greece and Libya in the west. As the academic disciplines developed in the eighteenth and nineteenth centuries, the Near East was a region that particularly attracted attention: it had formed the eastern part of the Roman Empire, and before it the Hellenistic kingdoms, the Persian, Babylonian and Assyrian empires, and their predecessors. There was also immense interest in the exotic world of Western Europe's main political rival, the Ottoman Empire, which was close, yet strikingly different. In the Near East, Western Europe rediscovered the physical remains of its cultural ancestry, which was already well known through Greek and Latin literature. For scholarship, there were numerous large standing monuments to be observed, inscriptions recorded, 'art works' to be transferred to museums, and, with the development of archaeology, there were cemeteries and town mounds to dig in. Archaeology in much of sub-Saharan Africa is much more recent, so there is still an enormous imbalance in our understanding of the greater part of the continent.

These two placings for Egypt, Africa and the Near East represent not quite opposed points of view. Locating Egypt raises issues about how Europeans, who are largely those who have written Egyptology, have viewed Egypt both as part of, and distinct from, 'Africa'. It is also a useful starting point for discussing issues of culture and influences which we consider in later chapters.

Modern perceptions of where Egypt is are very different to those of the past. All terminology is, of course, subjective. To the Greeks 'Egypt' was the land of the Nile Valley, bounded by Asia on the east, 'Libya' (their term for the whole of the rest of north Africa) on the west, and Aithiopia (a vast, ill-defined region at the southernmost limit of the world) to the south. The Greek name *Aigyptos* (L. *Aegyptus*) derives from the name given to the city of Memphis, *Hu(t)-ka-Ptah*, meaning 'The House of the *Ka* (-Soul) of Ptah'. In the languages of western Asia the country was known as *Musri* (modern Arabic *Misr*), and is found as such in biblical and Assyrian texts. To the Assyrians, Egypt was in the West. The Assyrian records of the Sargonid Period (721–626 BC) refer to the pharaoh as the 'King of the Westland'. To them, the 'Mediterranean' (the central sea) was not central at all; it was the 'Great Sea', the 'Upper Sea' (contrasted with Lower Sea, the Gulf) or the 'Sea of the Setting Sun'. Presumably, the Kushites thought of Egypt as, in some sense, 'north', lying downstream on the same river. To the Romans, and their cultural heirs, Egypt was in the East, the Orient.

NAMING EGYPT

All of these locations of Egypt have been established by other peoples, or in relation to other peoples and places. For the Egyptians, Egypt was, of course, the centre. But 'Egypt' itself is a name imposed from outside: imposed by the Romans as the name of a province of their empire. And this brings us to one of the key problems of Egyptology and studying Egypt. Because, as we shall see in Chapter 3, the early European reconstructions of ancient Egypt's history and geography relied on Greek, Roman and biblical sources, as well as contemporary Arabic names, the literature displays a confusing, not to say bewildering, array of variant name forms. In his attempts to decipher hieroglyphics, Champollion used names known from such Greek and

Roman sources to find the Egyptian forms. As the proper Egyptian pronunciation was unknown to the Egyptologists (and still is) the names used in literature were 'Latinized', so that we often find Latinized forms of Greek versions of Egyptian names. In recent years, many Egyptologists have preferred to use a written form of the Egyptian name that is closer to a direct rendering of the Egyptian hieroglyphic signs (although it may not resemble the way the name was pronounced in ancient times).

So, to take one common name, the old form derived from the Greek and Latin writers was 'Amenophis' but the form from the hieroglyphic is 'Amenhotep'. Similarly, we have 'Sethos' and 'Sety', 'Sesostris' and 'Senusret' or 'Senwosret', 'Ammenemes' and 'Amenemhat'. The problem persists, as some writers prefer to use the Latinized forms and some the more Egyptian forms. Some writers even prefer to use the Latinized forms for pharaohs and Egyptian forms for others in order to distinguish the pharaohs, resulting in sentences that talk about a pharaoh 'Amenophis III' and his official Amenhotep. Not all pharaohs are mentioned in Greek and Roman sources (Hatshepsut, Akhenaten and Tutankhamun being the three obvious ones) so they have no Latinized forms; consequently, those who use the old forms have to mix them with Egyptian forms.

The reasons for using a form which is derived directly from the Egyptian are obvious. While we still cannot be certain how names were pronounced (Egyptian lacks vowels, so we only have the consonants) the Egyptian forms are a more honest attempt at rendering what is written in the hieroglyphic.

The same problem occurs with names of gods and goddesses, some writers preferring, for example, the Greek 'Arsaphes' for 'Herishef', and 'Satis' for 'Satet' (or 'Satjet'). Most divine names, however, still appear in their Latin/Greek forms: Osiris (rather than the Egyptian Usir), Isis (not Aset), Nephthys (not Nebet-hat), and Thoth (not Djehuty).

With place names the confusion increases since parts of archaeological sites are usually known by the Arabic names for the particular mound (*kom* or *tell*) or area. Generally, Egyptologists still refer to ancient towns and cities by the Greek (or Latinized Greek) names. Heliopolis (*Helios-polis*, the city of the sun) was the Greek name for the ancient Egyptian Iunu (meaning 'the Pillar'); Thebes was a Greek name for Waset; Memphis was the Greek form of the Egyptian 'Men-nofer'; and Bubastis comes from 'Per-Bast' ('Temple/ Domain of Bast', the cat goddess).

The forms used here are generally the 'Egyptian' ones, although gods such as Isis and Osiris still appear in the more familiar Greek style. The 'Egyptian' forms of names are derived from a 'transliteration' of the original Egyptian (which is usually written in hieroglyphic). The Egyptian language was written with signs which give the consonants and some 'semi-vowels': there were no full vowels in Egyptian (as in modern Arabic). A transliteration of, for example, the name we read as 'Amenhotep' combines the signs and sign groups *I-mn-htp*. Conventionally, Egyptologists insert vowels to get 'Amen-hotep'. The transliterations can only be approximate, as Egyptian has, for example, four different sounds for 'h': in technical works these are identified with 'diacritical' marks (dots and lines under the letter).

This confusing system of names is the result of the way in which Egyptology, and the understanding of the Egyptian language, developed.

The Egyptians themselves used a number of names for their land, but most reflected duality, rather than unity. The Nile Valley, 'Upper Egypt', enclosed for most of its length by limestone cliffs, was 'Ta-Shemau' and was represented in hieroglyphic by a flowering sedge plant (or 'lily'). The broad expanse of the Delta, Lower Egypt, was 'Ta-Mehu', represented by a clump of papyrus.

By the time of the New Kingdom we find references to 'this land of KeMeT'. Kemet means 'black' and is generally taken to mean the land which is covered by the silt during the inundation of the Nile. Many Afrocentrist writers have argued that Kemet defines Egypt as the 'land of the black people', but this is a grammatically incorrect reading. That Kemet means the land rather than people is further confirmed by its use in contrast to DeSHReT, the 'red', a term for the areas beyond the cultivation, continuing into the deserts.

The Egyptians thought of their land as the result of the unification of two kingdoms, and Egyptian ideology emphasized this duality to the Roman Period. Each kingdom had its own crown and protective deities. Ta-Shemau, Upper Egypt, had as its symbol the sedge plant, and, as its ruler, the king wore the white crown. The protective goddess was the vulture, Nekhbet. Ta-Mehu, Lower

Figure 1.1 The king crowned by the goddesses of Upper and Lower Egypt. Ptolemaic Period, temple of Kom Ombo.

Egypt, was symbolized by the bee, or the papyrus, the Red Crown and the goddess Wadjet (Buto) (Figure 1.1).

Egypt was also divided into smaller districts which are generally known by the Greek-derived word *nome*, rather than the Egyptian term for them, *sepat*. Earlier Egyptologists thought that the division into nomes was a vestige of how Egypt had been before the unification, that each represented one of the chiefdoms which were eventually brought together into the two kingdoms. There were eventually 42 nomes, each represented by an androgynous figure symbolizing the fecundity of the flooding Nile (Figure 1.2). Outside the Nile Valley and Delta were regions that were ruled by Egypt, but not defined as nomes, notably the Oases of the Western Desert and the Wadi Natrun.

WHO WERE THE EGYPTIANS?

Did a 'Dynastic Race' sail from Mesopotamia along the Gulf and around Arabia then up the Red Sea? Or did they spread from some intermediate place such as Dilmun (Bahrain) in both directions? Few rational Egyptologists would nowadays subscribe to this idea. It was,

Figure 1.2 A fecundity figure with the sign of the nome of Khemenu (*Hermopolis*) in Middle Egypt: part of a procession in the temple of Ramesses II at Abydos, nineteenth dynasty.

however, very popular in the late nineteenth and early twentieth centuries. The leading British archaeologist of Egypt, Flinders Petrie, formed the 'Dynastic Race' theory to explain the rapid development of Egyptian civilization, assuming that Africans needed an external impetus. Deriving from nineteenth-century anthropological theories, Petrie's Dynastic Race theory was not fully accepted by Egyptologists, but it had a deep influence, notably on the American George Reisner in his reconstruction of Nubian cultures, and it was still being argued by W. B. Emery, excavator of important early royal cemeteries, in his study of early Egypt in 1961.

Speculation about the 'race' of the Egyptians began in the eighteenth century and increased during the nineteenth and early twentieth centuries, with the growing European influence over the Near East, Africa and Asia. Ideas about race were used as a justification for imperial expansion, and some of the developing academic disciplines were called upon to lend support to the racial theories. Notable among these were language studies, with languages soon being used to define peoples. The new theory of 'Evolution' too, was a major factor. Early anthropology proposed a 'unilinear' evolutionary development for humans, and claimed to produce scientific evidence for this by complex cranial measurements. The living 'races of mankind' were then ordered along a presumed scale of development. As a result, the Egyptians could be blackened or whitened according to the personal agenda of the writer.

The Dynastic Race theory was the 'scientific' (in that it was claimed to be based on archaeological evidence) exposition of the attitude that Egypt, being in Africa, was unable to produce a high culture, therefore the Egyptians (or, at least, the ruling class) must have come from somewhere else. As with every other significant cultural group (such as the Dorians in Greece) in late nineteenth-century interpretations, this place of origin turned out to be somewhere in central Asia, the supposed Indo-European/Aryan homeland. As the German Egyptologist, Heinrich Brugsch, put it in one of the most influential of late nineteenth-century histories of Egypt:

> according to ethnology, the Egyptians appear to form a third branch of the Caucasian race, the family called Cushite; and this much may be regarded as certain, that in the earliest ages of humanity, far beyond all historical remembrance, the Egyptians, for reasons unknown to us, left the soil of their early home, took their way towards the setting sun, and finally crossed that bridge of nations, the Isthmus of Suez, to find a new fatherland on the banks of the Nile.
>
> (Heinrich Brugsch, *Egypt Under The Pharaohs*, 1891: 2–3)

Brugsch here summarizes the European academic view that had developed during the nineteenth century, and which had completely overturned the view of Egypt as African. Egyptology generally adopted a view that the ancient Egyptians were a 'brown' north African race or the result of a mixture of black African and lighter-skinned peoples. Physical anthropology shows that there is a strong continuity in the appearance of the Egyptians from ancient to modern times.

The most extreme form of the Dynastic Race theory claims that civilization came from somewhere other than Earth itself. There is no good archaeological evidence that the ancient Egyptians or their culture came from Mars or any other distant planet or galaxy, through 'Stargate' or by spaceship! But whether or not Egypt was the creation of extra-terrestrial peoples, there are many writers who insist that Egypt was the repository of a 'Higher Culture' of, for example, the lost races of Atlantis. None of these ideas gets much sympathy from Egyptologists, but they do belong to the very broad range of uses and perceptions of ancient Egypt. These ideas may lack 'scientific' or archaeological authority, but that does little to diminish their popularity and indeed, just as biblical and classical literature before, they have resulted in archaeological investigations, if only to refute them. Egyptologists may ignore or despise these extreme uses of ancient Egypt and its culture, but they capture the public imagination in numerous books, newspapers and television programmes. They also represent that search for 'the other' that Egypt has represented to outsiders since ancient times.

WHO WERE THE ANCIENT EGYPTIANS?

Our knowledge of the prehistory of north Africa has changed quite dramatically in the past thirty years. Environmental studies now show that, rather than one phase of desiccation, the Sahara has had several wet and dry phases, and these have affected movements of animals and peoples. With the desiccation of the Sahara in the period 10,000–5000 BC peoples moved from the central regions in different directions, some coming into the Nile Valley – or initially settling along the desert plateau above the swampy valley. Current research suggests that the southern regions of Nubia may have fallen within the seasonal rain belt much later than we had previously thought, perhaps as late as the New Kingdom. The Wadi Howar, originally a tributary of the Nile which connected with it in the Dongola Reach, runs from Darfur, Kordofan and Chad. The Wadi may even have been able to support some arable production and pastoralism into the early centuries AD, and perhaps served as a route between the Nile and regions further west throughout ancient times. The complexity of climatic change suggests that for a long period before the emergence of Egypt as a unified state, there were peoples, probably pastoralists, ranging over large regions of what is now the Sahara.

Evidence from recent excavations in some Delta sites shows that there were very close contacts between that region and Canaan from the late prehistoric period into the Early Dynastic. There was considerable trade between the two regions, and there were Asiatic settlers in Egypt, and Egyptian settlements (probably trade based) in Sinai and Canaan.

The evidence of language is also relevant here. Ancient Egyptian belongs to a language group known as 'Afro-Asiatic' (formerly called Hamito-Semitic) and its closest relatives are other north-east African languages from Somalia to Chad. Egypt's cultural features, both material and ideological and particularly in the earliest phases, show clear connections with that same broad area. In sum, ancient Egypt was an African culture, developed by African peoples who had wide-ranging contacts in north Africa and western Asia.

WHAT DID THE ANCIENT EGYPTIANS LOOK LIKE?

The European idea of the ancient Egyptians has varied a lot in the past three hundred years, and has been the subject of much recent study. Martin Bernal in *Black Athena* shows how Egyptian culture and peoples were 'blackened' and 'whitened' according to racial prejudices, bolstered by changes in academic thought. This is epitomized in the quotation from Heinrich Brugsch above, which promotes the idea that the ancient Egyptians were Caucasians. Much nineteenth-century painting of biblical events or episodes set in ancient Egypt includes elite Egyptians who are remarkably European in colouring and appearance. 'Brown' and black people appear, but nearly always in the role of servants or slaves: the main characters of pharaohs and female royalty (such as the princess in the numerous pictures of the 'finding of Moses') are distinctly white. In these paintings ancient Egypt was used for all sorts of purposes. From the Egyptological perspective, these choices are certainly wrong: the ancient Egyptians were not 'white' in any European sense, nor were they 'Caucasian'.

So were they 'black'? This depends, in part, on your own point of view and how you would define 'black'. Much Afro-American literature promotes the view that the ancient Egyptians were essentially like modern Afro-Americans. The more extreme (and, it must be said, racist) versions state that the present-day Egyptians are

10

Figure 1.3 The Egyptian elite as they wished to be seen: Sennefer, the Mayor of Thebes, and his wife, depicted in conventional manner: Tomb of Sennefer, Thebes (Luxor), eighteenth dynasty.

'only' Arabs who came in later. Certainly, there have been migrations from Arabia throughout medieval and early modern times, and no doubt in ancient times as well. However, the Arab Conquest of CE (AD) 641 was, like the Roman or Norman conquests in England, essentially an elite conquest rather than a mass population movement. In Egypt, once the country had been taken over there were large-scale conversions to Islam, but the population remained essentially that of late Roman Egypt.

One major problem in discussing ethnicity is time. There is a tendency in both polarized extremes to dismiss the later historical phases (from the end of the New Kingdom onwards). Both groups say that by then the Egyptians were no longer 'Egyptian', having been replaced or 'diluted' by increasing numbers of 'foreigners'. Both assume some sort of ideal early-Egyptian race, in the one case 'black' and in the other perhaps less clearly defined. This ignores earlier non-Egyptians in Egypt, and places too much emphasis on the foreign ancestry of individual pharaohs. It raises the fundamental question of how *we* define ancient Egypt. Both professional Egyptologists and other interest groups impose a time limit on ancient Egypt. The attitudes of Egyptologists are of immense importance in forming the attitudes of secondary literature. For a long time the Ptolemaic and Roman Periods have been regarded as distinctly 'after', and the first millennium has not been given equal importance with the earlier 'kingdoms'. Yet if we look at Egyptian culture, there is much in Ptolemaic and Roman Egypt that is a direct continuation of the earlier periods. We cannot expect any society to remain monolithic and unchanging over five thousand years. The evidence, increasing in quantity and diversity from the earlier to the later phases, also puts our attempts to understand out of balance. There is a tendency in general works (such as this one) to illustrate aspects of Egypt by using evidence from different periods. This again is perhaps a problem of the timescale involved, and the apparently unchanging culture; we would not do this with, for example, Mesopotamia, much less with Greece or Rome.

At all periods there were 'foreign' populations absorbed into Egypt, most notably the Libyan tribes. There were settlements of Greeks (from Greece, the islands and Asia Minor) and Macedonians in the Ptolemaic Period. There were people from the south ('Nubia') in Egypt at all periods, and in the Aswan region they must always have been a significant element of the population. Similarly, Asiatic and other captives of war would have been integrated. In the New Kingdom we have good evidence for royal marriages with foreign princesses, who were accompanied by large numbers of female attendants, some of whom would have been given in marriage to courtiers. Not all of the sons of foreign rulers who were educated at the Egyptian court returned to their homelands, and many took up administrative offices and married Egyptian wives.

It is impossible to make a generalization about the appearance of a single population over a period of five thousand years, but we can say that the earliest population of ancient Egypt included African people from the upper Nile, African people from the regions of the Sahara and modern Libya, and smaller numbers of people who had come from south-western Asia and perhaps the Arabian peninsula. By the period of the unification of Egypt, and the beginning of 'Dynastic' history, these peoples had been living in Egypt for thousands of years: they were indigenous. Throughout the succeeding millennia individuals and groups (generally fairly small) of people from all of those same regions continued to settle in Egypt, but there were no mass movements of population that 'replaced' the original population.

So, what is the evidence for the appearance of the ancient populations? We have extensive human remains preserved as skeletons or mummies. The better-preserved mummies, particularly of royalty, require little imagination or restoration to give an impression of the appearance of the person when alive. Less well-preserved or skeletal remains require reconstruction, and considerable advances have been made in recent years in the re-creation of faces from skulls. This, of course, gives us the features of the person, but not necessarily skin, hair or eye colour. It should also be noted that the majority of the well-preserved remains are of members of the elite; relatively few non-elite cemeteries have been examined in detail.

There is a wealth of artistic representation in the form of statuary, relief sculpture and painting from all periods of Egyptian history, and depicting all social classes. As in all societies where portraiture is practised there are various conventions, idealizations and period styles which affect the image. The face of the reigning monarch frequently influences the portrayal of his subjects, perhaps most obviously in the reign of Akhenaten. There are certainly specific types of face at certain periods, but this does not necessarily indicate any ethnic change.

The most important conventions in Egyptian art are the distinguishing of male and female by colour: men are painted red-brown, women creamy yellow (Figure 1.3). These conventions clearly reflect a social ideal: that elite women are paler because they stay indoors and do not work in the fields. In the New Kingdom these conventions change slightly, and Nefertiti, for example can be coloured red-brown like Akhenaten; slightly later, pinkish tones were added to the palette and used for female figures (e.g. Nefertari, wife of Ramesses II). There is also an idealization of the figure, particularly the body. This is notable in, for example, statues of Senusret III where the face is lined and, if not old, at least 'careworn', yet the body is the ideal youthful image. Occasionally, royal images do not conform to the ideal, as with some statues of Amenhotep III and his son Akhenaten. But these deviations from the ideal are relatively rare, and were created with a specific ideological message.

Foreigners too are designated by conventions. At times these can be almost caricatures of racial stereotypes, but that is to emphasize their foreignness, and their difference, particularly when they appear as enemies of Egypt. In some instances, such as in the scenes of Nubian captives in the tomb of Horemheb at Saqqara, the foreign captives are portrayed with great sympathy, and it is the petty Egyptian officials who are shown unflatteringly. When a foreigner was absorbed into Egyptian society s/he could be shown as an Egyptian. For example in the tomb of Tutankhamun's Viceroy of Kush, Huy, a Nubian prince named Heqa-nefer, is depicted. Because he appears as a subject foreigner bringing the tribute of Nubia to the pharaoh, Heqa-nefer is shown wearing the feathered headdress and costume of a Nubian, and is painted black in colour. Yet, in his own tomb, where he was portrayed as a member of the Egyptian elite, Heqa-nefer was depicted as any other Egyptian official, painted red-brown in colour and wearing conventional Egyptian costume. Occasionally foreigners seem to emphasize their origins, such as the Nubian mercenaries depicted on stelae from Gebelein, the Asiatic soldier with his Egyptian wife and servant on a stela from Amarna, and the Kushite pharaohs of the twenty-fifth dynasty.

SELF-DEFINITION: WHO DID THE EGYPTIANS THINK THEY WERE?

Ancient Egypt had no myth recording the origin of the population or the foundation of the state dependent upon one 'people' as, for example, Rome and the Israelites had. Egyptian origins of both the people and the state are attributed to the creation of the gods. Insofar as they defined themselves at all, an Egyptian was simply someone who lived in Egypt and presumably conformed, to a greater or lesser degree, to Egyptian culture, and spoke the language. There does not appear to have been a view of being Egyptian based upon 'race' or 'ethnicity'. The descriptions of individuals in documents as 'the Kushite', 'the Syrian' or 'the Libyan' are usually due to the type of document and the context. There is also an unspoken assumption that, although we have rich evidence of 'foreigners' in the New Kingdom and later Egypt, there were fewer in the Old and Middle Kingdoms. It may be true that from the New Kingdom to Roman times 'foreigners' came from a greater range of countries, and from much further away than in earlier times, but there would always have been significant groups of people from the south ('Nubia'), the west ('Libya') and the east (the desert, Sinai and southern Canaan).

The Egyptians did distinguish themselves from other peoples. The lists of foreign or subject countries and city-states that can be found in temples from the New Kingdom onwards carry the name of the place surmounted by a figure representing it. The names are then grouped together, usually as northern and southern localities. The broad divisions of peoples that Egyptians recognized were established, like so much royal ideology, in the developing years of the state, and reflected those early direct contacts with their nearest neighbours to the south, west and east. These groups were called *remetj*, the 'people', representing the Egyptians themselves; *Nehesiu*, black-skinned southerners ('Nubians'); *Tjehenu*, 'Libyans', and *Aamu*, 'Asiatics' (originally representing the people of south Canaan). As Egyptian knowledge of the world expanded, new peoples and places were included in lists, but still clustered in the same groups. When, in the eighteenth dynasty, Egypt became involved with the kingdoms of Assyria and Babylonia, Mitanni in north Syria and Khatti (the Hittites) in Anatolia, along with the people of Cyprus,

Crete and Greece, they were all included in *Aamu*, as extensions of the north and east.

There is evidence for a form of xenophobia in Egyptian attitudes to foreigners, foreign places, food and cultures, but this, as in most ancient societies, is based on their being non-Egyptian, rather than on race or religion. As the 'Great Hymn to the Aten', written in the reign of Akhenaten (*c.* 1352–1336 BC), expressed it:

> You (the sun god) made the earth as you wished . . . you set every man in his place, you supply their needs; everyone has his food; his lifetime is counted. Their tongues differ in speech, their characters likewise; their skins are distinct, for you distinguished the peoples.
>
> (Lichtheim 1973: 131–2)

What did the Egyptians call themselves? By the Middle Kingdom official documents refer to the 'people of Kemet', but at the same time emphasize that they are all subjects of Pharaoh, and hence rank in the same categories as the 'Nine Bows' and any other of those groups that he must control. The people of Egypt are often called the *'rekhyt'* in texts. The word is written with the hieroglyph of a lapwing, and the bird appears as a symbol for the Egyptian people in numerous contexts. On the ceremonial mace head of King 'Scorpion', from the period of state unification, dead lapwings are shown hanging from standards, as a symbol of defeated peoples (perhaps here specifically the people of the Delta). Otherwise, the Egyptians are simply *remetj*, 'the people'.

In the rarer personal evidence, such as letters and 'autobiographical' inscriptions, it is clear that the Egyptians usually defined themselves by relation to their local town. This is shown by the use of theophoric names and invocations to local gods. Clearly some deities, such as the state gods Amun, Ptah and Re, and the funerary gods Osiris and Isis, were worshipped all over Egypt; others had more localized popularity. So the name Wepwawet-mose suggests that the man came from the region of Asyut, whereas the name Nes-Iusaas suggests that he came from Iunu (*Heliopolis*).

Letters such as those in the archive of the late twentieth-dynasty scribes of the Theban necropolis, the father and son Dhutmose and

Butehamun reveal their dislike of being away from their home town, whether elsewhere in Egypt or in Nubia. They use a term, colourfully translated by one Egyptologist as 'hellhole', for places in both Nubia and northern Egypt, and they constantly urge their families to pray to the gods of the home town for a safe return. While at certain periods the pharaoh provided burial places near his own pyramid or tomb for selected high officials, there was a distinct preference for being buried in one's home town. This is demonstrated by the burial of a Viceroy of Kush, named Hori, who served in the reign of Ramesses III. Hori came from the important town of Per-Bast (Bubastis) in the eastern Delta, and on several monuments he dedicated in the viceregal domain he included invocations to the patron goddess of his home town, Bast. Hori died in Nubia, and was probably mummified there before the long journey to his burial place in Per-Bast. A series of rock inscriptions records the journey of his body northwards, accompanied by officials of his retinue and professional mourners. It must have taken several weeks for the body to sail from Nubia to the Delta, where it was laid to rest in a massive sarcophagus of red Aswan granite in his family tomb.

In common with many other ancient peoples, the Egyptians acknowledged that there were differences in skin colour and language, but they did not define themselves by race. The Egyptians are perhaps best defined by cultural factors: those who lived in Egypt and belonged to the Egyptian system. We have generally assumed that the range of cultural values and religious beliefs documented by the written and material remains were common to the whole society. But we have to remember that most of our evidence comes from a very narrow sector of that society. Trying to penetrate ancient Egypt beyond the world presented by the elite is actually very difficult. Another factor that cannot be forgotten is the enormous timescale of ancient Egypt. From the developing period of the recognizable Egyptian state and culture to the Arab conquest is some five thousand years; there were certainly enormous changes during that time, but the Egyptians themselves chose to emphasize continuity.

Egypt was the first large nation state. It was a geographically well-defined unit with one dominant language, and culture, ruled by a king and centralized administration. It was also, in many ways different from the other countries with which it was involved. This difference was something that was emphasized by the Asiatic, and later by Greek and Roman writers: Egypt did things differently, and this has contributed to her enduring myth.

2

THE EGYPTIAN
WORLD

People entering Egypt from other parts of Africa usually came from
the south along the Nile, or by the desert roads. The ancient
evidence emphasizes the Nile route, but in medieval and early
modern times large numbers of people came, or were brought, along
the Darb el-Arbain, the 'Forty Days road', that crossed the desert
from the southern side of the Sahara, through several small oases to
Kharga, and thence to the Nile at Girga or Asyut. This was the
route favoured by official deputations from the Muslim kingdoms
of West Africa to Cairo, where they joined the Hajj to Mecca. It
was also the route used by the slave traders. How much of this route
was used in ancient times is still very uncertain, although parts of
it into, and from, Nubia certainly were. The major access to Egypt
from the west was along the Mediterranean coast, and this was,
in some periods, defended against Libyan attack with a chain of
fortresses.

   Most people arriving in Egypt before the advent of air travel came
by sea, or across the Sinai land bridge. They therefore arrived at one
of the mouths of the Nile or, later, at Alexandria, before travelling
upstream. The Delta and its cities were, therefore, the first places
encountered before approaching Heliopolis and Memphis. Viewing
Egypt this way helps us to appreciate that, despite the wealth of its
surviving monuments, Thebes was actually quite remote from the
ancient centres of population and production. This should perhaps
make us rethink our ideas of Thebes as a 'capital' and question the
emphasis that we place on its surviving monuments.

   To the Egyptians the orientation of their world was dictated by
the valley and the river flowing from south to north. The religious

world was on a predominantly east–west axis: dictated by the rising and setting sun.

The Herodotean view of Egypt as a long, narrow country defined by the Nile is endlessly repeated in books, but how far does it reflect an ancient Egyptian perception of the country? Certainly, the Egyptians abhorred the deserts, but we are now realizing that they did in fact use desert travel far more than we have previously acknowledged. Evidence from excavations in the western oases shows that Dakhla, and no doubt Kharga and Bahariya, were under Egyptian authority during the Old Kingdom: ancient Egypt as a state was never confined to the Nile Valley and Delta, even if that was its main focus.

Over the past thirty years there has been an enormous advance in our understanding of the changing environment of Egypt in prehistoric and historic times, notably through the work of Karl Butzer. We are now far more aware of climatic change and its far-reaching effects, and the fluctuations in the flooding of the Nile, and this has influenced our interpretations of state formation and state collapse at, for example, the end of the Old Kingdom.

To the Egyptians, the 'Nile' was known as *Iteru*, perhaps meaning 'the seasonal one'. When in flood it was *Hapy*. The Nile in Egypt and Nubia is a single stream carrying the waters of the White Nile, which flows from the lakes of Equatorial Africa, and the Blue Nile and the Atbara, both issuing from the highlands of Ethiopia. It was the Ethiopian waters that brought the rich silt that made Egypt fertile. In its very early history the Nile had other tributaries running in from the Sahara, and was fed by the water courses that ran from the hills of the surrounding desert (now forming the dry *wadis*). Throughout its history the annual inundation has varied, at times dramatically, dependent as it is on the rains in Ethiopia. Since the construction of the dams at Aswan, the inundation has been controlled, and the rich silt no longer feeds the land.

The flood waters began to rise in early June at Aswan (eight to fourteen days later at Memphis), their arrival predicted by the appearance of the star that we call Sirius and the Egyptians call Sopdet. The river rose slowly, gradually covering the whole of the broad flood plain, which remained under water for four to six weeks to a depth of 1.0–1.5 metres (3–5 feet). Grain was sown as the waters receded during October and November. The crops grew and ripened over winter and were harvested in March or April. This cycle gave the seasons: *Akhet*, 'the inundation'; *Peret*, literally, 'coming forth' – the growing season; and *Shomu*, the dry season. In earlier historical phases the Egyptians had little need to improve upon this natural flooding of the land. As the population increased, dykes were used to keep water in the fields for longer, and canals carried water to the edges of the flood plain. Additional watering of fields and gardens was by the simple method of filling two pots slung on a yoke. Irrigation by mechanical means only came much later: the *shaduf*, a bucket on a pivoting pole was not introduced until the New Kingdom, and the *saqia*, a type of water-wheel, not until Persian or Ptolemaic times.

Throughout its history the course of the river has moved in the broad valley, generally towards the east. Irrigation canals presumably ran throughout the flood plain, with larger waterways connecting to the river the bigger towns that were not set on the river itself. Settlements were built on pockets of higher ground, so that they did not get completely flooded, and they were presumably surrounded by dykes and walls to protect them.

Travel by river was fairly slow. The current moved downstream at a rate of one knot (1.85 km per hour), increasing to four knots during the inundation. Sailing upstream, against the current, required sails. The detailed accounts of early European travellers indicate that it took about ten days to sail from Luxor to Cairo in late August, although contrary winds and other problems could extend the time to sixteen days. In 656 BC the princess Nitoqert, daughter of Psamtik I, took sixteen days to sail to Thebes, probably from Memphis (or perhaps Sau in the Delta): but her progress was ceremonial, rather than urgent.

Nothing is really known of the ancient road system, but it may be assumed that roads would have been created on top of the field embankments. Such limited evidence that we have suggests that routes along the desert edge were used for donkey caravans, and later for swift courier communications using horses and chariots. The site of Akhetaten (Amarna), Akhenaten's city in Middle Egypt, is one of few where a road network can be identified. There, the main routes in the town, and roads leading to the tombs and other religious areas away from the centre, are still clearly visible. These were maintained with the larger stones being moved to the edges, defining the roads and creating a smoother surface. There is a clear preference for straight lines connecting points at Akhetaten, and we may assume that any major road system in Egypt would have been similarly planned.

UPPER EGYPT

The Egyptians themselves numbered the *sepat* (nomes) of Upper Egypt from the First Cataract to the apex of the Delta. There were 22 nomes in Upper Egypt, and these were clearly defined by the fifth dynasty. In the Delta the number of nomes changed at different periods, being fixed at 20 in Ptolemaic–Roman times. There are complete lists of the nomes on monuments from the Old Kingdom to Ptolemaic Period, and these show a little variation in the names.

In historical times, the southern border of Egypt was at the 'first' cataract of the river (actually the last from its sources) – modern Aswan. In the prehistoric periods (700,000–5000 BC), and perhaps to the late Predynastic Period (3500–3000 BC) the region of Gebel Silsila seems to have marked the southern border of the kingdom of Nekhen (Gk *Hierakonpolis*). The first nome of Upper Egypt, between the Cataract and Silsila, was called Ta-Seti. Usually understood as 'Bow Land', it was a name that was also given to the region south of the Cataract (Nubia), and archaeology shows that the early Nubian cultures did extend north of the Cataract towards the Kom Ombo basin. This southern frontier was political and practical: the Cataract is the most easily defensible point on the river. The main settlement was on the large island of Abu (Gk *Elephantine*), where the excavations of the German Archaeological Institute have uncovered the remains of the Early Dynastic town beneath the extensive remains of the later settlement. In Egyptian, Abu means 'elephant' or 'ivory'. Some writers suggest that the name derives from the massive granite outcrops that resemble elephants or that this was the northern limit at which elephants were encountered in the Predynastic Period; but it is more likely that the name derives from the function of the original Egyptian settlement: as an ivory trading centre in Nubian territory. The town was later dominated by the temples of the Cataract god, Khnum, and his associated goddesses, Anuqet and Satjet. In the Old Kingdom, the town's officials were important as controllers of the frontier and leaders of expeditions into Nubia. In the Middle Kingdom, a long wall enclosed the whole of the Cataract, protecting the road from the mainland settlement

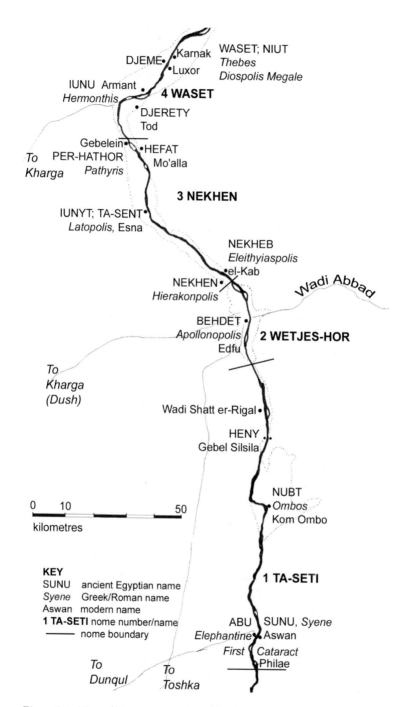

Figure 2.1 Map of Upper Egypt from the first to the fourth nome.

to the port, situated at the head of the Cataract on the plain of Shellal. In the New Kingdom, the Egyptian army sailed from here into Nubia, and there were numerous inscriptions recording the progress of the viceroy and his staff. With the loss of the Nubian domains at the end of the New Kingdom, Abu became a frontier town. In Persian times there was a Jewish garrison on the island, with its own temple. This garrison is well documented from a large archive. There is also good evidence for the developing mainland town, called in Egyptian 'Sunu', later Syene (modern Aswan), deriving from a word meaning 'trade'. Although the official frontier throughout the Ptolemaic and Roman Periods (until the reign of Diocletian) lay at Maharraqa in Nubia, there was a garrison at Aswan, and defence network stretching across the desert.

As well as its role as frontier town, supply base for the Nubian fortresses in the Middle and early New Kingdoms, and starting point for trading and military expeditions, Abu was important for the quarrying of granite. The islands in the Cataract, and quarries on the mainland, supplied huge quantities of red, black and grey granite for architectural and sculptural work throughout Egypt. The quarrying of stone on islands in the river had the added advantage of clearing the way for ships.

Abu had religious importance, too, since the Nile was believed to be controlled by the Cataract god Khnum and to flow from a cavern here. In the Late Period the cult of the goddess Isis was introduced to the island of Philae (Egn *Pa-iu-rk*), at the head of the Cataract, and under royal patronage the temples expanded, becoming a major pilgrimage centre in the Ptolemaic and Roman Periods.

The nome of Ta-Seti stretched northwards through the fertile Kom Ombo basin, where Nubt (Gk *Ombos*) was another major settlement. There are extensive prehistoric remains in the Kom Ombo basin. The crocodile god Sobek was worshipped here, and Nubt also had a temple dedicated to the god Horus 'the elder'. In the Ptolemaic Period, a new double temple was built for both gods and their consorts. Nubt stood at the end of desert roads into Nubia (as nearby Daraw served them in early modern times) and to the Red Sea.

The gorge at Silsila (Egn *Heny*) is a natural geological boundary, near the change of the valley from sandstone to limestone. It probably served as the southern border of the 'kingdom' of Nekhen in the Predynastic Period. In the New Kingdom Silsila was a major source of sandstone: the temples of Thebes are built largely of stone from here. As the narrowest point on the river in Egypt, it also served as a place where the Nile flood was measured and its god, Hapy, worshipped.

The second nome was Wetjes-Hor, 'Throne of Horus', with its capital at Edfu. The town was called by a variety of names in ancient times: Djeba 'the perch' (signifying the reed on which Horus as a falcon alighted); Behdet; and Mesen. Through the association of the chief god Horus with Apollo, in Greek times it was called *Apollonopolis Megale* (L. *Magna*). Horus took as his consort Hathor of Dendera, whose statue was brought here to celebrate the 'Feast of the Beautiful Meeting'. Their child was called Hor-sema-tawy ('Uniter of the two lands') or Ihy.

Edfu stood near the end of desert routes to Kharga Oasis and Nubia on the west bank, and through the Eastern Desert, along the Wadi Abbad, to the Red Sea. The town of Edfu is dominated by a massive Ptolemaic temple, built on an ancient site, with part of the New Kingdom temple preserved. Recent excavations in the extensive town mound have yielded important information on the Second Intermediate Period.

The third nome was Nekhen. The principal town, Nekhen, is often known by the Greek form *Hierakonpolis*, deriving from the local falcon god, who was here depicted as mummified. The importance of Nekhen as a major centre in the Predynastic Period was established by early archaeologists with the discovery of the ceremonial palette of Narmer and the mace head of king 'Scorpion'. Excavations directed by Michael Hofmann and his successors in the past two decades have considerably expanded our knowledge of this major Upper Egyptian town. Nekhen's early importance was probably associated with its position near the end of one of the routes across the Eastern Desert to the Red Sea.

Almost opposite Nekhen, on the east bank, lay another important town, Nekheb (Gk *Eleithyiaspolis*; Ar. el-Kab), home of the eponymous vulture goddess Nekhbet. Within the extensive remains of the great enclosure wall of this significant town are the temple of Nekhbet, patroness of the white crown of Upper Egypt, and a predynastic town. In the cliffs nearby are tombs of the early eighteenth dynasty with important autobiographical inscriptions of soldiers who fought in the campaigns against the 'Hyksos'.

Downstream from Nekhen, the Nile flows through a double bend with Iunyt, 'the Pillar', on the west bank. The town was later known as Ta-sent, the origin of its modern Arabic name, Esna. By Ptolemaic times this had become the capital of the nome, and was called *Latopolis*, after the fish sacred to the goddess Neith, who was worshipped here. The principal temple was dedicated to the ram-headed creator god Khnum. Iunyt stood at the end of desert roads to Kharga Oasis.

There were other smaller towns within the nome. A falcon god, Hemen, was worshipped at Hefat (el-Moalla). This town played a significant role in the First Intermediate Period when its ruler, Ankhtify, opposed the expanding power of Thebes. At the northern limit of the nome was Per-Hathor (Gk *Pathyris*), which served as a base for Nubian mercenary troops in the First Intermediate Period, and a well-documented garrison in the Ptolemaic Period; the Arabic name, Gebelein, refers to the two prominent hills that mark the boundary between the third nome and its northern neighbour.

The fourth nome, Wase(t), 'the divine sceptre', occupies rich country on a bend in the river. The small town of Sumenu (Gk *Krokodilopolis*, modern Rizeiqat), at the point where the river bends sharply to the east, was a cult-centre of the crocodile god Sobek, but the chief deity of the nome was the falcon-headed Montju, who had solar and warrior attributes. His main cult centres were Armant, Tod, Karnak and Medamud. From the late First Intermediate Period onwards, another sky god, Amun, became increasingly prominent with royal patronage of his temples at Ipet-sut (Karnak) and Ipet-resyt (Luxor). In the New Kingdom it was Amun and his sanctuaries that dominated the region, although Montju regained importance in the Libyan and Late Periods. Amun acquired a consort in the vulture goddess Mut, and the moon god Khonsu became their child.

In Ptolemaic times, Iunu, 'the Pillar', was known as *Hermonthis* (Ar. Armant) after Montju, who had a large temple here, and whose sacred bull, Buchis, was mummified and buried here. On the east bank, another temple to the god was built at Djerety (Ar. Tod).

The small town of Wase(t) (Thebes, modern Luxor) has one of the most beautiful settings on the Nile. The cliffs come close to the river, unusually on the west rather than eastern side of the river, and the whole is dominated by the natural pyramid of the Qurn.

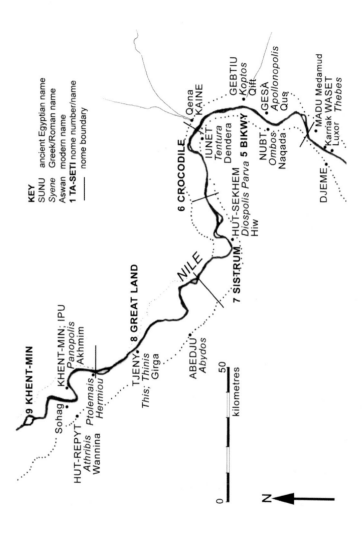

Figure 2.2 Map of Upper Egypt from the fourth to the ninth nome.

Prosperity began with the local rulers of the First Intermediate Period, who expanded their power to north and south, and reunited the whole of Egypt. The town received considerable royal patronage from the rulers of the eleventh and twelfth dynasties, and the temple of Amun was enlarged. In the Second Intermediate Period, Wase(t) was the capital of a kingdom that stretched from Aswan into Middle Egypt. Again, it was the local rulers who reunited Egypt and established the New Kingdom. The town and its temples were now elevated to a rank beside the great northern cities of Iunu (*Heliopolis*) and Memphis. Amun was merged with the sun-god Ra, and Wase(t) became Iunu-shemau, 'the Southern Iunu'. It was also known quite simply as Niu(t) (No) 'the City', and appears in biblical texts as 'No-Ammon', 'City of Amun', and in Greek as *Diospolis Megale* (L. *Magna*), through the equation of Amun with Zeus. Thebes was never the 'capital' of all Egypt in any modern sense – it was far too removed from the centre of Egypt's prosperity and population, but as a royal burial place it played a particularly important role. In the rich lands to the east of the city was the small town of Madu, another cult centre of Montju.

The importance of the fifth nome, Bikwy, 'Two Falcons', or Netjerwy, 'Two Gods', was in part due to its position, controlling access to the main routes through the Eastern Desert along the Wadi Hammamat to the gold mines, the quarries and the Red Sea. The town of Gesa (Ar. Qus) stood at the end of one branch of the desert roads. From the association of its patron god Horus with Apollo, it became *Apollonopolis Mikra* (L. *Parva*) in the Ptolemaic Period. Opposite Gesa, on the west bank, was Nubt (Gk *Ombos*), now generally known by the Arabic name Naqada. The extensive archaeological remains here became the 'type site' for predynastic Upper Egyptian pottery, and the name generally applied to the culture of Upper Egypt in that formative stage.

Although Gesa and Nubt may have been important early, the nome capital Gebtiu (Gk *Koptos*; Ar. Qift) remained significant throughout Egyptian history. Some of the earliest colossal sculptures were discovered here, representing the town's chief god, Min. Temples to Min and his consort Isis continued to be raised here until the Roman Period. Min combined his usual aspect of fertility god with a role as patron of the deserts.

Figure 2.3 The Nile near Qena.

The river, which has been flowing north-east, now turns west-ward, and the impressive range of the Eastern Desert plateau comes to the river, its sheer cliffs dominating the east bank throughout most of the valley to Cairo (Figure 2.3). Now the river runs close to the east bank, although it may have been farther west in ancient times. At the entrance to the sixth nome, 'the Crocodile', another town stood near the routes into the Eastern Desert, Kaine, or *Kainepolis* (Ar. Qena). The nome had Iun(et), 'the Pillar', as its chief town, later known as Ta-Iunu-ta-netjeret, 'the Pillar of the Goddess', and Tentura (Ar. Dendera). The presiding deity was Hathor who took as her consort Horus of Edfu. Their child was Ihy, the child god of music and jubilation. With origins in the Old Kingdom, the vast and imposing remains of the Ptolemaic–Roman temple of Hathor stand testimony to the ancient importance of Dendera.

The seventh nome was originally Bat, later Sesheshet, 'Sistrum'. The goddess Bat was depicted full face with the ears of a cow and curling horns. Quite early she was assimilated with the neighbouring goddess Hathor, and with her votive object the sistrum. The principal town was Hu(t)-Sekhem, abbreviated Hu, hence the Arabic Hiw. In Ptolemaic times it was called *Diospolis Mikra* (L. *Diospolis Parva*).

The eighth nome, Ta-wer, 'the Great Land', had as its chief town Tjeny (Gk *This* or *Thinis*) which is probably near (or the same as) the modern town of Girga. Little is known of Tjeny in ancient times, but it probably owed its importance to its position at the end of the desert road to Kharga. In the late twenty-fifth and early twenty-sixth dynasties, Tjeny was the seat of the Vizier of Upper Egypt. The town's principal god was Inheret-Shu, son of Ra.

The most notable archaeological remains in this district are at the great ancient centre of Abedju, *Abydos* (Ar. el-Araba el-Madfuna), perhaps the cemetery of Tjeny. The chief god here was Khentiamentiu, 'the Foremost of the Westerners'. By the late Old Kingdom he had been assimilated with and supplanted by Osiris. Abydos became one of the most important religious sites in Egypt, and by the Middle Kingdom the tomb of one of the earliest pharaohs in the vast desert cemetery was identified as the burial place of Osiris. Little has been excavated of the ancient city, or the chief temple of Osiris, although there are well-preserved temples of Sety I and Ramesses II at the edge of the cultivation. The Early Dynastic cemetery stretches out toward the entrance of a major wadi, which was clearly a religious focus (probably as the entrance to the underworld). The cemetery is still producing exciting new archaeological material, and it now seems likely that the seat of the Upper Egyptian kingdom had moved from Nekhen to Tjeny some considerable time before the unification.

North of Abydos the Nile flows close to the cliffs of the Eastern Desert plateau, often high and sheer. In the west the rise to the desert escarpment is more gradual, and the flood plain is broad. At Asyut the western cliffs do come closer to the river, and north of the city a branch of the Nile, the Bahr Yusef, begins its parallel journey, eventually turning into the Fayum basin. Although the ancient Egyptians regarded the whole valley from Memphis to Aswan as Upper Egypt, the region north of Asyut is now usually referred to as Middle Egypt, and its broad, rich agricultural lands are today planted with fields of sugar cane and cotton.

In times of internal weakness, a natural division in Upper Egypt appears to the north of Tjeny. In the First Intermediate Period, the princes of Thebes controlled this region, to the border with Asyut. In the Third Intermediate and Late Periods, the northern boundary of the Theban territory was in the same area, and at times the vizier of Upper Egypt had his power base at Tjeny, rather than Thebes. In the Ptolemaic Period a new administrative city for Upper Egypt was built at *Ptolemais Hermiou* (Ar. el-Mansha) in the same region.

The ninth nome, Khen(t)-Min, was probably bounded on the east bank by Gebel Toukh in the south and Gebel Haridi in the north. These are both places where the eastern cliffs come to the river; between them the plain broadens and the river makes several sharp turns. The chief town was, like the nome, called Khent-Min (the origin of the modern name Akhmim) or Ipu. Through the association of Min with Pan, it became *Panopolis* in Greek. On the west bank the large modern town of Sohag may be the ancient Neshau, and nearby lay Hut-repyt (Ar. Wannina), which has a Ptolemaic temple. Panopolis and the region to its south were important in the religious developments of the Roman Period.

The tenth nome, Wadjet, 'the Cobra', lay between Gebel Haridi and Gebel Selim. The capital of the nome was Tjebu (Gr. *Antaiopolis*), near the modern Qaw el-Kebir, where there are large, terraced and partly rock-cut funerary complexes of the local elite of the twelfth dynasty.

The emblem of the eleventh nome was the animal of the god Seth. The chief town was Shay-sehetep (Ar. Shutb) and its elite were buried at Deir Rifeh. It was the smallest nome, confined to the west bank.

The twelfth nome, 'Viper Mountain', was entirely on the east bank, facing the territory of the thirteenth nome. Its capital was Per-Nemty (Ar. el-Ataula), and the tombs of its elite were carved in hills near Deir el-Gebrawi. Nemty (Anti) is a rather obscure falcon god, later called Duen-anwy and Hor-nubti 'Horus of Gold'.

The thirteenth and fourteenth nomes have the same emblem combining a tree (a sycamore-fig or perhaps a pomegranate) and a viper, one nome being designated 'upper' (*khentet*) and the other 'lower' (*pehut*). Nedjfet-khentet was an important nome with Sauty (Ar. Asyut) as its capital. The chief deity was the canine Wepwawet, hence the Greek name *Lykopolis*. Asyut played an important role at many times in Egyptian history, ancient and medieval, although archaeological exploration has been concentrated on the rock-cut tombs and cemeteries.

Nedjfet-pehut had as its capital Qis (Gk *Cusae*) probably to be identified with el-Qusiya, although there are no significant remains.

KEY
SUNU   ancient Egyptian name
Syene   Greek/Roman name
Aswan   modern name
1 TA-SETI nome number/name
——   nome boundary

•Tihna
Akoris
Minya•
HEBENU Kom el-Ahmar
Zawiyet el-Maiyitin
16 THE ORYX

• Beni Hasan
• Istabl Antar *Speos Artemidos*

? NEFRUSY
KHEMENU•
Hermopolis
Ashmunein

• *Antinoopolis*
Sheikh Ibada
•Deir el-Bersha

15 THE HARE
•AKHETATEN
Amarna

• Hatnub

14 NEDJFET-PEHUT
QIS *Cusae*
el-Qusiya•
Meir•

Deir el-Gebrawi

**13 NEDJFET
-KHENTET**

12 VIPER MOUNTAIN
•PER-NEMTY
el-Ataula

SAUTY *Lykopolis* Asyut•
SHAY-SEHETEP Shutb• **11**
Deir
Rifeh

**DJEW-KA;
TJEBU**
Antaiopolis
Qaw el-Kebir

N

To

Kharga

10 COBRA

Gebel
el-Sheikh
el-Haridi

Aphrodito
Kom Ishqaw•

TA-HUT-TIY•
Tahta

0   50
kilometres

Akhmim

9 KHENT-MIN

Figure 2.4 Map of Upper Egypt from the ninth to the sixteenth nome.

The tombs of the nomarchs of the sixth and twelfth dynasties are carved into the cliffs at Meir.

Much more is known of the history and archaeology of the fifteenth nome, Unu, 'the Hare'. Lying at the heart of the rich agricultural lands of Middle Egypt, the Hare nome had the city of Khemenu (Coptic, Shmun, hence Ar. Ashmunein) as its capital. Khemenu could also be called Unu, like the nome, and through the identification of the principal god Thoth with Hermes, it became *Hermopolis Megale* in the Ptolemaic Period. The ruins of the ancient town cover a huge area, with the remains of several temples, and a basilica of the Roman Period. The tombs of the Old Kingdom nomarchs were in the steep cliffs at Sheikh Said, and those of their Middle Kingdom successors at el-Bersha, both sites on the east bank. An extensive cemetery in the desert west of Khemenu, at Tuna el-Gebel, was used from the Late to the Roman Periods, and also has the underground galleries where mummified creatures sacred to Thoth, notably ibises and baboons, were buried. Khemenu was a major religious centre, and also played a significant political role in a number of periods. In the later Libyan Period, an independent kingdom was centred on the city. The best documented of its pharaohs was Nimlot, who figures prominently in the inscription of the Kushite conqueror Piye (*c.* 735–712 BC).

Within the territory of the Hare nome two unusual towns were founded. At the southern end, Akhenaten chose a site on the east bank of the river for his new city, Akhetaten (usually known as 'Amarna'), built as an upper Egyptian administrative and religious centre to replace Thebes. The town area was clearly defined by a semi-circular bay in the cliffs, some ten kilometres long. Agricultural land for the estates of the officials was on the west bank, and defined by boundary stelae along the desert cliffs. Also on the east bank of the river, a little to the north of Hermopolis, the emperor Hadrian founded *Antinoöpolis* (also *Antinoë*, the modern el-Sheikh Ibada) in memory of his favourite, Antinous, who drowned in the Nile nearby. Standing at the river end of the Via Hadriana running through the Eastern Desert to the Red Sea ports, Antinoë was a flourishing centre throughout the Late Antique Period.

To the south-east of Akhetaten were the important quarries of Hat-nub ('House of Gold') where 'Egyptian alabaster' or calcite was extracted. Used as building material and for sarcophagi and statuary, ointment jars and small cosmetic containers, this easily worked stone was popular throughout Egyptian history.

To the north of 'the Hare' lay the sixteenth nome, Ma-hedj, 'the Oryx', with its early capital at Hebenu (Ar. Kom el-Ahmar) on the east bank and cemeteries nearby at Zawiyet el-Maiyitin (Zawiyet el-Amwat). The later capital seems to have been Menat-Khufu, the modern city of Minya, on the west bank. The nomarchs of the Middle Kingdom were buried at the south of the nome, in the east bank cliffs at Beni Hasan, with its magnificent views northwards over the territory they ruled. A little to the south of Beni Hasan was Seret, usually known by the Greek name *Speos Artemidos*, where the valley was a quarry, but also sacred to the local goddess Pakht, a wild cat. Here the female pharaoh, Hatshepsut, ordered a rock-cut shrine for the goddess, which carries a lengthy inscription alluding to the time of 'Hyksos' rule in Egypt. In the Late Period mummified cats were buried here as offerings to Pakht.

There has been much less archaeological work in the region of the seventeenth nome, Inpu, 'the Jackal'. It was an agricultural district on the west bank, and its principal town was Saka (Ar. el-Qais), which had temples to Anubis (Inpu) and later to Bata. The only significant historical event recorded is the attack on the town by the Theban ruler Kamose during his northward advance against the 'Hyksos'.

'The house of the king', Hut-nesut (Gk *Cynopolis*, Ar. Kom el-Ahmar Sawaris), was the capital of the eighteenth nome which lay on the east bank of the river. The nome took its name from the god, Nemty (Anti, later called Duen-anwy), the falcon with outstretched wings. At its southern limit was Dehen (Gk *Akoris*, Ar. Tihna) and at its northern, Ta-dehen-wer-nakhtu, 'The Crag-Great-of-Victories', also called 'the Crag of Amun' (also Teudjoi, Gk *Ankyronpolis*, Ar. El-Hiba). Both names signify rocky outcrops, which presumably served to delimit the nome. The northern town became a major fortress in the Libyan Period.

On the west bank the nineteenth nome, Wabwy, 'the Two Sceptres', is another relatively unexamined region. Its principal town, Per-medjed, modern el-Bahnasa, was called *Oxyrhynchus* in the Ptolemaic–Roman Periods after the cult of the fish. Nothing is known of the archaeology of the site before the Ptolemaic Period, but excavations between 1896 and 1907 produced huge quantities

Figure 2.5 Map of Upper Egypt from the seventeenth to the twenty-second nome, with the Fayum.

of papyri which describe the theatres, baths, temples and other public buildings associated with a Greek town. It continued to be important into late Roman times. The papyri, mostly in Greek, but with some in Latin, Demotic, Coptic and Arabic, are informative about the society, culture, economics and religion of the town throughout the Roman Period. There were also many fragments of literary texts.

The twentieth nome, Nar-khent, 'Upper sycamore-fig', stood in a commanding position at the entrance to the Fayum. The chief town was originally called Nenu-sut, or Nen-nesut, later becoming Hu(t)-nen-nesut, which is found in Assyrian texts as Khininshi and Hebrew as Hnes, and is the origin of the Arabic Ahnas or Ehnasya. The Greeks identified the chief god of the town, a ram-headed creator god, Herishef, with Herakles, hence the town's late name, *Herakleopolis*. The town became politically significant in the First Intermediate Period when it replaced Memphis as the principal residence city under the 'house of Khety': no significant remains of that phase have yet been recovered. The evidence of late New Kingdom papyri shows that there were many settlements in the nome, including significant numbers of veteran soldiers of Asiatic origin. In the later part of the Third Intermediate Period, the town was again important as the seat of Libyan pharaoh, Pef-tjau-awy-Bast.

The twenty-first nome, Nar-pehut, 'Lower sycamore-fig', included the residence city of the twelfth-dynasty pharaohs at Itj-tawy (el-Lisht), and the early fourth-dynasty pyramid and elite cemetery at Mer-tem (Medum). The northern boundary of the nome lay between Itj-tawy and Dashur.

The northernmost nome of Upper Egypt, the twenty-second, lay on the east bank. Called 'the Knife', its principal town was Tep-ihu (Ar. Atfih), and its patron deity 'the white cow', a form of the goddess Hathor (hence the Greek name, *Aphroditopolis*).

LOWER EGYPT

The broad expanse of the Delta presents a very different landscape to the valley. The shape of the Delta coastline has changed significantly since prehistoric times, with the formation of a series of large shallow lagoons separated from the Mediterranean by coastal sand ridges: from east to west these are el-Manzala, el-Buruillus, Edku and Maryut. In ancient times there was certainly extensive marshland and swamp along the southern edges of these lakes. Into Ptolemaic times the Delta was one of the major papyrus-producing regions. Used for a range of purposes as well as the manufacture of 'paper', the plant had to be processed quite close to where it was cut.

Immediately to the north of Cairo, the Nile divides into two main branches, the Rosetta and Damietta, but in ancient times there were three main rivers, and four branches from these. It is difficult to trace the ancient river courses accurately, and no doubt they changed over time, and were developed by clearing and digging. The main channels were the Pelusiac, the Sebennytic and the Canopic, known to the Egyptians as the waters 'of Ra', 'of Amun' and 'of Ptah'. The Mendesian and Saitic were lesser natural branches, and the Bolbitine and Bucolic artificial ones.

The eastern Delta was more developed and settled than the western. This was due to the spread of a natural feature across the eastern Delta: sandy islands, usually known by the Arabic term *gezira* (also called turtle-backs), that rise up to 12 metres (39 feet) above the surrounding land. These were ideal places for settlement.

The first nome of Lower Egypt was Inbu-hedj, literally the 'White Walls', but sometimes rendered as the 'White Castle' or 'White Fortress'. This was the name of the fortified enclosure founded by 'Meni' as the new capital for a united Egypt. It was also called Mekhat-tawy, the 'Balance of the Two Lands', from its position between the Delta and valley. This early settlement was probably in the vicinity of Abusir. Throughout the Old Kingdom the royal residence moved with the royal burial site, from Saqqara south to Medum and Dashur, north to Giza and Abu Rawash, and south again to Abusir and Saqqara. The name of one of the royal burial places, the Pyramid of Pepi I, called 'Mery-ra-men-nofer', 'Meryra is established and perfect', was abbreviated as Men-nofer (Gk *Memphis*), and by the time of the New Kingdom was generally applied to the whole town. Another name, that of the main religious complex, also became general: Hut-ka-ptah, used in the Ramesside Period for the town, became in Greek *Aigyptos*.

The principal gods of Memphis were: Tatjenen, representing the earth as it appeared from the flood waters; the bull Apis; the creator

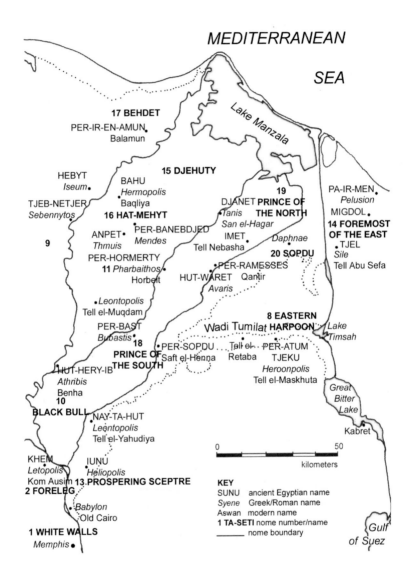

Figure 2.6 Map of Lower Egypt, eastern nomes.

god, Ptah, with his consort, Sakhmet, and child, Nefertum; Hathor, the 'Lady of the southern Sycamore-fig'; and the goddess Neith. The presiding deity of the cemetery region was the falcon, Sokar, who later merged with Ptah and Osiris.

Although the royal residence moved around in the Old Kingdom, in the New Kingdom the palace and temple quarters appear to have become anchored. An eastward movement of the river may have played a crucial role in the city's development, creating new land. In the Ramesside Period there was a quarter for traders from western Asia, and the cults of the Asiatic deities Baal, Qadesh, Astarte and Baal-Zephon were celebrated. Later, Herodotos refers to the 'camp of the Tyrians' as part of the city. Peru-nefer, the port of Memphis, probably lay in the northern part of the city.

Immediately to the north of Memphis was the second nome, 'Foreleg', which had a form of Horus, Khenti-irty, also called Khenty-Khem, as its presiding deity. The capital, Khem (Gk *Letopolis*, Ar. Kom Ausim) has not been fully explored. The tenth nome, the 'Black Bull', stood in a controlling position in the south central Delta, with its capital at Hut-hery-ib (Gk *Athribis*, Ar. Benha). Although it is known to have existed by the fourth dynasty, and statues of Middle and New Kingdom date have been found, the evidence for large architectural monuments is of the later periods. The town and its ruler played a key role in the conflict between the Saite chief Tefnakht and the Kushite king Piye in the eighth century BC. The surviving remains of the temple of the chief god, Horus-khenty-khety, date from the time of the Kushite pharaoh Taharqo and the succeeding twenty-sixth dynasty.

On the east bank of the Nile, controlling the major crossing point, was the thirteenth nome, 'Prospering Sceptre'. The nome's capital, Iunu ('the Pillar', Gk *Heliopolis*), was already a major religious centre in the Old Kingdom, and remained one of the three most important cities in Egypt. Here the forms of the sun-god, as Ra, Harakhty, Atum and Khepri, sometimes combined, were worshipped. Little remains of the vast temples: most of the obelisks and statues were removed to Alexandria, and later to Rome. In addition to the temples of the individual gods, there were other shrines such as the Hut-ben-ben, which had a sacred stone (*ben-ben*) in the form of an obelisk or pyramidion as its focus. The Hut-bennu honoured the manifestation of the sun-god as a heron ('phoenix'). The goddesses Ius-aas and Hathor were revered as consort and daughter of the sun. Iunu was also the seat of Egyptian law, and archives of documents were preserved there. The reputation of Heliopolis as the centre of Egyptian learning and wisdom was maintained through Roman literature into the European traditions about Egypt. Iunu stood on the route taken by invading armies approaching Memphis, and its decline seems to have begun with the Persian invasions of 525 BC and 343 BC. In the Roman Period the Persian fortress near the river at Per-Hapy played an increasingly important role. It was rebuilt as 'Babylon' (Old Cairo) and its fall was a key event in the Arab conquest of Egypt. To the north of Iunu was Nay-ta-hut (Gk *Leontopolis*). An important archaeological site, it has produced material from Middle Kingdom dates onwards. A large enclosure with Ramesside statuary and numerous glazed tiles marks the site of a late New Kingdom palace. The modern name Tell el-Yahudiya ('mound of the Jew') derives from the town and temple built in the reign of Ptolemy VI by the exiled Jewish high priest Onias and his followers: this flourished until the reign of Vespasian (AD 70).

For much of Egyptian history, the east was the more important and densely settled part of the Delta. This was due to the natural *geziras*, and also to the importance of the land and sea routes to Sinai and western Asia. In the New Kingdom a large area of the eastern Delta had its main centre at Imet (Tell Nebasha). The remains of a temple to the goddess Wadjyt survive, with reused Middle Kingdom sphinxes and statuary. A Late Period cemetery and Ptolemaic–Roman town site show the town's continued importance on the route to the eastern border. By the Ptolemaic Period the whole region was divided into the eighteenth and nineteenth nomes.

The chief town of the eighteenth nome, Imu-khenty, 'Prince of the South', was Per-Bast (Gk *Bubastis*, Ar. Zagazig), standing on the main routes from Memphis to Sinai and Asia. Extensive monuments from the Old Kingdom onwards reveal the town's importance. Ramesses II and his successors settled large numbers of Libyans in the vicinity, and Per-Bast's greatest prominence was during the Third Intermediate Period, when it was endowed by descendants of some of those Libyans who became pharaohs. In the ruins of the temple of the goddess Bast are numerous granite statues of

Ramesses II (perhaps brought from Per-Ramesses) and of the 'festival hall' of Osorkon II. Herodotos describes the temple as it appeared in his day and the celebration of the 'festival of drunkenness'.

East of Per-Bastet lay the Wadi Tumilat, the eighth nome, called 'Eastern Harpoon', connecting the Delta waterways with the Red Sea. At the western end of the wadi was Per-Sopdu (Ar. Saft el-Henna) where there are the remains of a large temple enclosure dedicated to the falcon god Sopdu, patron of the east. The wadi was used by seasonal migrants from Sinai into Egypt, and was always an important strategic zone. The evidence is richest from the later periods when the twenty-sixth dynasty pharaoh, Nekau II, constructed a canal along the length of the wadi. This was cleared and enlarged by the Persian pharaoh, Darius, and later by the Ptolemies. The main city, Tjeku, was also called Per-Atum (Gk *Pithom*, also *Heroönpolis*) after its principal god; it is generally identified with Tell el-Maskhuta. The canal was later extended to reach Babylon (Old Cairo).

To the north-east of Per-Bast was the twentieth nome, Per-Sopdu, and the nineteenth nome, Imu-pehu, 'Prince of the north'. This region played a key role in Egyptian history at different periods. The settlement at Hut-waret (Gk *Avaris*, Ar. Tell el-Daba) grew to become a major city and contact point between Egypt and Canaan from the later Middle Kingdom through the Second Intermediate Period. It was the capital of the 'Hyksos' rulers, and was eventually captured and destroyed by the Theban ruler Kamose and his successor, Ahmose. There was renewed building in the late eighteenth and the nineteenth dynasties, including a temple to the god Seth. The ruling family of the nineteenth dynasty came from this region, if not from the town itself. At nearby Qantir, extensive remains of a palace structure, including many glazed tiles, indicate that this was probably the site of the new residence city of the nineteenth-dynasty pharaohs completed by Ramesses II as 'Per-Ramesses Great of Victories'. It is described in a number of contemporary documents and had temples to the chief gods of Egypt. Some monuments remain on the site, but the majority were removed under the Libyan pharaohs to adorn their new residence city at Djanet (biblical Zoan, Gk *Tanis*, Ar. San el-Hagar). Djanet probably began as the port for Per-Ramesses, its importance increasing in the later twentieth dynasty when the Nile branch silted up. The city first appears prominently in the reign of

Ramesses XI, and was important in the trade with the Levant. Excavations at the site began in the mid-nineteenth century and have produced numerous reused Middle Kingdom and Ramesside statues and sphinxes. The huge temple complex that has been excavated represents only one small part of the whole site. It was dedicated to Amun and was built by Pa-seba-kha-en-niut ('Psusennes'), Osorkon II and Sheshonq III. All three pharaohs were buried in tombs in an area adjacent to the temple.

The fourteenth nome, Khenty-iabty, 'Foremost of the East', was Egypt's most vulnerable point. In the Old Kingdom there was a defensive system named the 'Walls of Sneferu', perhaps a chain of forts; in the Middle Kingdom a similar line was called the 'Walls of the Ruler'. There is more detail from the New Kingdom, including a depiction in the temple at Karnak, showing small forts with access to wells, and a crocodile-infested canal. The main frontier fortress was Tjel (Gk *Sile*, Ar. Tell Abu Sefa), which controlled access to the 'Ways of Horus' which then ran through Pa-ir-men (Gk *Pelusion*, Ar. Tell el-Farama) and along the coast to Gaza.

The central Delta has only recently become the subject of major archaeological survey and excavation. The risks posed by environmental changes and increased farming have now directed attention to the region, with remarkable results. The eleventh nome, 'Ox Count', was originally administered from the cult centre of Hor-merty, called Per-Hor-merty (Gk *Pharbaithos*, Ar. Horbeit). In Ptolemaic times, the capital was Leontopolis, the extensive archaeological site of Tell el-Muqdam. This had probably achieved prominence earlier as the seat of Libyan princes and the pharaoh Iuput. Its temple was dedicated to the 'fierce-eyed lion' god, Mahes (Gk *Mihos*), son of the goddess Bastet.

To the north lay the sixteenth nome, with a fish as its emblem, named after its early goddess Hat-mehyt. A ram became the most important deity in later times. The Egyptian word *ba* can mean both 'ram' and 'soul', the god becoming the 'Ram (or soul) Lord of Djedet', Ba-neb-djedet. There are extensive remains at two sites very close together, Anpet (also Djedet, Gk *Thmuis*, Ar. Tell el-Timai) and Per-Ba-neb-djedet (Gk *Mendes*, Ar. Tell el-Ruba), the power-base of the pharaohs of the twenty-ninth dynasty. The earliest evidence is from the fourth dynasty, with other remains of the New Kingdom to Ptolemaic–Roman Periods, including a necropolis of sacred rams. To the west, the fifteenth nome, Djehuty (Thoth) or 'Ibis', had Bahu (also Per-Djehuty-wep-rehwy, Gk *Hermopolis*, Ar. el-Baqliya) as its capital, where the surviving monuments are mostly late. The seventeenth nome, Behdet, was close to the sea. At Per-iu-en-Amun, 'The island of Amun' (Ar. el-Balamun), evidence for an enormous Late Period temple enclosure has recently been found, attesting the significance of some of these previously ignored sites.

The ninth nome was originally sacred to Andjety, but he was soon merged with Osiris, who gave his name to the later town, Busiris (Ar. Abusir). To its north lay the twelfth nome, with the calf and cow as its emblem. The chief deity was Inheret-Shu (Onuris). The principal town, Tjeb-netjer (Gk *Sebennytos*, Ar. Samannud) was the ancestral home of the pharaohs of the thirtieth dynasty, and of the priest Manetho who wrote a history of Egypt in the reign of Ptolemy II. The surviving monuments reflect this period of the town's importance, the temple of Nakhthorheb being completed by Alexander IV, Philip Arrhidaios and Ptolemy II. A little to the north of Tjeb-netjer, the pharaohs of the thirtieth dynasty constructed a large temple to their patron goddess, Isis, at Hebyt (Gk *Iseum*, Ar. Behbeit el-Hagar). A block from this temple was later removed to the temple of Isis on the Campus Martius in Rome, and along with the other Late Period sculptures which were found in that temple, helped to form the Western image of the Egyptian artistic style.

The nome of the 'Mountain Bull' had Khasu (Gk *Xois*, Ar. Sakha) as its capital, although little is known of this area of the north central Delta. To the north-west the two mounds, Tell Farain, mark the twin cities of Pe and Dep, later known as Buto. Sacred to the cobra goddess Wadjyt, one of the patron deities of Lower Egypt, it was an ancient city, and early Egyptologists thought that it was the capital of Lower Egypt prior to the unification. Recent excavations have shown that in the later Predynastic Period there were strong contacts between Buto and western Asia.

The nome of the goddess Neith was divided into two parts in the twelfth dynasty. By the Ptolemaic Period, the southern part, the fourth nome, 'Southern Shield', was called *Prosopis*, after its main town. The fifth nome, 'Northern Shield', contained the former nome capital and ancient city of Sau (Gk *Sais*, Ar. Sa el-Hagar). This was dominated by the temple of Neith. In the Third Intermediate Period the western Delta came under the rule of Libyan princes with the

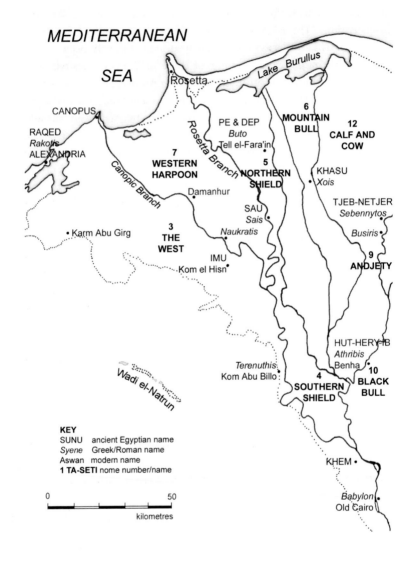

MEDITERRANEAN

SEA   Rosetta   Lake Burullus

CANOPUS   6
                        PE & DEP   MOUNTAIN
RAQED   Buto   BULL   12
Rakotis   Tell el-Fara'in   CALF AND
ALEXANDRIA   COW
                  7
              WESTERN   5   KHASU
              HARPOON   NORTHERN   Xois
                          SHIELD
                  Damanhur   TJEB-NETJER
                                           Sebennytos
                       SAU
                       Sais   Busiris
   • Karm Abu Girg   3
                    THE   Naukratis   9
                    WEST   ANDJETY
                       IMU
                    Kom el Hisn

                                          HUT-HERY-IB
                                           Athribis
                    Terenuthis   Benha   10
                    Kom Abu Billo   4   BLACK
                                     SOUTHERN   BULL
Wadi el-Natrun   SHIELD

KEY
SUNU   ancient Egyptian name
Syene   Greek/Roman name
Aswan   modern name   KHEM •
1 TA-SETI nome number/name

0   50   Babylon
                                           Old Cairo
        kilometres

Figure 2.7 Map of Lower Egypt, western nomes.

title Great Chief of the Libu. Under Prince Tefnakht they extended their power east towards the central Delta, and south to Memphis. Tefnakht's ambitions to reunite Egypt were thwarted by the Kushite ruler of Thebes and Upper Egypt, Piye. Tefnakht appears to have assumed royal style, as did his successor, Bakenranef, who also captured Memphis, but was defeated (c. 709 BC) by Piye's successor, Shabaqo. The Saites eventually succeeded in their ambitions, with Assyrian support, and Psamtik I asserted his control over the whole country. His long reign, and those of his successors (dynasty 26, 664–525 BC), was a period of renewal in Egypt. Sau was lavishly endowed by the pharaohs, who were buried in tombs adjacent to the temple of their city goddess. Many monuments from the city were later taken to Rome.

Under the early Libyan rulers, Sau may have been able to take advantage of trade with the Phoenicians, who had established colonies in Libya and the western Mediterranean. Later, the twenty-sixth-dynasty pharaohs fostered trade with the Greeks, allowing them to build a city on one of the main branches of the river, and eventually granting them a trade monopoly. *Naukratis* (the archaeological sites of Kom el-Gieif and Nibeira) was probably on the site of an earlier Phoenician trading centre. It had temples to the Greek deities, and was reputedly visited by many eminent Greeks, including Solon, Plato and Herodotos.

The third nome lay on the west side of the Rosetta branch of the river as far as lake Mariotis. Called Imentet 'the West', it was presided over by the goddess Hathor, who took the title Nebet-Imu, Mistress of Imu, from the principal town of the New Kingdom and later periods, Imu (Kom el-Hisn). Hathor was also worshipped at *Terenuthis* (Kom Abu Billo) as Nebet-mefket, the 'Mistress of Turquoise'. The site has produced archaeological material from the fourth dynasty to the Ptolemaic–Roman Periods, although it is for the latter that it is best known.

To the far west lay the seventh nome, the 'Western Harpoon', presided over by the god of the deserts, Ha. Lake *Mariotis* (Ar. Maryut) is a long narrow lagoon, parallel to the sea and separated from it by a strip of land. The small town of Ra-qed (Gk *Rakotis*) stood on this coastal strip, and was refounded as Alexandria in 332 BC. The Ptolemies connected the lake to a branch of the Nile, forming a major navigation link with the Delta and valley. On the south of the lake there was rich agriculture, with wine and olive production.

Egypt spread out from the valley and Delta into the deserts. The Wadi el-Natrun is a depression to the west of the Delta, some 60 kilometres (about 40 miles) long. It is all that remains of an ancient lake, now reduced to a number of small lakes 23 metres (70 feet) below sea level, fed by the water table of the Nile. The wadi's major importance was, as its name indicates, as a source of natron. This combination of sodium carbonate and sodium bicarbonate occurs naturally, forming a crust around the edges of the lakes. It was used for cleansing in ritual and in the process of mummification.

The Fayum, often described as an 'oasis', is a large basin immediately to the west of the Nile Valley. Lake Qarun, ancient Mer-wer, 'great lake' (Gk *Moeris*), is now some 65 kilometres (40 miles) long from east to west and 44 metres (135 feet) below sea level, but has shrunk considerably since ancient times. The lake originally filled the entire depression, and the earliest human evidence in Egypt, from Palaeolithic sites, is from sites on the margins. Rather than a simple process of shrinking, the lake appears to have had considerable fluctuations in its size throughout historical times. In the Middle Kingdom, the pharaohs of the twelfth dynasty founded settlements on the southern edge of the depression, perhaps part of a land reclamation project. They also constructed a large barrier at el-Lahun which directed flood waters into the basin. The major residences and burial places of these pharaohs were near the entrance to the Fayum, at Itj-tawy (el-Lisht), Hawara, and el-Lahun. With the exception of Shedyt (Medinet Fayum), most pre-Ptolemaic settlements are on the southern edges of the basin. There were settlements of army veterans in the Fayum from New Kingdom times onwards. The first were Asiatics, then, in Ptolemaic times, Greeks and Macedonians. The major development of the region began with Ptolemy II, who founded numerous new settlements, most with temples to forms of the crocodile god Sobek (Gk *Souchos*). The whole of the Fayum flourished throughout the Ptolemaic and Roman Periods, and life there is detailed from finds of papyrus documents.

Further out in the desert there are other depressions of the desert with lakes and wells. There has been an increase in archaeological investigation of these regions in recent years, and evidence now ranges from prehistoric (including dinosaur fossils) to Roman times.

The northernmost oasis, Bahariya, was reached easily from the Fayum and northern Middle Egypt. The archaeological evidence excavated so far ranges from the New Kingdom to the Late Period. Bahariya was renowned for its wine production in ancient times.

From Bahariya it was possible to travel through a series of small oases to Siwa. Whether this route was regularly used in dynastic times is unknown, although there is Roman evidence for settlement in these inhospitable places. Egyptian evidence from Siwa begins in the Late Period, when temples were constructed by the pharaohs of the twenty-sixth and thirtieth dynasties. During this time the oracle of the local god Ammon rose to international fame, its advice regularly sought by the Greek city-states, and eventually by Alexander the Great.

Another road led from Bahariya south to Farafra, the westernmost oasis, standing on the edge of the Great Sand Sea. Most archaeological evidence from Farafra is of Roman date, although it is referred to in texts of earlier periods. Much more important was the oasis of Dakhla, where excavations have uncovered the Old Kingdom administrative centre and governors' tombs. In the early Libyan Period some members of the Theban elite were exiled to Dakhla. There was extensive development in the Roman Period, reflected in the large sites and temples still well preserved.

Kharga was the oasis closest to the Nile Valley, with routes across the desert plateau connecting it with the important towns of Upper Egypt, Edfu, Esna and Tjeny. Little has been discovered earlier than the Persian Period, and the largest sites are of Roman date, but the oasis certainly played an important role much earlier. In the sixth dynasty, the official Harkhuf set out on his long journey into Nubia from Tjeny, passing through Kharga, and this route was no doubt important at all times. In the late New Kingdom groups of Libyans from further west, possibly Cyrenaica, entered Egypt through the oases, as far south as Kharga, threatening Thebes and the towns around Abedju and Tjeny.

In the complex relationship with the lands to the south of the First Cataract, the Egyptians continued to use natural barriers along the river as defensible frontiers. In the Middle Kingdom the new southern border was the Second Cataract; in the early New Kingdom it was the third, and finally the fourth. Egyptian activity in Nubia was not confined to the Nile Valley, and the wadis that scour the

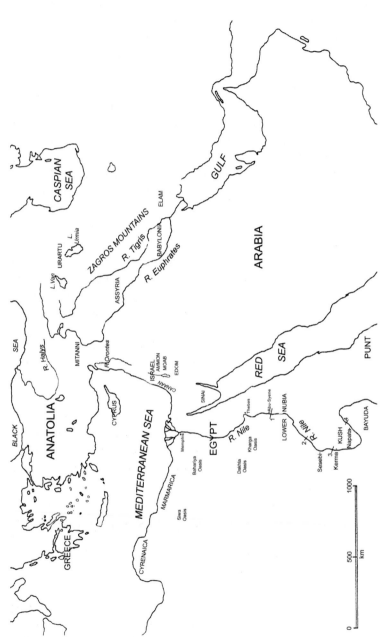

Figure 2.8 Map of the Egyptian world.

Eastern Desert were a major source of gold: they also connected Upper Egypt and Wawat (Lower Nubia) with lands much further south. The pharaohs of the New Kingdom maintained a river frontier at the Fourth Cataract and desert frontier in the region of Kurgus, but their military, economic and political activities went further south, into the savannah lands between the Nile and Atbara. Possibly by this land route, and certainly by the Red Sea routes, the Egyptians intermittently sent trading expeditions to the land of Punt. Once thought to be the 'Horn of Africa', Punt was probably in the northern part of Ethiopia or Eritrea. Egyptian activities in Africa certainly ranged as far as they did in western Asia. These regions of north-east Africa supplied incense, ivory, ebony, ostrich feathers and eggs, cheetah skins and a range of other 'luxury' commodities that played a vital role in international trade.

To the east and north-east, Egypt was active in Sinai from the Predynastic Period, the main lure being the exploitation of the turquoise and copper mines. From the second dynasty there were direct contacts by sea with the coastal cities of Tyre, Sidon, Byblos and Ugarit, and the island of Cyprus. Of these, Byblos was probably the most important trading partner, controlling the cutting of valuable timber, cedar and pine, in the Lebanon range. The range of direct and indirect contacts spread much further, to the lands beyond the Jordan, to north Syria, Anatolia and eastwards into Mesopotamia. The farthest limit is represented by the trade in lapis-lazuli, mined in Badakhshan in Afghanistan, and traded through Iran and Mesopotamia. Major contacts with India and Ceylon did not come about until the Ptolemaic and Roman Periods, with the opening of the routes along the Red Sea to the Arabian Sea and Indian Ocean.

WHAT DID ANCIENT EGYPT LOOK LIKE?

It is easy to be beguiled by the landscape of modern Egypt, and by nineteenth-century orientalist paintings that depicted it as an unchanging 'biblical' world. Ancient Egypt *may* have looked much as parts of rural Egypt do today, but it is actually quite difficult to reconstruct the appearance of the landscape. The scenes in Egyptian tombs are highly selective in what they depict, and 'landscapes' are extremely rare. We know that there were extensive areas of marsh and papyrus swamp in the Delta and Fayum. There was presumably reed and papyrus at the river margins elsewhere in the valley. In this brief survey of the country and its divisions, the important 'towns' have been named, perhaps suggesting a landscape that we are familiar with in the West: larger towns with smaller outlying villages and hamlets in the surrounding countryside. Unfortunately, our knowledge of how the population was spread throughout the land is still very limited, and most Egyptian 'towns' were rather different from our expectations of urban settlements. But if it is difficult to assess what the Egyptian world actually looked like, it is even more difficult to understand what it sounded like. From the vocalization of the Egyptian language to the form of its music, the Egyptian sound world largely eludes us.

3

ESOTERIC KNOWLEDGE AND ORIENTAL MYSTERY
The lure of Egypt

Why are we drawn to study ancient Egypt? However our interests may develop, whatever branches of the subject we may ultimately study, we are nearly all drawn initially (even if we deny it) by something that is romantic, exotic or thrilling. It may be the stories of 'great discoveries', such as the tomb of Tutankhamun; it may be the 'mystery' of the pyramids; it may be mummies; it may be 'esoteric knowledge'; it may be the pursuit of black heritage; it may be, although perhaps less now than ever before, the biblical stories. In 'the West' there is a wide range of traditions, images and interpretations of Egypt that make it part of our cultural background. Some of these visions of Egypt are spurned by academic Egyptology, but they all have their roots in the Western traditions associated with the country.

Egyptology is generally said to begin with the French ('Napoleonic') expedition of 1798. The opening of Egypt to the West, the 'discovery' of the 'Rosetta Stone', and, more precisely, the decipherment of hieroglyphics, first announced in 1822, enable Egyptologists to mark the 'birth' of their subject and to draw a very clear line between 'true' Egyptology and everything that went before. Many Egyptologists will say that pre-Napoleonic views of Egypt, and particularly attempts to understand hieroglyphics, are at best mere antiquarianism, more likely downright nonsense. We might acknowledge the works of Greek and Roman writers on Egypt, but generally point out where they are 'wrong', and, perhaps with some surprise, credit them when they are 'right': the Greeks and Romans, after all, had the advantage that they were close enough in time to observe what many Egyptologists still regard as the death throes of ancient Egypt. The interest of medieval and Renaissance writers in Egypt, particularly in the 'Hermetic Corpus', is usually dismissed by Egyptologists as being of no worth. A little more attention might be paid to the seventeenth century, emphasizing the attempts of Athanasius Kircher to decipher hieroglyphic: he will probably be lampooned. So, generally, these early writers will be referred to only to provide quotes to make an entertaining lecture, or chapter, in which we can reveal just how silly our predecessors really were, and how 'advanced' we are, because, after all, 'we know better'. Serious interest in Egypt, we will be told, began in the mid-eighteenth century with 'travellers' going south of Cairo and bringing back some small objects, and publishing accounts of their travels. This 'empirical' observation of Egypt and its artefacts laid the foundations that were to motivate the scholarly expedition of 1798, and even if the histories begin earlier, the authors will still state that 'scientific' Egyptology really begins with that expedition.

In the history of Egyptology, the Napoleonic expedition is certainly a pivotal point, and it makes a convenient starting point for written studies, but we rarely ask the question *why* was Napoleon in Egypt with an army of scholars? (The political issues are separate.) The intellectual background to Napoleon's expedition owes much more to what Egyptologists have dismissed as 'esoteric' than we might readily acknowledge. Another important factor is that, in terms of interest in, and knowledge about, ancient Egypt, the Napoleonic expedition is not the beginning, but marks the culmination of three centuries (at least) of Western European fascination with the country.

We can, for convenience, use the Napoleonic expedition as a beginning, but we should not dismiss out of hand what went before, nor assume that what followed was purely 'scientific' and 'transparent'. Traditions relating to Egypt are part of the foundation of European culture. There are numerous historical 'facts' and descriptions of the people, the country and its monuments, its customs and, particularly, its religion preserved by Greek and Roman writers. Egypt also figures in Greek myth, epic and drama. Many of the novels, or romances, written in the Hellenistic and Roman Periods have an Egyptian episode, deliberately used to add a touch of the exotic. Egypt is equally important to the biblical traditions, both Old and New Testaments, and to early Christianity, as the desert

home of monasticism and numerous saints. Despite this important role in European culture, Egypt has always been a fine example
of the 'Other'. The Greeks and Romans, while acknowledging its
cultural importance, also pointed out the ways in which Egypt
differed from them. Later, throughout medieval and modern times,
Egypt has been part of the Islamic world, and from AD 1516 specifically of the Ottoman Empire, distancing it from Western Europe by
religion as well as politics. The attraction of this exotic 'oriental'
location is clear in Western writing and painting throughout the
eighteenth and particularly the nineteenth centuries, in the works
of figures as various as Gérôme, David Roberts, Edward Lear,
Gustave Flaubert, Gerard de Nerval and Amelia Edwards.

So, despite the 'birth' of Egyptology in the early years of the nineteenth century, we should not think that the *attitude* had changed
dramatically overnight, that the shroud of mysticism had suddenly
been rent asunder and that Egypt was now seen within the clear
light of a new scientific dawn. The founders of Egyptology in the
nineteenth century brought to their studies, as *we* still do, all of the
preconceptions, prejudices, strengths and failings of their education,
their time and their personality. And their education was rooted in
the classical and the biblical traditions.

THE CLASSICAL TRADITION

For the ancient world of Greece and Rome, Egypt was exotic and
different in many ways. This appears quite clearly in the writings
of Herodotos, Diodoros and many others. But although it was
different, Egypt was culturally immensely influential. The Greeks
were quite explicit about the influence of Egypt on their philosophy
and religion, and many leading Greek politicians and thinkers were
said to have travelled there, among them the Athenian lawgiver
Solon, the mathematician Pythagoras, the philosopher Plato and
Thales of Miletos, one of the important early scientists. Herodotos
of Halikarnassos is the first Greek traveller, in the fifth century BC,
to have left an extensive account of Egypt, an account that has
inspired numerous readers and generated considerable scholarly
debate as to its accuracy. Ancient tradition claimed that most of
these Greeks had visited the trading centre of Naukratis, in the
western Delta, and the chief centre of sun worship, *Heliopolis* (the

ancient Iunu), which was also thought to be the major centre of Egyptian learning.

The 'classical' literature on Egypt was, and generally still is, treated in a very different way from the literature of the Medieval Period, the Renaissance and the Enlightenment. Egyptologists state that, while they did get things wrong, misinterpret, or were deliberately misled, the Greek and Roman authors include 'facts' that can be used in the reconstruction and interpretation of ancient Egypt. Of course, deciding what is and is not 'fact' is a source of constant argument. But 'fact' was not necessarily what the reading (or read to) public of the Hellenistic and Roman worlds sought: Egypt provided a touch of the 'other', of fantasy. The regions beyond Egypt were treated in the same way, and the relative lack of direct experience meant that their human and animal occupants became the ancient equivalent of science fiction. 'Things Egyptian' found their way into the world of interior decoration, and numerous villas throughout the Roman world were decorated with mosaics and paintings that included 'Egyptian' animals and birds – ibises, crocodiles and hippopotami – and episodes from myth, such as the battle of the pygmies with the cranes. They may have been chosen for religious reasons (if the owners were devotees of Isis and the Egyptian cults) or they may have been purely decorative.

One particular question fascinated the Greeks and Romans: where was the source of the Nile? It is a key element in Herodotos's description of Egypt, and is said to have motivated Alexander the Great of Macedon in his world travels. Indeed, at the time of his death, Alexander was reputed to be arranging a further expedition into *Aithiopia* (modern Nubia, Sudan and Ethiopia) expressly to find the source. Later, both Ptolemy II (reigned 285–246 BC) and the emperor Nero (reigned AD 54–68) sent fleets beyond Meroe (in Sudan) with the same mission, and this subject remained one of interest for (classically educated) Europeans, and was a factor in the 'exploration' of Africa in the eighteenth and nineteenth centuries.

Under the rule of the Ptolemies (323–30 BC), Egypt's new capital, Alexandria, became one of the greatest seats of learning in the Hellenistic world. The works housed in Alexandria's libraries included translations of older Egyptian literature into Greek. There were also new works that contained 'information' and speculation on Egypt and the regions around, covering their history, political philosophy, geography, ethnography and zoology. Much that was contained in these works was then digested in the great encyclopaedic works of the first two centuries AD, such as the *History* of Diodoros of Sicily, the *Natural History* of Pliny and the *Geography* of Strabo, and through them was passed into the European cultural tradition, preserved in Byzantium and in the monasteries.

In the late Ptolemaic and early Roman Periods, there were increasing numbers of visitors to Egypt, some on official visits, others as tourists. The visit that had the most impact, internally and externally, was undoubtedly that of the emperor Hadrian in AD 130. On the journey south, the emperor's lover, Antinous, was drowned in the Nile in Middle Egypt, near the city of *Hermopolis* (Egn Khemenu), the centre of the worship of Thoth, the god of writing and wisdom. Antinous was deified and associated with Osiris. Hadrian founded a new city and cult centre in his honour. Little survives of *Antinoöpolis* (also called *Antinoë*), the modern site of Sheikh Ibada, although its splendid columned streets and temples were well preserved at the time of the French expedition of 1798. Antinous was well known to the *savants* who accompanied Napoleon, as many statues of him had been excavated around Rome from the Renaissance on, notably at the site of Hadrian's imperial villa at Tivoli. These statues, blending Egyptian pharaonic imagery with classical forms, were widely imitated as representing the Egyptian style.

Hadrian represents the interest in Egypt and the considerable enthusiasm that there was for the Egyptian gods in Rome and its empire. The Egyptian cults had spread around the Aegean and eastern Mediterranean in Hellenistic times and had spread to the west by the first century BC. The most popular of the Egyptian cults was that of Isis which, by the early Roman Period, had adopted all the characteristics of a 'mystery religion' requiring initiation.

With Isis came a number of other gods, notably Serapis, who was the Hellenized form of her Egyptian husband Osiris. Serapis, from the Egyptian names Osiris and Apis (the sacred bull of Memphis), combined his Egyptian role as god of the underworld with his Greek counterpart, Hades, with another god associated with resurrection, Dionysos, with Zeus/Jupiter and with Asklepios, god of medicine and healing. The child of this divine couple, Horus, and the god of mummification, Anubis, were two of their chief companions. The satirist, Juvenal (reputedly exiled to Aswan by the emperor Domitian) mocked the Roman lady who was prepared to travel as far as Meroe (in modern Sudan) to bring holy water for the Isiac rituals: but this also emphasizes the importance of the cult among the elite of the Roman world. Priests of Isis (and of other cults) travelled around the empire, and the goddess had her devotees and temples from Cyrene and Sabratha in Libya to London. The temples of Isis at Pompeii and Herculaneum, with their painted scenes of religious rites, were of particular interest after their rediscovery in the eighteenth century, and there were claims that Paris had possessed a major temple to the goddess.

Outside Egypt, one of the most important of the temples of Isis, and certainly the most lavishly endowed, was that in the Campus Martius in Rome. The complex, adjacent to the temple of Serapis and the Pantheon, was decorated with statuary and obelisks. The emperor Caligula (AD 37–41) built the temple, which was also favoured by Vespasian (AD 69–79), Domitian (AD 81–96), and Hadrian (AD 117–38). Caracalla (AD 211–17) built another temple to Isis on the Quirinal hill. The cult of Isis became one of the dominant ones of Late Antiquity.

This Roman interest in Egypt and its religion was to be important in the development of Egyptology in a very practical sense. Augustus and his successors removed obelisks and many other Egyptian sculptures to adorn their capital and other cities of the empire. Rome still has thirteen standing obelisks, some brought from Alexandria (themselves removed from other cities), Sau (*Sais*), and from Iunu (*Heliopolis*), the major centre of the solar gods. There are also obelisks commissioned and inscribed for the emperors, notably that re-erected by Pope Innocent X in the Piazza Navona, which was carved at Aswan for the emperor Domitian, and set up outside the temple of Serapis on the Campus Martius. The sculptures that were recovered from the site of the temples on the Campus Martius during the Renaissance and the eighteenth century were of great importance for the study of Egypt, and for the European idea of what Egyptian art was like.

The world of Late Antiquity was indeed a religious melting pot in which the 'mystery' cults, notably those of Isis, the 'Unconquered Sun' (Sol Invictus), Mithras and Christianity, were blended with the dominant philosophical movement, Neo-Platonism. Egypt, particularly Upper Egypt around *Panopolis* (Akhmim), played an important role in the development of religious ideas, both Christianity and what is generally known as 'Gnosticism'. The ideas preserved in these early Christian and Gnostic texts embraced both Egyptian and non-Egyptian, including Persian, ideas. Many of the religious books produced claimed to be much older than they actually were, and authorship was often attributed to sages of the past or divine figures. The most important of these was Hermes 'Trismegistus' – the 'thrice great', the Hellenized form of the Egyptian god of wisdom, Thoth. Books supposedly written by Thoth were taken to Western Europe in the early Renaissance. This 'Hermetic Corpus' was central to the development of ideas about ancient Egypt until the eighteenth century.

Egypt also figured prominently in novels of the Hellenistic and Roman Period, not only as an exotic location, but also with more than a hint of this religious world. The *Metamorphoses* of Apuleius (more familiar by its alternative name *The Golden Ass*) is set in Greece rather than Egypt, but its underlying theme is initiation into the mysteries of the cult of Isis, and the ultimate redemption of the hero during a festival in honour of the goddess, who then joins her priesthood. The *Aithiopika* of Heliodoros exploits the exotic locations of Egypt and Meroe, but is also an early 'historical novel', being set in the time of Persian rule in Egypt (*c.* 500–400 BC). It owes much to Herodotos's account of Egypt and Meroe, which was, no doubt, familiar to its readers. Heliodoros, whose name means 'gift of the sun', wrote in the third or fourth century AD, and may have included an allegory of initiation into the sun cult in his work. The *Aithiopika* begins at Delphi in Greece, centre of the cult of Apollo, and ends at Meroe in Aithiopia, the place on earth regarded by Greek tradition as being closest to the sun. Commentators from the Renaissance into modern times have understood the narrative as embodying Neo-Platonic ideas, with the incidents in the plot representing the journey through life and the stages of initiation, culminating in the return of the soul to the land of the sun; others have preferred to read it more straightforwardly as a ripping yarn.

This intellectual world was fundamental to the development of Christianity, which became the state religion of the Roman Empire in the early fourth century. Egypt, particularly Alexandria, played an important role in the doctrinal disputes that divided the church during these decades. This was the religious atmosphere in which the powerful force of Christian monasticism emerged in Egypt, notably under the influence of St Anthony. The Christian form of monasticism itself owed much to the Gnostic monasticism of Upper Egypt. Conflict over religious ideas within the church was balanced by the pagan reaction, notably in the reign of Julian (AD 361–3). Christianity triumphed, and the Edict of Theodosius (AD 391) closed the temples within the empire. But that of Isis standing on the Egyptian–Nubian border was left open – for political reasons: the Blemmye peoples of Nubia had been attacking the frontier since the time of Diocletian (AD 286–305) and closure of their major sanctuary would have invited more conflict. Philae remained open until the reign of Justinian (AD 527–65), but by then, even in Nubia, great Isis had been toppled from her seat, and Christianity reigned supreme. However, Christianity in Egypt, as in so many parts of the empire, built on local traditions: nobody would deny the influence of the images of Isis and the infant Horus on those of the Virgin and Child. But other Egyptian gods also found their Christian saintly counterparts: Anubis with St Christopher, Horus with St George and St Michael Archangel. Paradoxically, it was the monastic libraries that played such an important role in preserving the literature of the classical world through the Medieval Period.

THE BIBLICAL TRADITION

Although very few pharaohs are specifically named in the Bible, Egypt figures large. Indeed, in the nineteenth century, the biblical overtook the classical tradition in importance in the early years of archaeology. Egypt and its nameless pharaohs were familiar to the church-going public. There was the pharaoh whose dreams were interpreted by Joseph, and there was the pharaoh of the oppression (generally assumed to be Ramesses II) who ordered the Israelites to build the cities of Pithom and Ramses. Later there was 'Shishak' who sacked Jerusalem, 'So, king of Egypt' and 'Tirhakah' the Kushite pharaoh who came to the aid of Hezekiah of Judah during the Assyrian siege of Jerusalem; there was Necho who fought the Babylonians; and finally there was Hophra (the twenty-sixth-dynasty

pharaoh Wahibre, *Apries*). Egypt occurs in many other biblical contexts, frequently being invoked by the Jewish prophets. Egypt was
also the refuge of the Holy Family in their flight from Herod – so the
biblical attitude towards Egypt was not entirely negative – unlike,
for example, its attitude towards Assyria. In the 1880s, Amelia
Edwards and Flinders Petrie both thought that excavation of sites
with biblical connections would bring in money for the newly
founded Egypt Exploration Fund, and the membership lists show
that they were right.

Christianity had developed rapidly in Egypt in the fourth century
AD and the country had become the great centre of monasticism,
but in AD 642 Egypt was conquered by the Arabs. Gradually,
a process of Islamization, conversion and immigration restricted
Christianity and the native Egyptian language, known as Coptic.
However, Coptic remained the language of the Egyptian church,
and this was to be of great importance in attempts to decipher
hieroglyphic.

Under the rule of the caliphs and sultans, many ancient monuments suffered destruction, but no more than under the pharaohs
themselves. The great ruins of Memphis and Heliopolis, close to
the new centres of al-Fustat and Qahira, were used as quarries. But
there was also an Arab interest in ancient Egypt and its monuments,
and writers of the period provide us with much information. This
has generally been ignored by Egyptology, and is only now being
addressed properly. The medieval Arab scholars also translated
Greek and Roman literature, influences of which can be found in
their accounts of Egypt.

Egypt was not completely cut off from the world of medieval
Europe. The Crusades involved conflict in Egypt; Alexandria
and, to a lesser extent, Cairo were visited by pilgrims *en route* to the
Holy Land. Such monuments as were accessible to European visitors,
or which were remembered from the classical tradition, acquired
a biblical association. As early as the fourth century AD Julius
Honorius claimed that the pyramids were the granaries of Joseph;
this was generally followed and was satisfying for the pilgrims
who passed through Egypt. The idea that the pyramids were Joseph's
granaries became widely accepted even if there was the occasional
dissenting voice, one being the ninth-century Patriarch of Antioch
who claimed that the pyramids were 'astonishing mausoleums, built

on the tombs of Ancient Kings; they are oblique and solid, and not hollow and empty'. But it was as Joseph's granaries that the pyramids were first depicted in Western European art – in the thirteenth-century mosaics of the Basilica of St Mark in Venice – and the interpretation remained popular in succeeding centuries.

FROM RENAISSANCE TO ENLIGHTENMENT

With the Renaissance, there was a renewed interest in Egypt. The literature of Greece and Rome was being printed, widely disseminated and studied anew. In it there was an enormous amount about Egypt. This interest was increased by the statements of ancient authorities that such revered figures as Plato and Pythagoras had visited Egypt and studied there. The works of Plato and the Neo-Platonic school were fundamental to the Renaissance, but, following the fall of Byzantium, more ancient texts were brought to Western Europe. One of the most influential of these 'new' texts was the so-called 'Hermetic Corpus', supposed to have been written by Thoth (Hermes) himself. The Greek manuscript containing the *Corpus Hermeticum* was brought to Florence from Macedonia in 1460. The *Corpus* was widely believed to be genuinely Egyptian in origin, a basic source for Egyptian philosophy and a precursor of Plato's. Whether or not it is of ancient Egyptian origin, the significance of the *Corpus* to Western scholarship and the formation of ideas about Egypt becomes clear when we realize that the translation by Marcilio Ficino appeared in eight editions between its first publication in 1471 and 1500, and that there were 22 editions before 1641.

Around the same time – in 1488 – the new pavement in Siena Cathedral included, as one of the dominant images, 'Hermes Mercurius Trismegistus, the contemporary of Moses'. Typical for its time, Trismegistus is depicted in a costume of loosely oriental type. Trismegistus was thought to have revealed his knowledge to Moses, and he is shown in Siena, like Moses, as a lawgiver. The 'Hermetic Corpus' also tells about the perfect sun-city founded by Hermes Trismegistus. The Hermetic tradition remained important in European constructions of ancient Egypt until the nineteenth century, but since then it has been rejected by Egyptology as, at best, of little value. Indeed, many Egyptologists still doubt its Egyptian origin.

The renewal of interest in Egypt naturally embraced Isis and Osiris, stimulated particularly by study of Plutarch's *On Isis and Osiris*. There were obvious parallels to be drawn between the god's death and resurrection and Christ's, and it was interpreted as an imperfect prefiguring of the passion, even being used to decorate the Papal Apartments in the Vatican.

Egyptian hieroglyphic texts also attracted considerable attention. Renaissance scholars thought that hieroglyphic writing was not simply alphabetic but allegorical. This idea was to have enormous influence until the decipherment of hieroglyphic in the early nineteenth century. A manuscript found in 1419 on the Greek island of Andros and which arrived in Florence about 1422 apparently confirmed the allegorical nature of the Egyptian script. Called *The Hieroglyphics of Horapollo*, it probably dates from the early fourth century AD and comprises 189 chapters, each describing the allegorical meaning of an individual hieroglyph. *Horapollo* is correct in many meanings, if not their explanations. Although there is clearly the vestige of some correct tradition in *Horapollo*, there is no doubt that some of what is preserved belongs to the interpretation of the Egyptian priesthood in the Roman Period. After the invention of printing, *The Hieroglyphics* was one of the first books published, in Venice in 1505, and its allegorical interpretation of hieroglyphs continued to be influential for the next two centuries.

The Renaissance also saw the translation and publication of some of the Hellenistic romances in which Egypt had a prominent role, as well as the philosophical and historical works *The Golden Ass* and the *Aithiopika*, both of which enjoyed a wide circulation.

The spectacular renewal of Rome by the Renaissance popes, culminating in the pontificate of Sixtus V Peretti (1585–90), brought large numbers of ancient statues to light which now form the core of the Vatican collections. Sixtus V had a number of obelisks re-erected, notably those in front of the Basilicas of St John Lateran and St Peter, and the Quirinal Palace. Of course, many of the monuments and works of art uncovered were Roman or Roman copies of Greek and Hellenistic originals, but there were also many Egyptian and Egyptianizing pieces. The major source of these was the area of ancient Rome called the Campus Martius, near the Pantheon and the Church of Santa Maria sopra Minerva, the ancient site of the temples of Isis and Serapis.

The rediscovery and re-erection of obelisks in Rome continued throughout the seventeenth century, and became the basis for hieroglyphic research by Athanasius Kircher (1602–80), a Jesuit with a wide range of expertise. In the 1630s two large collections of manuscripts in the Coptic language arrived in Western Europe, and Kircher was encouraged to work on them. Coptic itself, although still widely spoken in Egypt in the fifteenth century, declined significantly in the sixteenth and seventeenth centuries. As a result of his studies, Kircher, who is held up to ridicule by some Egyptologists, was to make one immensely important claim: that Coptic and pharaonic Egyptian were essentially the same language, and that a knowledge of Coptic was essential for understanding hieroglyphic. Kircher himself went on to publish several volumes on Egyptian hieroglyphic. Kircher's major work, the four-volume *Oedipus Aegyptiaca* (1652–54) did contain some brilliant observations, but, unfortunately, he did not pursue this rationalistic line and generally he identified signs with a philosophic concept rather than a phonetic value, thus following his Renaissance predecessors, the Neo-Platonists, and the Hermetic literature.

Kircher's failure to decipher hieroglyphs discouraged others from following him, but his other works ensured that Coptic became established as a philological discipline, continuing throughout the eighteenth century and supplemented with new manuscripts, resulting in a new dictionary in 1775. The connection between Coptic and pharaonic Egyptian became widely accepted and was to provide the key for Champollion.

Another thread which owes much to the Renaissance Hermetic literature and seventeenth-century Rosicrucians is freemasonry, which in the late seventeenth and early eighteenth centuries began to evolve into its modern form. Throughout the eighteenth century the supposed Egyptian origins of masonry were emphasized, Mozart's *Magic Flute* perhaps being the most renowned expression.

TRAVELLING

The early eighteenth century saw more travellers passing upstream from Cairo and publishing accounts of the monuments. Paul Lucas was sent by Louis XIV to visit Siwa, Thebes, the antiquities near Lake Moeris and the Labyrinth, and 'he will open a pyramid in order to find out in a detailed manner all that this kind of edifice contains'. The places are all those prominent in the classical tradition. Lucas arrived in Alexandria in 1716, but failed to see most of the things he was sent to examine. Others were more successful and by 1740 one French writer commented: 'the only things talked about are the ancient cities of Thebes and Memphis, the Libyan Desert, and the caves of the Thebaid. The Nile is as familiar to many people as the Seine. Even the children have their ears battered with its cataracts and openings.'

In France, enthusiasm for things Egyptian manifested itself in the Abbé Terrasson's *Sethos*, published in 1731. Purporting to be translated from Greek, the work of an Alexandrian of the second century AD, this influential work claimed to reveal the mysteries of Isis and Osiris. It was a fabrication, but nevertheless it was used as a model for the rituals of the Freemasons in the eighteenth century. It also served as the source for a number of musical works, most notably Mozart's *singspiel*, *The Magic Flute* (*Die Zauberflöte*), first performed in Vienna in 1791. The work was a collaboration between Mozart and his friend, and fellow Freemason, Emanuel Schikaneder. The original stage sets and costumes for the production were a mixture of classical and 'oriental' rather than Egyptian, but following the publications of the French expedition, spectacular, and distinctively Egyptian, sets were introduced.

One of the most significant early eighteenth-century travellers was the English clergyman Richard Pococke (1704–65), who arrived in Egypt in 1737 as part of an extended visit to the eastern Mediterranean, including Palestine, Asia Minor and Greece. He visited the 'mummy pits' of Saqqara and the temple of Dendera; he measured the gates of Karnak, and continued on to Armant and Aswan. His account of his travels, published in 1743, included plans of various monuments and a view of the Valley of the Kings with the tombs that were accessible at the time.

Pococke's journey coincided with that of Frederick Norden, quite literally: their boats passed in the night in Upper Egypt, one going upstream, the other downstream. Norden was a Danish artist and naval marine architect who went as far as Derr in Nubia, and his account, published in 1755, was one of the first to give detailed descriptions of monuments. Norden came to England and both he and Pococke were present for the dinner in the Lebeck's Head

Tavern, Chandos Street, Charing Cross, on 11 December 1741 ('the Feast of Isis') to form the first Egyptian Society. At its meetings a sistrum, 'the rattle of Isis', was placed before the President, who was known as 'the Sheich'. One of its founder members, Colonel William Lethieullier, had brought a small collection of antiquities, including a mummy and coffin, reputedly from Saqqara in 1721, and these were bequeathed to the British Museum (as it was to become) in 1756, ranking among its first Egyptian acquisitions.

The Scottish traveller James Bruce arrived in Egypt in 1768 to search for the source of the Nile, which he 'discovered' in 1770 (although a group of Jesuits had been in the same place in 1615). Among his other exploits he described and illustrated scenes in a tomb in the Valley of Kings (that of Ramesses III), which was for a long time after known as 'Bruce's tomb'. He returned to England in 1774 and retired to his Scottish estates, eventually publishing five volumes of his travels in 1790.

Although there were other 'explorers' of this type, as well as merchants dealing with Alexandria and Cairo who brought back small objects, Egypt remained off the 'Grand Tour' – it was too far, and too difficult, to get to. The classical world, particularly Rome, remained the focus; artists and travellers were descending on the city and Italy from all over Europe, forming the collections which now adorn galleries, castles and country houses.

The late eighteenth century also saw further excavations within Rome itself and in the neighbourhood, particularly at Hadrian's Villa, producing quantities of Egyptian and Egyptianizing sculpture. Visitors to Naples saw the first excavations at Pompeii, including the temple of Isis. Although for most visitors to Italy the classical world was their principal goal, things Egyptian were also keenly observed. More travellers were going to the Ottoman Empire, and the political situation was about to open the whole region to the Western gaze.

EGYPT REVEALED

The work of the scholars who accompanied Napoleon's military expedition to Egypt in 1798 is usually regarded as the beginning of modern Egyptology. Their mission was to make a systematic study and publish any and all records of ancient and contemporary

Egypt. Egypt was to be catalogued, from its insects and fish to the social classes of its people, from its ancient remains to its modern condition. Although the scholars who were to do this were part of the empirical movement from which modern academic disciplines have developed, they were also imbued with the traditions about Egypt that can be traced back to the Renaissance.

During the first year or so of their time in Egypt, the French formed a large collection of Egyptian antiquities, which was seized by the British in 1801. The most significant of these was, of course, the 'Rosetta Stone' (now in the British Museum in London). It was 'discovered' in the Delta town in 1799 and its importance immediately recognized. The inscription is written in two languages and three scripts: Egyptian hieroglyphic and Demotic, and Greek. The Greek text was translated and revealed it to be a decree made in 196 BC by a conclave of priests in Memphis in honour of Ptolemy V. The whole text was engraved and published in 1803 and scholars throughout Europe immediately focused their attention on it.

A number of publications resulted from the French expedition, the most significant being the massive folio volumes of the *Description de l'Egypte*. Reasonably accurate illustrations of the monuments of Egypt – ranging from panoramas of the vast temples to details of tomb and temple decoration and small objects – were published in this, and the other accounts, for the first time.

The British and French clash in Egypt was followed by significant political changes in the country. At the start of the nineteenth century, Mohammed Ali, ruling Egypt as the Ottoman viceroy, opened the country to Europeans. Since it was not difficult to obtain an excavation permit, the newly appointed European consuls, diplomatic agents, engineers and businessmen also became archaeologists and antiquities dealers overnight. The treasures they accumulated became the nucleus of dazzling collections in European museums, and 'finds' made while digging major temples and pyramids out of the encroaching sands became the source of new excitement and impetus for the students of Egyptology.

Notable among those who formed large collections were Henry Salt, acting for the British; Bernardino Drovetti, the French vice-consul; Giuseppe di Nizzoli, working for the Austrian consulate; Giuseppe Passalacqua; and Alessandro Ricci. Their acquisitions form the foundations of the museum collections in London, Paris, Turin,

Vienna, Berlin, Dresden and Florence. These new collections included many large statues, architectural elements and small objects and immediately became the focus of scholarly and public interest. As a result, in the period from 1815 to 1840 many Europeans travelled in Egypt and Nubia, some for extended periods. These included significant numbers of artists and architects, some in the employ of wealthy gentlemen, copying scenes from tombs and temples, and producing romantic views of the monuments. Franz Gau, Hector Horeau and David Roberts all published copies of their paintings of Egyptian monuments. These combine keen observation of the architecture and landscape with a romantic and orientalist sensibility, creating some of the most popular and enduring images of the period.

Many writers and artists were lured as much by the 'oriental' present as by the ancient past, and orientalist literature and paintings remained popular throughout the nineteenth century. Painting frequently combined archaeological precision from the new Egyptological publications with landscape (from personal travels or works of other artists) and traditional themes: the death of Cleopatra was always popular, as it merged the orientalist and erotic; biblical stories such as Joseph and the pharaoh, and the finding of Moses appealed to a church-going public. Although background detail might be accurate, the contemporary racial views also had their influence: the Egyptians – at least, the rulers – are nearly always depicted as Europeans.

In the rush to decipher hieroglyphic following the discovery of the Rosetta Stone, it was Jean-François Champollion who was ultimately the most successful, because of his knowledge of the Coptic language. Decipherment of the script was not, however, the same as translation of the texts, and Champollion's sudden, early death in 1832 left his work to be completed by others.

Although remembered for his decipherment, Champollion was also the leading figure behind the joint Franco-Tuscan Expedition of 1828–9. With Ippolito Rosellini, Champollion drew up a detailed plan for the study of the monuments. Rather than publishing the reliefs and tomb paintings in a geographical order, they were now organized historically and culturally. The result was an enormous synthesis of the material completed by Rosellini. In the volumes dealing with Egyptian history, Rosellini brought together all of the ancient classical and biblical sources on Egypt, and tied them, as far as was possible, to the cartouches containing kings' names that had formed the basis for Champollion's decipherment.

The last major expedition to record (and collect) monuments was that of the Prussian Expedition of the Imperial Academy of Berlin, led by Karl Richard Lepsius. From 1842 to 1845, Lepsius and his assistants travelled the entire valley of the Nile far into Sudan, and the deserts surrounding it, surveying monuments and copying inscriptions and scenes in temples and tombs. The publications resulting from all of these expeditions excited considerable interest and rapidly increased knowledge of Egypt and Sudan and their monuments. These volumes still remain important as a record of preservation at the time, and of some monuments that have been completely destroyed since.

A significant development in the subject came with the career of the French Egyptologist Auguste Mariette, who began working in Egypt in 1850. Having seen the irreparable damage that antiquities dealers and art collectors were causing, Mariette urged the establishment of a national service for the care and conservation of standing monuments, and the creation of a museum. As a result, he was appointed Director of Egyptian Monuments in 1858, and a house at Bulaq was set aside to serve as a museum and storage place for excavation finds. This represented a major step towards the eventual formation of the Egyptian Museum of Cairo. Mariette conducted clearing, consolidation and excavation operations all over Egypt.

Mariette's career also symbolizes another important change in attitudes to Egypt. Mariette wrote the plot for the opera *Aïda*, with music by Verdi. *Aïda* was first performed in Cairo on 24 December 1871. The Egypt of *Aïda* is very different to that conjured up by Mozart and Schikaneder in *The Magic Flute*. Mariette's plot and characters belong much more to the world of 'history painting' exemplified by artists such as Laurence Alma-Tadema. Mariette managed to create a classical romance with historical detail culled from the most recently discovered monuments. The conflict between Egyptians and 'Ethiopians' reflects the narratives of several historical inscriptions that had been found at Gebel Barkal in the northern Sudan in 1862, and the names of the Ethiopian king, Amonasro, and the Egyptian princess, Amneris, are those of historical characters (although we would read them differently nowadays). There may be romance, but there is no mysticism or magic.

By the third quarter of the nineteenth century, the confidence of Egyptologists had grown so much that they began to reject the classical writers, and attempted to write 'history from the monuments'. This period saw the discipline of Egyptology distance itself from many of the aspects of the subject that interested its lay audience. Flinders Petrie, Amelia Edwards and their colleagues might exploit the interest of the public in the biblical aspects of ancient Egypt, as a means of gaining funding for excavation, but the more esoteric aspects of the European tradition were now largely rejected by the new university-based and museum-based academic Egyptologists.

It was normal practice for the finds from excavation to be divided between the excavator and the Cairo Museum, with any particularly important pieces remaining in Egypt. This policy considerably enriched museum collections abroad. It also had the effect of preserving material that had previously been ignored or discarded. The wily Flinders Petrie found that there was considerable benefit from saving a range of artefacts that could be given to his sponsors, thereby encouraging their future generosity (many of the artefacts eventually made their way into museum collections). Petrie himself was interested in pottery and other types of artefact that had previously received little scholastic attention. He was also pioneering in his work on the prehistoric phases of Egyptian archaeology.

Egyptology in the nineteenth century was a rapidly developing and dynamic subject. It was a mere half-century between the decipherment of hieroglyphics and the first attempt to write a history entirely from the Egyptian monuments without recourse to the classical tradition. Living in an age of European self-confidence, the pioneers of this period – Egyptologists such as Ipollito Rosellini, Emmanuel de Rougé, Richard Lepsius, Gaston Maspero, Heinrich Brugsch, James Henry Breasted and Flinders Petrie – constructed the framework for Egyptian chronology and history that we still use today. Their ideas were influenced by the increasingly analytical and scientific approaches of many other disciplines, and they generally rejected the esoteric in favour of the 'factual'. A hundred years further on, we know vastly more about ancient Egypt, but we also view the development of Egyptology rather differently. We now acknowledge that medieval, Renaissance, and Enlightenment views of Egypt are interesting in their own right, and that imperialism and racism have played significant roles in the development of academic thought. Perhaps we lack the confidence of our late nineteenth-century and early twentieth-century predecessors, but perhaps we are also more open to what Egypt represents to a wider public.

4

CONSTRUCTING THE EGYPTIAN PAST

The vast span of Egyptian prehistory and history is divided up by Egyptologists into a series of periods – how and why we consider shortly. The basic unit is the dynasty. The most recent literature may have as many as thirty-three of these, numbered from '00' to 31. These dynasties are then grouped together into Kingdoms and Intermediate Periods, preceded and followed by other unnumbered dynasties and periods (in some nineteenth-century works the Ptolemaic and Roman dynasties were given numbers as well). The result (detailed further in the Appendix: King List) is:

— Prehistoric Period
— Predynastic Period
— Early Dynastic Period (older books call it Archaic): dynasty '00' to dynasty 2
— Old Kingdom: usually beginning with dynasty 3, but lasting until dynasty 6, 7 or 8 (depending which book you look at)
— First Intermediate Period: dynasty 7/8 to dynasty 11 part 1
— Middle Kingdom: dynasty 11 part 2 to early dynasty 13
— Second Intermediate Period: dynasty 13 to dynasty 17
— New Kingdom: dynasty 18 to dynasty 20
— Third Intermediate Period: dynasty 21 to dynasty 24 (or 25)
— Late Period: dynasty 25 or 26 to dynasty 31.
— Macedonians
— Ptolemies
— Roman Period
— Byzantine (or Late Antique) Period
— Arab Conquest

Egyptian archaeology during the Dynastic Period has always been tied to the king list. This is a fundamental point because, ultimately, all artefacts in Egypt are tied directly, or indirectly, to material that is dated by royal association. This material is used to date Egyptian material in contexts outside Egypt, and also the cultures in which that material appears.

The basic tool for establishing a chronology for ancient Egypt is the king list because the Egyptians themselves dated by regnal years. Some other ancient societies used an 'era' system ('x years' since a certain event). In classical Greece a system of dating from the first Olympic Games (supposedly 776 BC in our terms) was used along-side local dating systems. In Rome the era system was dated *ab urbe condita* 'from the foundation of the city', which was placed at (what we call) 752 BC, although the exact date was controversial even in ancient times. Another system, used in Mesopotamia as well as Greece and Rome, was to name the year after the chief magistrates (eponym lists). In 1862 Henry Rawlinson found an Assyrian eponym list which runs from 911 BC to 660 BC. The king was one of the officials in his first year, so this tied together the king and the eponym lists. Other ancient societies also used eponym lists; in Athens the eponyms were the archons, and in Rome the consuls. Egypt used none of these other systems, only regnal years, hence the importance of the king list to our interpretation of its historical and cultural development.

The first process for Egyptology was to establish a complete king list. Before the decipherment of hieroglyphic it was not possible to do this directly from the monuments, and scholarship relied on the evidence of Greek and Latin authors. Of these, two were of major importance: the *History* of Manetho and the *Royal Canon* of Ptolemy. To these outline chronologies could be added the evidence of Herodotos and other Greek and Latin writers.

The first 'History of Egypt' was written by the Egyptian priest Manetho in the reign of Ptolemy II around 280 BC. Called *Aigyptiaka* ('On things Egyptian') it was written for the new Ptolemaic ruling dynasty just as a near contemporary Babylonian, Berossos, wrote a history of Babylon for the new Seleukid dynasty. Each historian was setting out to prove that his country was the oldest, a matter of prestige for their new Macedonian rulers.

Manetho is said to have been a priest from Sebennytos (modern Samannud) in the Delta. He may have served at Sebennytos or Heliopolis and is reputed to have written a number of works, most on Egyptian religion. Manetho divided Egyptian history into 31 dynasties, each being a ruling family from a particular city. Undoubtedly, Manetho based his work on Egyptian written sources and traditions, and his dynastic framework probably has some sort of Egyptian tradition behind it. However, no complete version of Manetho's *Aigyptiaka* survives, only abridgements, and the king lists are preserved in the writings of later authors. All ancient books were multiplied by hand copies, and when books such as Manetho's, with its lists of kings and of regnal years, were copied and quoted, error soon crept in. The most important writers to preserve sections of Manetho are Flavios Josephos and the Christian chronographers Africanus and Eusebius.

Flavios Josephos was a Jewish historian of the late first century AD. He was author of *The Antiquities of the Jews*, a history of the Jewish people from the creation to the mid-first century AD. Sextus Julius Africanus of Aelia Capitolina (Jerusalem), was a Christian philosopher who wrote around 217/221 AD. His major work was the *Chronographies*, which covered history, both sacred and profane, from the Creation to AD 221. Eusebius, the Bishop of Caesarea in Palestine (lived *c*. AD 260–339), was the first writer on the history of the Christian church. There are also fragments of Manetho's work preserved in other writers, much of it garbled. A Byzantine monk, George Syncellus (*c*. AD 800), used 'Manetho' in his chronicle of the world from Adam to the reign of the emperor Diocletian (AD 284–305). Syncellus actually used the epitomes of Africanus and Eusebius and the even more inaccurate versions called the *Old Chronicle* and the *Book of Sothis*.

With copying, abbreviation and corruption of texts, by AD 800 the preserved versions of Manetho were so far removed from the original that they were virtually useless. It is, perhaps, hard to see why Egyptologists put so much value on Manetho, but the first Egyptologists had little choice. The texts of Manetho were available to European scholarship, along with much other Greek and Roman literature, from the Renaissance onwards. Without direct access to monuments, and unable to read the hieroglyphic texts, scholars found in Manetho an outline chronology of ancient Egypt, which was then supplemented by information gleaned from Herodotos, Diodoros and many other authors. Indeed, Jean-François Champollion (1790–1832), who is generally regarded as the founder of modern Egyptology, increased Manetho's authority when, in 1828, he announced that he could read the names of some of the Egyptian kings recorded by Manetho on the monuments. Those kings were Achoris (Hakor), Nepherites (Nefaurud), Psammetichos (Psamtik), Osorcho (Osorkon), Sesonchis (Sheshonq), Ramesses and Tuthmosis (Thutmose).

As well as using (sometimes extremely confused) Greek forms of Egyptian names, and occasionally repeating kings, the preserved king lists of Manetho also omit many rulers, and the reign lengths rarely agree in the different versions. As his work survives, it is hopelessly garbled in places. But, despite all of the problems associated with the dynastic divisions, Manetho's system is so ingrained in Egyptology that it is now impossible to discard it; and, despite the problems, the dynastic system is still useful as a building block for Egyptian history. Although there are overlapping dynasties, it is safe to assume that the higher the number, the later the dynasty; and remembering which important rulers – or monuments, such as pyramids – belong in which dynasty does help to form a broad cultural-historical framework.

In the early nineteenth century, scholars attempting to decipher hieroglyphic realized that the cartouche contained royal names, and therefore began to assemble collections of all of those that were visible on monuments. One of the first collections published was in the *Description de l'Egypte*, the result of the French scholarly expedition of 1798. It was also recognized that cartouches were usually paired; one carrying the personal name of the pharaoh, and the other the name that he assumed when he ascended the throne. As European activity in Egypt increased, a number of important ancient lists of kings were found that aided in the reconstruction of the historical framework.

The *Turin Canon of Kings* is preserved on papyrus (now in the Museo Egizio, Turin) and dates from the time of Ramesses II. It was reputedly virtually intact when acquired by the French consul Bernardino Drovetti in 1823 or 1824, but by the time that Champollion looked at it, it was a mass of fragments. A German scholar, Gustav Seyffarth, began to examine the fragments in detail in 1826.

By looking closely at the fibres of the papyrus he was able to reconstruct sections of it. Despite the efforts of other scholars, the papyrus has still not been completely restored to everybody's agreement. It carries a king list divided into groups, with totals of regnal years.

A fragmentary king list carved on a wall in the temple of Ramesses II at Abydos was unearthed by the scholarly traveller William Bankes in 1818, but left there. In 1837 it was removed and later acquired by the British Museum. This list carried cartouches of 52 kings, with the throne-names of rulers, beginning with Meni and ending with Ramesses II. In 1825 another, similar list, the *Karnak Table of Kings*, was recognized, carved on the walls of a small chamber in the temple of Thutmose III at Karnak. The walls carry images of 61 kings, with their cartouches, of which 48 were legible. In 1843 it was removed to the Louvre Museum.

The most important of these king lists was found carved on the wall of a corridor in the temple of Sety I at Abydos during the clearance of the temple by Auguste Mariette. Richard Lepsius published a copy in 1863. The whole scene shows the pharaoh Sety I and the crown prince Ramesses (later Ramesses II) making offerings to the names of the ancestral kings, beginning with Meni and ending with Ramesses I and Sety I. This list is perfectly preserved, but there are political omissions, such as the entire Second Intermediate Period, Hatshepsut, Akhenaten and his immediate successors.

The *Table of Saqqara* was found in 1861 in the tomb of an official of Ramesses II named Tjuneroy. It originally had 57 cartouches, some of which were damaged by the time of the relief's discovery.

It is significant that most of these king lists are early Ramesside and that such lists do not survive from other periods. In addition to the king lists, some temples and tombs at Thebes depict processions of royal statues in a similar chronological arrangement.

At the Festival of the god Min there was a procession of royal statues. This is depicted in the temples of Ramesses II (the Ramesseum) and Ramesses III (Medinet Habu). The earliest ruler shown is Meni, the founder of the Egyptian state; he is followed by Neb-hepet-ra (Mentjuhotep II) who reunited Egypt and founded the Middle Kingdom. These two pharaohs stand as shorthand for the whole of the Old and Middle Kingdoms. Neb-pehty-ra (Ahmose) reunited Egypt and is thought of as founder of the New Kingdom.

He is followed by the statues of nearly all of the pharaohs of the eighteenth and nineteenth dynasties to the reigning sovereign, Ramesses II or III; as is usual, Hatshepsut and the immediate successors of Amenhotep III are omitted.

In addition to these New Kingdom sources, fragments of an Old Kingdom list survive. This is generally known, after the largest surviving piece, as the 'Palermo Stone'. The original monument appears to have carried a complex historical text that recorded Old Kingdom rulers with information on their reigns, such as height of inundation, the foundation of temples and military activities.

One of the major early organizers of the evidence from the monuments alongside the Greek, Roman and biblical traditions was Ippolito Rosellini (1800–43), leader, with Champollion, of the joint Franco–Tuscan expedition to Egypt 1828–9. Following Champollion's untimely death, Rosellini published the vast amount of material gathered by the expedition in three parts: historical, religious and social. His synthesis of the historical evidence gathered all of the known ancient sources that could be read (in Greek, Latin and Hebrew), attached them to Manetho's chronology, and, wherever possible added the newly read hieroglyphic cartouches and the monuments where they were to be found. Rosellini included the standing monuments in Egypt and Sudan and inscribed artefacts in museum collections. Although Rosellini did not get everything correct, for the first time Egyptian monuments had been ordered chronologically.

THE PERIODS: OLD, MIDDLE, NEW AND LATE

Manetho ordered his kings in dynasties, or ruling families, associated with a town of origin. The dynastic system has some problems (mostly in the 'Intermediate Periods'), but is generally fairly useful, and we now have little chance of eradicating it. In further defence of the dynastic system, it can be said that the Egyptians themselves must have employed a similar form in some of their records. The Turin Canon divides the rulers into groups, and gives totals, although they do not correspond to Manetho's dynasties. Manetho himself was basing his work on ancient Egyptian records, which must have used the system.

The broader scheme into which the dynasties are clustered – Old Kingdom, Middle Kingdom, New Kingdom and Late Period, separated by the First, Second and Third Intermediate Periods – has no ancient authority and is the invention of Egyptologists. However, this division of Egyptian history into kingdoms was not, as one might expect, done by one person (such as Champollion or Rosellini); it developed gradually throughout the nineteenth and twentieth centuries. For example, the Third Intermediate Period became a popular term for the dynasties 21–25, previously called the 'Libyan' and 'Ethiopian' periods, only in the 1960s.

The division into kingdoms and periods began in the mid-nineteenth century as an art historical method of ordering antiquities in the new museum collections (notably those of the Louvre and Berlin) and for publications of monuments. The main periodic divisions were established by the late nineteenth century and became canonized in the immensely influential histories of Heinrich Brugsch (1827–94) and James Henry Breasted (1865–1935).

In papyrus archival documents, of which only the Turin Canon survives as an example, the Egyptians presumably did cluster their kings into 'dynasties', but in the official king lists carved on temple walls the pharaohs appear as if they ruled in unbroken line of succession from the foundation of a united Egypt by 'Meni' (the Menes of Manetho). In abbreviated lists, Meni is followed directly by the rulers who reunited Egypt, Mentjuhotep (Nebhepetra) and Ahmose, founding what we call the Middle and New Kingdoms. This is a tacit acknowledgement that there were periods of breakdown. None of the surviving king lists is later in date than the New Kingdom, but Psamtik I would perhaps have been accorded a similar honour to Mentjuhotep and Ahmose, as reuniter of Egypt in the twenty-sixth dynasty.

EXPANDING THE KING LISTS

The early Western constructions of ancient Egypt relied on Greek and Latin writers, and on the books of the Bible. The decipherment of hieroglyphic, and the increasing ability to read and understand the Egyptian texts, opened a new world in which the Egyptians themselves spoke to us. For a long time Egyptologists took the texts that were preserved rather literally, and 'text criticism' was limited.

As in other branches of ancient history, in recent years there have considerable changes to our understanding of the ways in which the Egyptians (or Greeks, or Romans) used 'texts'.

We no longer view the ancient Greeks as rational, observant people whose texts are to be trusted implicitly. We acknowledge that their writings are riddled with textual problems, biases, xenophobia and straightforward misunderstanding. Nevertheless they also contain a huge amount about Egypt, and are worth discussing, but we now ask more questions about literary genres and the function of individual texts. Many of the literary sources surviving from the Roman Period were written by scholars from the Greek-speaking eastern Mediterranean, and continue that tradition. Therefore, in the most recent narrative chronicles and more detailed studies, the Greek and Roman writings on Egypt have largely been dropped by Egyptologists, or at least discussed in a more text-critical manner. And new studies have appeared that discuss the perception of Egypt by the Greeks and by the Romans – no longer mixing them together as a single entity.

The biblical texts were the great favourites of early archaeologists who 'excavated with the Bible in one hand', but now most archaeologists acknowledge that the biblical books are very difficult documents to use for the reconstruction of historical narratives. There is a vast scholarly literature discussing the texts and their problems. None of the books was written down in its existing form until well after it was composed. The 'Bible' as it stands is a collection of books that illustrate the religious history of the Jewish people, and there are many references to other sources, now lost, such as the annals of the kings. Like all ancient sources, they are riddled with textual problems and biases. That is not to say that they cannot be used, but we must question how we should use them.

In the mid-nineteenth century, in addition to the Egyptian hieroglyphic texts which were being read for the first time, another group of ancient texts was being deciphered and translated. These were the records of the Assyrian, Babylonian and Persian kings. The Annals of the Assyrian kings of the Late Assyrian empire (also known as the Neo-Assyrian and Sargonid periods) are extremely important as sources for the political history of western Asia from the ninth to the seventh centuries BC. Of course, the Assyrian records suffer from the same biases as Egyptian sources. They also exist in several versions, but this is valuable in letting us see how royal annals were adapted as a reign advanced: things which were important in the early years might pale into insignificance by the end of the reign. The same can be said of the official records of the rulers of Babylon and Persia. Much rarer, but immensely valuable when they do survive, are documents such as letters. The Assyrian palaces have yielded vast archives of clay tablets that include prayers to the sun-god Shamash, oracular pronouncements, astrological predictions, administrative documents relating to the palace and letters between the rulers and their high officials. Of course, these also suffer from numerous problems, such as the lack of a date or the lack of a named ruler, but they provide valuable additions to the officially published records of reigns. The archives of the Hittite rulers of Anatolia are another important ancient source, particularly for the conflict between Egypt and the Hittite kingdom culminating in the battle of Qadesh.

WRITING THE HISTORY OF EGYPT

In the later part of the nineteenth century, when large numbers of hieroglyphic texts were being translated, writing history from the Egyptian sources – rather than Greek, Roman and biblical sources – became, quite rightly, the ideal. The style of narrative royal chronicle first popularized by Heinrich Brugsch (1877) and James Henry Breasted (1905) has continued to be written by leading Egyptologists, from Flinders Petrie (1894), Étienne Drioton and Jacques Vandier (1938) to Alan Gardiner's classic, *Egypt of the Pharaohs* (1961). In approach, these histories are essentially the same, the newer updating the older works by adding newly discovered material and incorporating new interpretations of the evidence. The process is a simple, empirical one. First, a chronological framework is established from the surviving ancient Egyptian king lists, with only a sideways glance at Greek, Roman and biblical sources. This is then supplemented by other monumental records, putting in the rulers such as Hatshepsut and Akhenaten who were omitted, for a variety of reasons, by the official lists. To this basic outline, detail can then be added from royal inscriptions recording military and building activities, along with evidence for the officials for each reign, and archaeological evidence, such as that for the early kings of 'dynasty 0'. Occasionally, detail of specific events or phenomena can be found in what might be termed 'real' historical texts, such as the economic, juridical and other texts of the 'Wilbour Papyrus', the 'Harem Conspiracy' trial records, the Deir el Medina archives and the Amarna archives. For almost any period before the Ptolemaic, this form of narrative chronicle is about the best that can be achieved because we are severely limited by the evidence available.

These popular histories of Egypt have been enormously important in establishing a view of ancient Egypt and turning theories (some of them highly dubious) into 'facts'. In the later nineteenth century, Egyptology was developing rapidly (along with other branches of archaeology and ancient history) and many ideas were being proposed to explain the evidence. Unfortunately, as often happens, these ideas were quoted in, for example, Brugsch's volume and then repeated in later histories (having been taught in classrooms) and by the time Breasted, Drioton and Vandier or Gardiner wrote their histories, they were no longer theories but accepted truths. One good example is the case of the 'Sea Peoples', who were thought to have been instrumental in the collapse of the great empires of the Late Bronze Age. A theory explaining their supposed migrations was put forward by Gaston Maspero; this theory soon gained currency, and by Breasted's time it was virtually a 'Fact'. Another of Maspero's theories was that the right to the throne passed through the female line in the eighteenth dynasty; this idea can still be found in recent books, although it is quite certainly wrong.

The early histories were also important in establishing the periodization of ancient Egypt into Kingdoms and Intermediate Periods. This has had significant repercussions for assessing and writing history. It generally introduces the idea of rise, high point, decline or collapse. This is usually applied to both dynasties and Kingdoms. The Kingdoms – Old, Middle and New – are, quite rightly, viewed as periods of unity and high cultural achievement. The Intermediate Periods are thought of as times of disunity and generally regarded as culturally 'poor'. In the past the 'Late Period' has suffered from being precisely that – 'late' – although at times there has been some grudging acceptance that the plastic arts, particularly sculpture, were of very high technical excellence then. For a long time the Ptolemaic and Roman Periods were more usually the province of classicists than Egyptologists, although this has changed significantly in recent years.

In some senses, and in specific instances, the system of periods may be legitimate, but there is usually a lot of moralizing attached to decline and collapse. The nineteenth century developed a whole array of characterizations of historical phases, both long and short, which colour, consciously or subconsciously, the way we interpret. Beginning (rise) is associated with vigour and dynamism – and to some extent, perhaps, with austerity. The high point frequently introduces luxury and opulence, which itself will ultimately lead to decline. Decline, which the nineteenth-century writers were particularly fond of, can manifest itself in 'tired blood', corruption (economic and any other type), luxury and dissipation, reliance on mercenary troops (who will ultimately overthrow the state), neglect of frontiers and barbarian invasions.

Looking at the eighteenth dynasty, this simple scheme seems to fit nicely. The vigorous and dynamic rulers Kamose and Ahmose reunited Egypt, followed by the warrior pharaohs Amenhotep I and Thutmose I–III who established the empire. High empire under Amenhotep II and Thutmose IV began to turn to luxury under Amenhotep III, with decline setting in under Akhenaten, the dynasty fading away with child (Tutankhamun) and elderly (Ay) nonentities. In this case an internal military leader, Horemheb, seized power. The overarching view of the whole New Kingdom can also be fitted into this scheme with relatively little alteration. In writing history, the scheme satisfies the need of narrative, and serves a didactic purpose – the 'lesson of history'.

This type of royal chronicle was largely abandoned, for a period, in the 1960s, and attempts were made to write social history with greater emphasis on 'ordinary' people. These suffered from problems of evidence, too, since it was the elite who left the records. The past two decades have seen some interesting developments in Egyptology, particularly in the Prehistoric–Predynastic, and Ptolemaic–Roman Periods. For the Prehistoric–Predynastic phases, much new archaeological material has been recovered, radically changing our interpretations. For Ptolemaic and Roman Egypt the rich evidence from all sectors of society has been reconsidered by scholars who combine expertise in Egyptology and Classics, and all forms of history – political, religious, art, economic, social, gender – can now be written using the range of materials and methodologies that have been developed for more recent historical periods.

For pre-Ptolemaic Egypt, the traditional narrative chronicle is now widely seen as not particularly desirable, although it serves as a useful – indeed necessary – framework for discussion of other cultural and archaeological phenomena. Increasingly, attention is paid to specific periods, or places, in more detailed discussion of the surviving evidence. The most popular archaeological site, simply because of the wealth of information available, is the village of Deir el-Medina, home to the artisans who carved the royal tombs. In the past they were seen as a microcosm of the life of the 'ordinary' people, but we now acknowledge that they were a special and, in many ways, elite, group. Nevertheless, the quantity and quality of evidence from the site does allow analyses that cannot be made elsewhere in Egypt.

There has also been more serious interest in, and a less dismissive attitude towards, the writings of Europeans from the Renaissance to the early nineteenth century. Their constructions of ancient Egypt were perhaps not 'correct' to our modern understanding, which has a more direct contact with ancient materials, but we recognize that they have a legitimacy. Even the 'Hermetic Corpus', once dismissed by Egyptologists as irrelevant, is now seen to reflect important aspects of Egyptian religious practice of Late Antiquity.

WHEN WAS ANCIENT EGYPT?

Placing exact dates on ancient Egypt is still a very difficult and a contentious subject. Most recent discussions of chronology (with a few notable exceptions) have been concerned with detail, perhaps moving the reign of a particular pharaoh by a few years, at most a couple of decades. This reflects a (possibly misplaced) sense of certainty about the backbone chronology. But if we look at the work of Egyptologists in the late nineteenth and early twentieth centuries, we find that they were quite happy to revise their dates by tens, or even hundreds, of years.

Egyptologists have generally agreed on the dates for the main periods and dynasties. Suggestions that we have got Egyptian chronology wrong – by 250 or even 400 years – are dismissed out of hand and consigned to the 'loony fringe'.

When academic Egyptology really began in the nineteenth century, there were few methods of calculating *when* it all happened. The king lists establish an internal and relative chronology for Egypt: who came before whom. The most obvious method to achieve the exact dates for those dynasties and kings, therefore, is 'dead reckoning' . . . simply adding up the reign lengths of the pharaohs. Dead reckoning was the method used by Manetho, and it was also used in the other fundamental source for reconstructing the history of the ancient world, the *Royal Canon* of the mathematician and astronomer Claudius Ptolemy. Writing in the second century AD, Ptolemy included a *Royal Canon* that named all of the kings of Babylon, with their reign lengths, and gave a running total from Nabonassar (ascended the throne 747 BC) to Alexander the Great who died in the city in 323 BC. After Alexander the kings listed are the Ptolemies of Egypt and the Roman emperors. This anchored the latter part of the chronology to the first century AD. We do not know what sources Ptolemy used, but they apparently contained a variety of astronomical information, including dates of eclipses, which was his main interest. The sources were certainly Babylonian in origin, although Ptolemy may have used an Alexandrian copy of the original. The importance of Ptolemy's list is that it contains not only kings who were Babylonians but Assyrian conquerors of the city and, later, the Persian kings. The Persian kings also appeared in Manetho as dynasty 27, and the Bible provided a synchronism between the Babylonian king Nebuchadrezzar and the pharaoh Hophra (Apries of Manetho's dynasty 26). Ptolemy's *Royal Canon* thus tied Manetho's dynastic list firmly to the known chronology of Western Europe.

Manetho gives totals for his Book I (dynasties 1–11) as 2,300 years 70 days, for Book II (dynasties 12–19) as 2,121 years and for Book III (dynasty 20 to Alexander the Great (332 BC)) as 1,050 years, which gives a total of 5,803 years from the first dynasty to the birth of Christ. This, of course, presented a problem to a nineteenth-century Western biblical tradition which (largely) believed that the world was created in 4004 BC!

Even if we do not accept that the world was created in 4004 BC, this method of calculating has problems: Manetho's regnal years are unreliable, but he also masks the overlaps between dynasties, particularly in the Intermediate Periods. The idea of dead reckoning is still good, but it requires an accurate set of regnal years from the contemporary monumental and documentary records. The chronological relationship between Ptolemaic Egypt and Rome is secure from a whole range of ancient sources. The conquest of Egypt by Octavian (later the emperor Augustus) – following the defeat of Kleopatra VII and Marcus Antonius – is certain (30 BC). Ptolemy I seized Egypt after Alexander the Great's death (323 BC), reigning first as governor (satrap) before proclaiming himself king. Working backwards, the conquest of Egypt by Alexander the Great took place in 332 BC. Prior to that, the conquest of Egypt by the Persian king Cambyses, which took place in 525 BC, is another key synchronism. Cambyses defeated Psamtik III, but did not acknowledge that king's reign, backdating his own to the death of Ahmose (Amasis), Psamtik's father. The twenty-sixth dynasty is known not only from Manetho but also from Herodotos and from the Egyptian monumental record. A number of texts allow us to be precise about the lengths of the reigns of the twenty-sixth-dynasty pharaohs, bringing us to 664 BC, for the accession of Psamtik I. We know that Psamtik ascended the throne on the death, probably in battle, of his father, Nekau I. We also know that Nekau was defeated by the twenty-fifth-dynasty Kushite king Tanwetamani in the first year of his reign. Tanwetamani became king at the death of Taharqo. As the length of the reign of Taharqo is certain, at 26 years, we can state that Taharqo ascended the throne in 690 BC. Unfortunately, the process of retrocalculation ends here. Uncertainties about the reign lengths and synchronisms of the Kushite and Libyan dynasties hinder a straightforward adding up.

To move further back in time, Egyptology has relied on one synchronism that has been accepted since Champollion began to read royal names. The biblical record tells us that the Pharaoh 'Shishak' sacked Jerusalem, and the year can be calculated as around 925 BC. Champollion identified Shishak with Sheshonq I who left a large record of an Asiatic campaign at Karnak (in which Jerusalem is notable only by its absence). The equation is still accepted by most Egyptologists and, right or wrong, forms another key date.

To establish when ancient Egypt happened, Egyptologists tried another method: astronomical dating.

CALENDARS AND ASTRONOMICAL
DATING

One of the most controversial subjects in chronology is the role of calendars. The Egyptians dated by regnal year of the pharaoh, but alongside that there was a civil calendar, so texts will carry, for example, the date line: 'year 23, first month of *shomu* (summer), day 1, under the majesty of . . .'. The system relating to regnal year change appears to have varied at different times. In some periods a king might 'back-date' his accession. So, for example, if he ascended the throne near the end of the civil year, his first regnal year might last a matter of weeks or days, and the second year begin on New Year's Day. At other periods the regnal year changed on the accession day during the year, so the date we had above ('year 23, first month of *shomu* (summer), day 1,') might be followed immediately by 'year 24, first month of *shomu* (summer), day 2' if that was the feast of the accession of the pharaoh. An example of this occurs in the Annals of Thutmose III.

The civil calendar began with New Year's Day, which was dictated by the rising of the star Sirius (Egn Sopdet; Gk *Sothis*), and relates to the rise of Nile flood, in late June. The year was divided into 12 months of 30 days. At the end of the year there were five days added on (the 'epagomenal' days), to bring the total to 365. This did not take into account the quarter day, and the Egyptians did not introduce the Leap Year, so, theoretically, their calendar moved out of sequence by one day every four years.

In the nineteenth century, scholars argued that the Egyptians never brought their calendars back into line, and that the realignment came only at the end of the natural 'Sothic cycle' of 1,460 years. But it is the key to the dates that we now accept for the reign of Ramesses II. It has to be emphasized that if only one king in the entire span of pre-Ptolemaic history decided to reform the calendar, those dates are wrong.

Achieving the accepted dates for Ramesses II has been a relatively long process. We now acknowledge 'High', 'Middle' and 'Low' possible dates for the accession of Ramesses II: these are 1304, 1290 and 1279. Most Egyptologists prefer the lowest. The earlier Egyptologists were actually quite happy to revise their chronologies frequently. This is notable in the dates for the Old Kingdom: Petrie lowered his original dates for the Old Kingdom by several hundred years. The main problems occur in the Intermediate Periods; the internal chronologies of the Old, Middle and New Kingdoms are fairly secure. Petrie and others ascribed a much longer time span to the 'Hyksos Period' (Second Intermediate) than we would now – and similarly with the First Intermediate Period.

By the middle of the nineteenth century astronomical data were being used to calculate the Egyptian dates. This is the method known as Sothic dating. Richard Lepsius wrote lengthily on the Sothic cycle, and it became accepted as the principle of Egyptian chronology. Some writers went so far as to say that Egyptian history actually began at the commencement of a Sothic cycle (hence Petrie's high dates for the Old Kingdom).

Some eminent Egyptologists have recently rejected the validity of Sothic dating, and many more would say that we no longer use it. However, the dates we use are actually calculated using this method as a starting point! Unfortunately, Sothic dating is extremely complex.

One of the problems that emerged from this reconstruction of Egyptian chronology was the lack of early links with western Asia. Eduard Meyer's *Aegyptische Chronologie* of 1904 was funda-mental in relating Egypt to the Near East and for lowering the dates of the Old Kingdom (which were accepted by Petrie). Meyer's work also established Sothic dating as a tenet of Egyptology. More recent studies have made only relatively small alterations to the overall span of Egyptian history.

Table 4.1 selects some significant dates given by a number of Egyptologists in classic, and influential, histories of Egypt to show how we have radically changed our dating for ancient Egypt. The key dates selected here are: the unification of the state (beginning of dynasty 1); the Great Pyramid (reign of Khufu, first pharaoh of dynasty 4); the end of the sixth dynasty; the twelfth dynasty (Middle Kingdom); and the beginning of the New Kingdom (dynasty 18). From dynasty 21 onward, the dates are fairly generally the same as there were the synchronisms from western Asia (the Persian Empire), and most Egyptologists accepted the identification of the biblical king Shishak with Sheshonq I (giving him a date of around 925 BC). The most notable reductions are in the lengths of the First and Second Intermediate Periods.

Table 4.1 Dating differences: significant dates given by a number of Egyptologists

	Heinrich Brugsch (1891)	Flinders Petrie (1894)	Alexandre Moret (1927)	Alan Gardiner (1961)	Ian Shaw (ed.) (2000)
Dynasty 1	4400	5546	3315	3100	3000
Dynasty 4	3733	4777	2840	2620	2613
Dynasty 6 (end)	3033	4077	c. 2400	c. 2200	2181
Dynasty 12	2466–2233	3579–3368	2000–1785	1991–1786	1985–1773
Second Intermediate Period	2233–1733	3366 onwards	1786–1575	1785–1580/1552	1650–1550
Dynasty 18	1700–1400	1587–1328	1580–1345	1575–1308	1550–1295
Dynasty 19	1400–1200	1328–1202	1345–1200	1308–1194	1295–1186
Dynasty 20	1200–1100	1202–1102	1200–1100	1184–1087	1186–1069

Note: all dates are BC

Because of the interconnections with the other states of the eastern Mediterranean and western Asia, the chronology of Egypt can be calculated fairly precisely back to the accession of the twenty-fifth-dynasty pharaoh Taharqo in 690 BC. Unfortunately, because of the uncertainties regarding the predecessors of Taharqo and the problems relating to their connections with the Libyan pharaohs of the dynasties '22' and '23', any date preceding 690 is uncertain. Nevertheless, nearly every Egyptologist has accepted the identification, first proposed by Champollion, of the biblical pharaoh 'Shishak' with Sheshonq I. 'Shishak' is stated in the *Book of Kings* to have sacked Jerusalem in the reign of Rehoboam. This event can be placed around 925 BC.

If astronomical dating presents problems for establishing an exact chronology, surely modern scientific methods of dating, such as radiocarbon, can provide accurate dates? The main problem stems from the fact that faith in the Egyptian chronology was such that Egyptian objects were used to demonstrate that the radiocarbon technique was actually correct.

We might well ask: 'Does it matter?' There are Egyptologists for whom exact chronology does not matter: the relative chronology is the important thing. But getting dates right for Egypt has huge implications in ancient Mediterranean history and archaeology. There are still many disagreements and fundamental problems with the specifics of certain sites throughout the whole region. Ultimately, whether directly or indirectly, this usually comes back to a reliance on Egyptian chronology. Because Egyptologists claimed that their dates were achieved astronomically through Sothic dating and qualified with the king lists, they were correct for the second millennium BC. Objects associated with a pharaoh's name can be used to date pottery in sites in western Asia. The same pottery can occur in Cyprus. Mycenaean pottery of specific types occurs in the reign of Akhenaten in Egypt, hence relating the later eighteenth dynasty to Mycenaean Greece; the wider ramifications spread to northern and Western Europe.

5

ORIGINS AND FIRST
FLOWERING

Egyptologists in the early twentieth century interpreted the formation of the Egyptian state as a Darwinian process: the desiccation
of the Sahara forced people into the Nile Valley, which gradually
led to the development of villages, then 'chiefdoms'. These early
chiefdoms, it was suggested, were preserved in the administrative
system of dynastic times as the nomes. Over time, the chiefdoms
were absorbed into two major kingdoms, Upper Egypt (the Nile
Valley) and Lower Egypt (the Delta). The two kingdoms were
then united by the king Meni (the 'Menes' of Manetho) who heads
the Egyptian king lists. Egyptologists identified him with the
pharaoh known from monuments as Narmer. This process was
assumed to have been achieved largely through military action,
ultimately sealed by a political marriage. The complex religion of
the Egyptians was also seen to embody this division into numerous
small chiefdoms. Each nome standard was thought to represent
the original 'fetish'. This conveniently explained why there were
so many gods with the same creative functions but different names
and associations. Archaeological work carried out over the past
three decades has revolutionized our understanding of early Egypt.
Indeed, there has been so much work on the Prehistoric and
Predynastic phases that these have emerged as disciplines in their
own right. Excavations at the major sites of Abu (*Elephantine*),
Nekhen (*Hierakonpolis*), Abedju (*Abydos*) in Upper Egypt and at
Buto in the Delta, have yielded particularly significant material.
Equally important are the publications of excavations carried out
in Nubia during the UNESCO salvage campaign of the 1960s
and 1970s. These have radically revised our understanding of the

development of cultures there that are contemporary with the Egyptian Predynastic Period.

PREHISTORIC AND EARLY PREDYNASTIC EGYPT (700,000–4000 BC)

We tend to forget the vast spans of time during which Egyptian civilization developed before the unification of the state. People settled in Egypt from 700,000 BC. In the succeeding millennia, there were major climatic changes in North Africa, with alternating dry and wet phases. The dry phases forced people and animals to move from the increasingly arid central Sahara to its margins; during wetter periods they moved back. The Nile, too, changed, being at times high and at times very low, its seasonal flood pattern developing by around 20,000 BC. Settlements along the river margin were constant from around 17,000/15,000 BC. The Delta changed more dramatically, affected by sea levels as well as the river, reaching its present limits and formation by the late Predynastic Period.

From 12,000 BC, the people of southern Upper Egypt and northern Nubia were collecting and grinding wild wheat, even if hunting and fishing remained the basis of subsistence. Another major climatic change around 9000 BC forced more people towards the Nile Valley, which was still probably swampy and uninhabitable along much of its length. In Nubia, the Early Khartoum culture (c. 7400–4900 BC) was also based predominantly on hunting and fishing, but also made the earliest pottery known in the Nile Valley.

There were further changes between 6000 and 5000 BC. In Egypt, the farming economy was influenced by that developing in the Near East, with cultivated wheat, flax, oats and goats. There are also connections with the Sahara, where domesticated cattle were herded and barley grown. Egyptian pottery shows influences from both areas.

At the important Lower Egyptian site of Merimde, the flint and pottery technologies, the types of domesticated animals and the manufacture of human and animal figurines all indicate close connections with the Near East during the earliest phase (c. 5000–4500 BC). Although there is a clear continuity in the following phases, the dominant influences seem to be coming from further south in Egypt, notably the Fayum, with cattle herding becoming important, as well as the cultivation of wheat and sorghum (millet), and perhaps barley.

THE FORMATION OF THE STATE
(c. 4000–3000 BC)

The emergence of Egyptian civilization should be seen within a context of evidence from the whole of north-east Africa and western Asia. The evidence from Nubia shows a parallel development of stratified society there and strong contacts with Upper Egypt, just as the evidence from the Delta indicates trade and contacts with western Asia and Mesopotamia. In Upper Egypt the phases are named after the important site of Naqada, a little to the north of Thebes.

Our knowledge of this period of state formation is changing rapidly due to work at Nekhen (*Hierakonpolis*) and Abedju (*Abydos*). The study of the Predynastic Period really began with the work of Flinders Petrie in various cemeteries, principally in Upper Egypt. Petrie acquired a large amount of pottery which he organized by sequence dating or 'seriation' from earliest to latest, based upon the increase and decrease of types within graves, along with other objects. While not allowing exact dates BC to be attached to graves, this allowed a relative chronology for the Predynastic Period to be constructed. Our knowledge has expanded considerably since Petrie's day, due to many more excavated sites, better archaeological techniques for recovery of material and the development of tools such as radiocarbon and thermoluminescence dating. In more recent years, settlement sites, rather than just cemeteries, have been examined, considerably expanding our understanding of the cultural influences.

Early excavations at Nekhen found major monuments, such as ceremonial mace heads and slate palettes, which had been dedicated by the early 'proto-pharaohs', 'Scorpion' and Narmer. Many of the attributes and regalia of the pharaonic monarchy appear in the later Naqada phases: crowns, the bull's tail attached to the belt, sandals, mace or club, flail and staffs. The evidence suggested that Nekhen rose to be the dominant kingdom of Upper Egypt and eventually conquered the north. More recent material excavated in the cemetery at Abedju suggests that the region of Tjeny may have supplanted Nekhen as the most important place in Upper Egypt a century or more before the unification.

In the Naqada II Period (*c.* 3800–3300 BC), there were major centres throughout Upper Egypt from Nekhen in the south to Abedju and Matmar, extending into northern Middle Egypt. By this phase, there was increasing social stratification, to be seen in the cemetery sites at Abedju, Naqada and Nekhen. The elite burials are increasingly large and complex, employing mud-brick in their construction, and their contents reveal wide-ranging trading contacts with Nubia and the Delta, and through the Delta with western Asia and Mesopotamia.

What brought this social change about is controversial. Some archaeologists suggest that the more limited land available in Upper Egypt (compared with the Delta) could have led to conflict and competition, hence providing the impetus for social complexity. The Naqada culture appears to have developed as the environment became more arid, forcing the cattle herders of the margins into the Nile Valley where the population consisted predominantly of hunter-gatherers and fishermen. As a number of anthropologist-Egyptologists have argued, the Egyptian kingship displays strong similarities with that of East African cattle cultures. This tradition is now being re-examined by Toby Wilkinson in the light of newly discovered rock drawings in the Upper Egyptian deserts.

Another important factor was the development of long-distance trade, and the exploitation of resources. The Naqada II phase shows the beginning of urban centres as elite residences and also ceremonial and production centres. There is considerable evidence for craft specialization and for trade in gold and copper from the Eastern Desert. Seal impressions suggest the beginning of the administrative system. In the second half of the Naqada II phase, the towns at Naqada and Nekhen were enclosed with walls, protecting the new centres of wealth.

The external contacts of Upper Egypt are important. The old idea of the 'Dynastic Race' has been abandoned, but contacts with Sumer and Elam are revealed by artistic motifs. How these contacts were effected is still controversial, and they may have been indirect. It is easier to document the very strong links with the 'A-Group' culture of Lower Nubia. Reassessments of the Nubian archaeological material by Bruce Williams and Harry Smith show that hierarchical societies were developing in Nubia, just as they were in Egypt, and that important kingdoms appeared there, one based in the region of Qustul and one at Seyala.

In the Delta the dominant culture is named after the two sites of Maadi near Cairo and Buto in the western Delta. This Maadi-Buto culture is characterized by phases of strong contact with south-western Asia (Canaan). There were also settled groups of people from the same regions, indicated by the local production of south Levantine vessels at Buto itself, and the evidence of a small number of houses of the Canaanite Beersheba culture on the outskirts of the Maadi settlement. There were certainly trading links across Sinai, and exploitation of Sinai's resources.

In the late Naqada II period, the Upper Egyptian culture expanded northwards into that of Maadi-Buto. There is no evidence to indicate whether this was a military conquest as early Egyptologists assumed. The result was a single state (the Naqada III phase) and a homogeneous culture throughout Egypt. Large quantities of imported Canaanite storage and wine jars are now found in tombs. Vine cultivation was introduced into the Delta towards the end of the Naqada III period, and became an important feature of Egyptian agriculture. The Egyptian bureaucratic system also manifests itself at this time, with standardized and locally made Egyptian wine jars in royal and elite burials.

EGYPT UNITED

Early Egyptologists assumed that the unification was the result of the conquest of the kingdom of Lower Egypt by the rulers of Upper Egypt. The concept of two kingdoms united is central to the ideology of the state for the rest of its history, but there is no archaeological evidence from Lower Egypt to show that it was a single unified kingdom. Even the significance of military activities in the unification has now been questioned. What is clear is that in the period immediately preceding the emergence of the single unified state, there was increasing homogeneity of culture throughout the Egyptian Nile Valley.

In Egyptian tradition, the unification was defined by the founding of Inbu-hedj (*Memphis*) at the strategic point just south of the apex

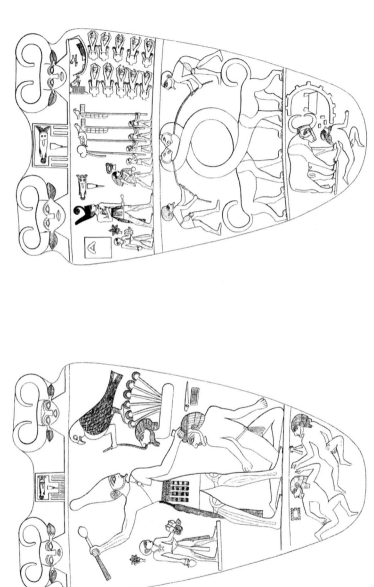

Figure 5.1 The ceremonial palette of Horus Narmer which is the first to show a ruler wearing the White Crown (left-hand image) and the Red Crown (right-hand image) (after W. M. F. Petrie, *Ceremonial Slate Palettes*, London: British School of Archaeology in Egypt).

of the Delta. The unification is represented monumentally by the ceremonial palette of Horus Narmer, which is the first to show a ruler wearing both the White and Red Crowns (see Figure 5.1).

As a result of unification Egypt appeared as a single nation state, with a homogeneous culture, probably single language, administration and religious system. It was centralized with a God King and a narrow elite, the most powerful being members of the royal family. The principal royal residence, administrative centre and burial place was at Memphis. The dominant characteristics of this state were the control of irrigation and agriculture. During the centuries of the developing state, there must have been an increasing understanding of the Nile flood, crop yields and quantities of grain produced. Records of Nile levels were probably kept, as they were in later times. Such knowledge enabled forward planning for years of low inundation and famine. The natural benefits of the annual inundation were now extended by a system of dykes and canals. The agricultural surplus supported specialist production, full-time artisans and a controlling elite. There were wide-ranging trade contacts with western Asia and Nubia.

The ruler ('pharaoh') exercised the key administrative functions: the organization of the irrigation and of the food surplus. The royal progress throughout the land was associated with the biennial 'cattle count'.

Large-scale building projects are already found associated with the royal burials of the Predynastic Period. Surviving large building works from the Early Dynastic Period and Old Kingdom are also funerary: the royal mastaba and pyramid complexes with the surrounding tombs of the elite. This is due to their desert location: there must also have been large buildings in settlements, perhaps concentrating on defensive enclosures to protect the storage of food and other wealth. Unlike early Mesopotamia, Egypt has no surviving evidence of massive religious structures as the focus of settlements, and Egyptian state resources do seem to have focused on the royal person and burial at this period.

Writing developed quickly for both ceremonial and accounting purposes. Seal impressions and labels on objects indicate ownership and quantity. The names of Egyptian rulers on vessels in Palestine and Nubia were probably used as indicators of who was important as the controller of goods. Writing was also used to record and celebrate royal activities, such as temple building and warfare, and then for religious texts. The materials that survive are primarily those from funerary contexts, where ownership and detailing of contents of vessels was important. Papyrus was manufactured from a very early date, the earliest surviving example being from a tomb of the first dynasty. No doubt papyri were soon used for a wide range of records, not just economic and administrative purposes, but the early centres of administration have not been located, and in any case, papyri would not be preserved in the alluvial plain.

ARCHITECTURE AND ART

One result of the hierarchic society that developed in the Predynastic Period was a specialized artisan class. Monumental architecture in mud-brick, and then in stone, became a feature of the Early Dynastic Period and the Old Kingdom, culminating in those most imposing of Egyptian remains, the pyramid complexes.

The characteristics of the Egyptian artistic style also emerge during the Predynastic Period. Many of the most impressive images of early kingship were excavated in the temple at Nekhen. The large ceremonial mace head of the Horus, 'Scorpion' (Oxford, Ashmolean Museum), is one of earliest large royal monuments to survive. The relief sculpture decoration depicts a ruler performing a rite associated with the irrigation. The image of the ruler already uses the conventions that will be characteristic of Egyptian art for the remainder of its history. The king wears the white crown and bull's tail, and is surrounded by the pharaonic paraphernalia of fan bearers and standards on poles. The development of the classical modes of representation of the royal image, royal iconography both human and zoomorphic, and the appearance of registers of scenes is found on a whole range of painted and carved objects. The most notable is the group of ceremonial palettes. Some of these display distinctly Mesopotamian influences in their details. Large-scale sculpture was also being made in the Late Predynastic Period. Among the most notable are the images of the fertility god Min from Gebtiu (*Koptos*), 4 metres (13 feet) high (Oxford, Ashmolean Museum), and three colossal lion statues.

Architectural construction was sophisticated, and survives in the elaborate brick tombs and cenotaphs of the rulers at Saqqara and

Abedju. Large blocks of hewn stone, both limestone and granite, were used within the construction. Stone vessels were produced in very elaborate forms, some imitating basket work, others with remarkably thin walls in the shape of leaves. The easily worked 'schists' and 'alabaster' were favoured for larger vessels, amethyst for unguent vases. The fine quality of the jewellery from the tomb of King Djer at Abydos (now in Cairo) shows characteristics of later work, and is made of gold, lapis lazuli and turquoise, indicative of foreign contacts. Ivory carving was also of high quality, being used for statuettes and furniture.

THE EXPANDING STATE

The early united state appears to have embarked on a rapid expansion both in trade and colonization. There is evidence of considerable activity in northern Sinai during the long reign of Horus Narmer. There are even indications of Egyptian settlements in southern Canaan and, for a brief period, Egyptian administration. Egyptian pottery found in Canaanite sites was both imported and locally made. The region produced agricultural products that were in demand in Egypt, such as olive oil and vines. Coastal trade increased northwards to Lebanon and Syria, and the trade eastwards to Transjordan and south to the Negev and southern Sinai brought copper.

This phase of Egyptian expansion was short. From the reign of Djer onwards, Egyptian settlements disappear and there was less imported Canaanite pottery in Egypt. This appears to relate to the increase in maritime trade with Byblos, which, from the second dynasty, became Egypt's main trading partner supplying Egypt with cedar. Trade with Canaan did not cease entirely, but it was now conducted through elite exchange between rulers, rather than by colonies.

Egypt also expanded southwards. The southern limit to the Predynastic kingdom of Nekhen was probably Gebel Silsila, with Abu (*Elephantine*) as a trading station within Nubian territory. By the late Predynastic Period two or three significant kingdoms had emerged in Lower Nubia, and they were perhaps later united under the rulers of Qustul. They controlled the wealth of the south, particularly ivory and gold. There are increasingly large quantities of Egyptian imports in the 'royal' graves at Qustul, but this ceases at the time of Djer. It seems very likely that the Egyptian pharaohs moved to take control of the trade themselves and crushed the Nubian kingdom.

There is considerably less evidence from the second dynasty. There are massive mud-brick tombs at Saqqara and some rulers may have been buried there rather than at Abedju. There is evidence for disunity between Upper and Lower Egypt. This is assumed to lie behind the changes visible in the reign of Khasekhem, the last king of the dynasty. He succeeded Peribsen, who appears to have ruled from Nekhen, but only over Upper Egypt. Brief inscriptions of Khasekhem suggest military activities in Nubia and the reconquest of Lower Egypt. Statues of the king have figures of slain enemies and the claim that 47,209 northerners were killed. To mark the reunification the king changed his name to Khasekhemwy and adopted the double title 'Horus and Seth'. He also made Memphis his main residence. Some massive building works in mud-brick survive from his reign, most notably at Abedju where the king was buried in a 58-chamber tomb with the huge enclosure known as 'Shunet el-Zebib' probably serving as a temple for the royal funerary cult.

THE OLD KINGDOM (c. 2686–2125 BC)

The Old Kingdom is generally regarded as beginning with the first ruler of the third dynasty, and continuing until the end of the sixth or eighth dynasty. Our knowledge of this period, lasting for some 550 years, is in some ways still quite limited. The principal source for 'history' is the 'Palermo Stone' which is devoted to royal activities. There is an increase in the number of both royal and private elite inscriptions during the Old Kingdom, and by the fifth and sixth dynasties there are significant religious documents (the 'Pyramid Texts') and 'autobiographical' inscriptions.

At the transition of the second and third dynasties, Queen Ni-maat-hep, the wife or daughter of Khasekhemwy played a significant role. She was the mother (or mother-in-law) of Netjer-khet (Djoser) who ordered her burial. There is little that can be said of the historical events of the third dynasty, which seems to have been a relatively short period of about 55 years. It is memorable for the spectacular architectural developments found in the royal funerary complexes. Only that of Netjer-khet was completed. Netjer-khet, more usually known by the name given to him in later times, 'Djoser', was buried in the first large-scale stone monument, the Step Pyramid of Saqqara. The pyramid and surrounding temple was a revolutionary structure designed by the king's son and architect, Imhotep, who was, in later times, revered as a god. The pyramid itself began as a mastaba tomb of the type used for earlier kings, but was enlarged and turned into a stepped pyramid. Surrounding it was a massive enclosure wall with courtyards and a series of chapels, all 'dummies', built of rubble with dressed limestone façades. These represented the temples of the gods of Upper and Lower Egypt, and translated the architecture of reeds and tent shrines into stone. This monument not only shows the wealth and political control exerted by the monarchy but the range of skills that had been developed in engineering, surveying, mathematics and astronomy. These skills were also employed in the irrigation system: a dam at Sadd el-Kafara, near Helwan, was planned and begun at the end of the third dynasty, and large canals were dug in Middle Egypt in the sixth dynasty.

The new monumental style of stone architecture rapidly developed. Hard stones were brought enormous distances – granite from Aswan and diorite-gneiss from the quarries of the Nubian Desert – to be used for statuary or as architectural elements. The geometrical austerity of the pyramid complexes was offset by the contrast of stones employed and the statuary and reliefs which decorated them. Private tombs had delicately painted (Medum) or carved relief (Saqqara and Giza) decorations, as well as numerous statues. Funerary monuments and sculpture dominate our perception of the Old Kingdom, but the refinement of court taste can be seen in the objects from the burial of Queen Hetep-heres, mother of Khufu, discovered at Giza (now in the Egyptian Museum, Cairo).

The fourth dynasty lasted some 150 years. It began with the reign of Sneferu, which later literary tradition viewed as a golden age, portraying the pharaoh as an ideal ruler, with human feelings. Sneferu is now generally credited with the building of three pyramids. The first of these was the pyramid at Medum, near the original royal residence of Djed-sneferu. This began as a stepped pyramid, but it was altered to turn it into a 'true' pyramid. Also notable is a change in the orientation of the pyramid and its associated temples. The mas-

Figure 5.2 Giza, the pyramid and sphinx of Khaefre.

sive enclosure with courts and temples oriented north–south is replaced with a very small temple adjacent to the pyramid, a causeway and a 'valley temple', all on the east side. Sneferu later constructed two pyramids at Dashur, the 'Bent' pyramid, so called because of the acute change in angle (forced on the builders by a fault in the foundations), and the 'Red Pyramid', completed shortly before the king's death. These, too, have small temples. All three pyramids were constructed using massive blocks of stone.

Datable to the end of the third or beginning of the fourth dynasty are seven small pyramids erected at a number of sites along the length of the Nile from Abu to Sila (south of Medum). These may have formed the focus of centres of the administration and of the royal cult.

Sneferu's successor was Khnum-khufwy, usually referred to as Khufu (or 'Cheops', from the Greek form). He transferred the royal residence to the northern end of Memphis, to Giza, where his tomb, the Great Pyramid, formed the centre of a large cemetery of subsidiary pyramids and elite mastaba burials. In the brief reign of Khufu's successor, Djedefra, a pyramid was built a little to the north of Giza, at Abu Rawash. Although little survives of the complex, some magnificent royal statues were excavated.

Khaefra, brother and successor of Djedefra, built the second pyramid at Giza with a massive temple adjacent to it, connected by a covered causeway to a valley temple. The carving of a rocky outcrop into the sphinx is also attributed to his reign. The notable features of the complex are the blocks of red granite used to line the valley temple (and used for its pillars) and the statues of diorite-gneiss brought from Nubia. The pyramid of Menkaura was dramatically smaller in scale than those of his predecessors, although the statue groups from its temple are some of the finest surviving from ancient Egypt.

Again, a queen was the central figure at the change of dynasty. Queen Khentkawes I was probably a daughter of Menkaura, and mother of one or more of the fifth-dynasty pharaohs.

The fifth dynasty lasted for perhaps 150 years, but the relationship of the rulers to each other is not clear. The later story preserved in the 'Westcar Papyrus' says that the first three kings were sons of the wife of the high priest of Re of Sakhebu in the Delta. The solar cult was certainly of great importance in this dynasty. Some of the pharaohs were buried at Saqqara, but others chose a site a little to the north, at Abusir. Here Userkaf built a sun temple comprising a valley temple, a causeway and an upper temple with an open court with an obelisk. Most kings of the dynasty built temples here or at Abu Ghurob, a short distance to the north. They must have had similarities with the temples at Iunu (*Heliopolis*) and would have been visible from there. Sahura built both a solar temple and his pyramid tomb at Abusir. The pyramid is rather small and poorly constructed compared with those of the fourth dynasty, but there was a large and elaborate temple complex attached to it. This was decorated with fine relief sculpture showing events of the reign, including a sea expedition to Byblos, conflict with Libyans and the presentation of Nubian produce. A wide range of contrasting stones was used in the temple's construction: basalt for the floor, hard white limestone for the ceilings and red granite for the date-palm pillars.

In the fifth dynasty the chief offices of state were no longer held by the sons or brothers of the reigning pharaoh, although a number of such officials were married to royal daughters. This is not really evidence of a decline in royal power since there is a possibility that these officials were more distant relatives of the pharaoh. Descendants of the pharaohs of the fourth dynasty were still living and playing a significant role in the administration. One such prince was Sekhemkara, a son of Khaefra, who served as vizier under Userkaf and Sahura.

An increase in the power of provincial officials is notable during this dynasty, and this eventually did challenge royal power. The nomarchs were no longer based entirely at the court, and these elite families gained hereditary control of their offices and of the lands and income that went with them. They now began to site their tombs near their main towns, rather than near the burial place of the reigning pharaoh. At the same time the monarchy was losing control of wealth, as the royal funerary estates of earlier pharaohs were permanent and inalienable. There is evidence from the fifth and sixth dynasties that such funerary estates did continue to function, and this must have had a considerable effect in diminishing the land available to the monarchy for new projects.

The sixth dynasty, lasting for perhaps 155 years, was a period of long reigns, but also one in which the power of the 'provincial' elites increased even further. The first ruler, Teti, was married to two daughters of Unas, last king of the fifth dynasty, but the title he adopted – 'He who reconciles the two lands' – suggests that there may have been some crisis at his accession. The (unreliable) tradition preserved in Manetho's history says that Teti was murdered, but there is no contemporary evidence. His son, Pepy I, did face a conspiracy organized by one of his wives, which was investigated by a high official, Weni, who has left veiled allusions to it. This is the earliest record of such family-based attempts at usurping the throne, a phenomenon that was probably far more frequent than official inscriptions would allow. Pepy married two daughters of a powerful provincial official, Khuy of Abedju: both were called Ankhesenmeryra. There is evidence for building throughout Egypt in the reigns of Teti and Pepy I. These include royal *ka*-chapels, which were associated in later times with the temples of the principal gods of each nome.

Pepy II ascended the throne at the age of six, and reigned for perhaps 94 years. The decline of centralized royal power is often attributed to this extraordinary longevity. Certainly such a lifespan could cause dynastic problems, as it did with the 67-year reign of Ramesses II. There is a likelihood that many, if not all, of Pepy's sons predeceased him, opening the way for rivalry between more remote descendants. Tradition actually records the reign of a female pharaoh, Nitoqert, as the end of the dynasty, but there is no contemporary evidence for her.

Exactly what caused the 'end' or 'collapse' of the Old Kingdom has been disputed for a long time. One idea favoured by many, and argued in detail by Barbara Bell, was that it was environmental factors, notably a series of major failures of the Nile inundation bringing famine and sudden change to a hotter, drier climate, destroying marginal pastureland. Other Egyptologists prefer to see the rising economic power of the elite and the excessive growth of the bureaucracy as major factors: weakened royal authority led to fragmentation as local elites took ever greater control of resources.

The later part of the Old Kingdom certainly shows the control of resources by an elite no longer entirely reliant on royal favour. This manifests itself particularly in funerary religion. Called by some the 'democratization' of funerary beliefs, the evidence culminates in the 'Coffin Texts' of the Middle Kingdom and shows that everyone could look forward to the afterlife, not just the pharaoh.

EXTERNAL AFFAIRS

Throughout the Old Kingdom the pharaohs sent prospecting, quarrying and mining expeditions to Nubia and Sinai. Following the campaigns of Djer that appear to have destroyed the Nubian kingdom based on Qustul, the Egyptians moved to gain direct control of the country's trade and resources. The Palermo Stone records that a military expedition in the reign of Sneferu brought 7,000 captives and 200,000 cattle, but it is unclear whether this was aimed at the Nubian deserts or south of the Egyptian limit of influence at the Second Cataract. A permanent town was constructed at Buhen which functioned as a trading centre throughout the fourth and fifth dynasties. At the same time there was extensive activity in the diorite-gneiss quarries in the desert to the north-west of Buhen. The stone from here was used most notably for the statues in the pyramid temple of Khaefra at Giza.

There was a change in the Egyptian–Nubian relationship in the later Old Kingdom, recorded by a long autobiographical inscription in the tomb of Harkhuf at Aswan. From this, and from archaeological evidence, it is clear that a settled population had returned to Lower Nubia during the fifth dynasty, and that small states were forming, eventually, in the sixth dynasty, being brought under the rule of one king. The town at Buhen was abandoned, and trading expeditions avoided the river route, preferring to travel through Kharga Oasis and the smaller Nubian wells to reach the kingdom of Yam, source of the luxury commodities they sought. The location of Yam is still a matter of dispute. Many Egyptologists would identify it with the region of Kerma, just south of the Third Cataract, although some would place it further south. Kerma became Egypt's major trading partner in Nubia during the Middle Kingdom, and it does seem to fulfil all of the requirements for Yam. The Egyptians did go further south in Africa: there were occasional expeditions to Punt during the Old Kingdom, one in the reign of Sahura. Punt was usually reached by the Red Sea routes, and lay somewhere in the region of the modern Sudan–Eritrea border. The inscription of Harkhuf also gives evidence for long-distance trade within Africa south of Nubia. Harkhuf records how the ruler of Yam gave him a 'dwarf' or 'pygmy' (Egn *deneg*), who must have been brought from further south. It was a rare event, and Harkhuf notes that the previous time such a person had been taken to Egypt was in the reign of Isesi, about a hundred years before.

Egyptian trade with western Asia increased throughout the Old Kingdom. After the brief period of colonization, trade with Canaan was conducted through gift exchange, but increasingly Egypt sailed to Byblos, which controlled the cedar timber of the Lebanon mountains. The most impressive surviving examples of this cedar are in funerary monuments and the Khufu ('*Cheops*') boat. Through the Levantine ports Egypt also gained access to the trade routes that passed through north Syria to Mesopotamia. Fifth- and sixth-dynasty Egyptian objects have been excavated at Ebla. Some fifth-dynasty objects have also been found at Dorak, near the Sea of Marmara, but it is uncertain whether we should understand them as products of long-distance trade or as objects that arrived there much later. Lapis lazuli was one material that came through Mesopotamia. Originating in Badakhshan in Afghanistan, the lapis trade appears to have suffered a severe disruption, as lapis does not appear in tombs of the first to third dynasties and the contemporary period in southern Mesopotamia, but it does occur in the later Old Kingdom.

EGYPT IN TRANSITION: THE FIRST INTERMEDIATE PERIOD (*c.* 2160–2025 BC)

Aside from any problems of interpreting the evidence, calculating the length of the First Intermediate Period has been a major problem for Egyptologists. Some sources, such as the Turin Canon and Manetho, record large numbers of rulers, but other ancient sources (such as the Saqqara list) omit the period completely. The seventh and eighth dynasties are said to have ruled from Memphis, which is why some Egyptologists prefer to regard them as 'Old Kingdom'. The ninth and tenth Dynasties ruled from Nen-nesut (*Herakleopolis*) and were acknowledged throughout the country by the nomarchs. The only major opposition to Nen-nesut came from the rulers of Thebes in Upper Egypt, one of whom assumed royal style, as Intef I.

Egyptologists such as Flinders Petrie proposed a very long First Intermediate Period. The length of the period has more recently been calculated by archaeological means. Stephan Seidlmayer suggests that the Herakleopolitan pharaohs ruled for three or four generations before conflict with Thebes broke out. With the conflict lasting for between 90 and 110 years, Siedlmayer proposes a total of some 200 years for the entire period from the end of the eighth dynasty to the reunification of Egypt by the Theban ruler Nebhepetra Mentjuhotep.

Although the struggle ultimately became that between Thebes and Nen-nesut, other centres had significant rulers. Most of the powerful nomarchs of Middle Egypt, south as far as Sauty (Asyut), owed their allegiance to the pharaohs of Nen-nesut. For a period, most of Upper Egypt south of Thebes was ruled by another adherent of the Herakleopolitans, the nomarch Ankhtify. Given their economic and military power, it is remarkable that, apart from the Thebans, the nomarchs did not adopt the royal style, even if they actually performed the duties of a monarch. This is clearly seen in one of the key monuments of the period, the tomb of Ankhtifi at el-Moalla (ancient Hefat). In a long autobiographical text Ankhtifi refers only once to the Herakleopolitan pharaoh to whom he was loyal. He tells us how he cared for people in times of food shortages and when the nomes under his control were threatened by the princes of Thebes (immediately to the north), but although many of his duties are 'royal' and he presents himself as the sole ruling figure in the region, he did not claim kingship.

The rise of Thebes began in the fifty-year reign of Wahankh Intef II. He adopted the titles of the dual kingship, 'King of Upper and Lower Egypt' and 'Son of Ra', but not the full five-fold titulary. Intef extended his rule to the southern border, building chapels at Abu (*Elephantine*). He then led his army northwards, attacking the nome of Tjeny, but his advance was checked by the nomarchs of Sauty (Asyut). This may have been followed by a northern counter-attack which resulted in the recapture of Abedju (*Abydos*). The reunification of Egypt under Theban rule was halted.

In the period of conflict there was extensive use of 'mercenary' troops, mostly from regions of Nubia. They are particularly well documented from Gebelein south of Thebes, where stelae reveal their high status, some with Egyptian wives and servants. A wooden model of a large contingent of Nubian archers, with a companion group of Egyptian spearmen, was found in the tomb of the nomarch Mesehti of Asyut, suggesting that Nubians from different regions were employed by rival factions.

In trying to understand the First Intermediate Period, Egyptologists were deeply influenced by a number of documents of Middle Kingdom origin. The most important are known as the *Admonitions of Ipuwer* and *The Prophecies of Neferti*. They paint a picture of chaos and disorder in which everything is inverted:

> See, he who had nothing is a man of wealth,
> . . . the poor of the land have become rich,
> . . .the man of property is become a pauper.

Lo, magic spells are divulged, spells are made worthless through being repeated by people.

Lo, offices are opened, their records stolen, the serf becomes an owner of serfs.

Lo, [scribes] are slain, their writings stolen, woe is me for the grief of this time!

> (For full text, see Miriam Lichtheim, *Ancient Egyptian Literature*, vol. 1, 1975: 157)

We no longer read these as historical records, but as a literary genre showing the fears of the elite: that the mass would gain control of wealth and the uninitiated would destroy knowledge.

In some ways, both socially and culturally, there were quite significant changes, although the underlying Egyptian system was not altered: there is no evidence for any form of mass or popular uprising, and the elite still maintained control, even if the power of the pharaohs was reduced. There is, so far, little archaeological or textual evidence from Memphis or Nen-nesut, and no major royal funerary monuments are known. Elsewhere, the 'provincial' centres saw an increase in the number of workshops that were not under direct royal control and instead served the local elites. This led to the development of more obviously regional styles, although all continued to work within the conventions of Egyptian depiction. In Middle Egypt, the influence of the Memphite traditions is clear, but at Thebes, for example, figures tend to be slim and attenuated. Also at Thebes, a distinctive local style of tomb was created for the rulers, with an open court cut into the low hills, colonnades of square columns, a chapel and a burial shaft. The artists who painted the tomb of Ankhtifi at el-Moalla, and contemporary tombs at Aswan, used vivid colouring and a distinctive style. Although the artistic production of the First Intermediate Period is often seen as cultural decline, it does appear that more people were able to acquire status objects, such as funerary stelae, than in the Old Kingdom.

One of the most significant developments is the more widespread Osirian burial customs, with coffins and other equipment, such as wooden figures of boats, offering bearers (later butchers' yards and houses), made specifically for the burials. Coffins carry funerary prayers and texts that derive from the royal pyramid texts of the late Old Kingdom. These developments come to full fruition in the Middle Kingdom, but certainly begin with the expansion of elite provincial cemeteries and family tombs during the First Intermediate Period.

6

IMPERIAL EGYPT
The Middle and New Kingdoms
(*c.* 2025–1069 BC)

The Middle Kingdom is undoubtedly one of the high points of Egyptian civilization. It was a period of four hundred years of, apparently, peace and prosperity, and of high cultural achievement. Through its literature, its people speak to us in a more direct way than those of the Old Kingdom, and the surviving administrative documents and letters permit an insight into the daily workings of palace and farm, and the tedium of service on the desert frontier.

THE REUNIFICATION OF EGYPT

The Middle Kingdom spans the latter part of the eleventh, the whole of the twelfth, and the first part of the thirteenth dynasties. It has a very clearly defined beginning: the reunification of Egypt by the Theban ruler, Nebhepetra Mentjuhotep II. This event, which took place part way through the king's 51 years of reign, probably around his 39th year, was the culmination of many years of conflict with the kings of Nen-nesut (*Herakleopolis*), and their allies in Middle Egypt, notably the nomarchs of Sauty (Asyut). During the long years of war, Mentjuhotep suffered losses: the burial of 60 soldiers whose part-scavenged bodies were reclaimed from the battlefield after an attack on a walled town is one of the most striking testimonies to the events.

As well as campaigning in Middle Egypt, Mentjuhotep II led his army into Nubia. There is some evidence that the king founded some of the main fortresses, but his activities are somewhat obscured by the extensive building work of the twelfth-dynasty pharaohs. Mentjuhotep's actions may have been part of a rear defence and expansionist programme before, or alternating with, his northward thrust. The Theban king appears to have formed a close relationship with the Medja people of the Eastern Desert, probably employing them as troops, and at least one of his wives may have been Medja. Undoubtedly, one of the major factors of Egyptian involvement in Nubia at this time was the renewal of intensive trade in the luxury traffic from further south. The fortresses were probably built as storage and supply depots connected with trade before becoming major military strongholds for the imposition of Egyptian rule. Egyptian activities appear to have stimulated an immediate response in Nubia, and during the reigns of Mentjuhotep II's successors an indigenous Lower Nubian kingdom emerged. Inscriptions of the early twelfth dynasty refer to twenty years of opposition by a local ruler in Lower Nubia, and this may have forced a more aggressive policy than had prevailed before.

Immediately following the reunification of Egypt, Mentjuhotep II began to centralize the administration, a process that continued in the succeeding dynasty. Some of the nomarchs were removed from office, notably the nomarch of Sauty who had been a major supporter of the rulers of Nen-nesut.

Mentjuhotep II's successors, Mentjuhotep III and IV, had quite short reigns, leaving few 'historical' records. Mentjuhotep III sent an expedition to Punt, and there was a concentration of building in the Theban region, some showing considerable architectural innovation. The last king of the dynasty, Mentjuhotep IV, had a brief reign of seven years, the only notable records being quarrying expeditions at Hatnub and in the Wadi Hammamat. The latter was led by the vizier Amemenhat whose inscription records two 'miracles' that occurred during the expedition. The vizier is generally thought to be the same as the pharaoh Amenemhat I who succeeded Mentjuhotep IV. How he achieved the throne is unknown, but a *coup* may be suspected: the 'miracles' that occurred during the quarrying expedition would have served to point out his favour with the gods.

THE TWELFTH DYNASTY (*c.* 1985–1773 BC)

The twelfth dynasty was one of the most stable dynasties to rule in Egypt, and the kings reasserted central authority. They reduced the power of the nomarchs through appointment of royal officials and by emphasizing the role of the mayors of towns. Egyptologists once thought that Senusret III had removed the nomarchs from office, but it is now clear that their disappearance is part of a longer process, which has its origins with Mentjuhotep II. Senusret III did institute a new administrative division of Egypt, with two departments, for north and south. All Egyptian pharaohs had to tread a fine line in controlling the power of the elite, and the twelfth dynasty used the policy of education – schooling elite children in the palace – and integrating elite families into the wider, rather than local, administration. There was a larger bureaucracy and greater specialization than in the Old Kingdom, reflecting the increasing complexities of government. The evidence from a large number of monuments raises the possibility that some of the pharaohs of this dynasty ensured a smooth transition of the kingship by associating a son as co-regent. However, the arguments for and against co-regencies are still keenly debated and Egyptologists remain divided.

Amenemhat I, the founder of the twelfth dynasty, may have had to use force to assert his authority. He built a new residence and administrative town called Amenemhat-Itj-tawy, meaning 'Amenemhat the seizer of the Two Lands', which itself suggests power by force. The town was probably situated near Lisht where his pyramid tomb stands. During his reign, the king also changed his Horus name to Wehem-mesut, 'Repeater of Births', a phrase that heralded a new beginning and was used at several other significant points in Egyptian history. After a reign of thirty years, Amenemhat I was murdered. This is clear from the *Tale of Sinuhe* and the didactic text called the *Instruction of Amemhat I* in which the king describes his own death. The story of Sinuhe implies a palace conspiracy involving some of the king's sons. His successor was Senusret I, who reigned for a total of 45 years, with or without a co-regency with his father.

Senusret I's reign saw two major Nubian expeditions, in years 10 and 18, and the initial phases of building in the fortress of Buhen at the foot of the Second Cataract. The reign also saw extensive royal patronage for temples throughout Egypt, notably at Karnak and Abydos. The reign of Amenemhat II provides evidence for Egypt's involvement with western Asia, including treaties with some of the Levantine cities. The tomb of the nomarch Khnumhotep at Beni Hasan has a fine painted scene depicting a 'bedouin' leader, Abisha, and his entourage dressed in brightly coloured clothes. Earlier interpretations used this scene as evidence of the immigration of Asiatics into Egypt, but this could be a seasonal movement of peoples or a specific trading expedition. Egyptian objects of this period are found throughout sites in the Near East, and Tunip in north Syria is specifically documented as a trading partner. There was some military action in Sinai, perhaps associated with expeditions to the turquoise and copper mines, and there was an expedition along the Red Sea to Punt.

The most important evidence from the reign of Senusret II, recently suggested to have lasted for nineteen years, relates to the development of the Fayum. The pharaoh ordered the construction of a massive serpentine dyke and canal system connecting the Bahr Yusef, a tributary of the Nile, with the Fayum basin. This channelled excess flood water and allowed the more intensive cultivation of the region. The king's pyramid complex at Lahun overlooks the dyke and the entrance to the Fayum. At the edge of the cultivation stood a large town, known to Egyptology as Kahun, which served as the centre of the king's mortuary cult, but was probably also a major royal residence and administrative centre.

The reign of Senusret III marks the high point of the dynasty in many ways. The highest date on royal monuments is year 19, but the Turin Canon grants Senusret over thirty years and recent research suggests that he may have reigned for thiry-nine years. There were fierce Nubian campaigns in years 6, 8, 10 and 16 associated with a change in Egyptian policy, and the expansion of the fortress system around the Second Cataract. The Cataract itself was defended with a series of massive fortifications. The largest, Buhen and Mirgissa, at the foot of the Cataract, acted as storage and supply depots for food, and for trade items brought from Egypt and Kush. The smaller forts, several on islands, were defensive and for the control of traffic, situated within signalling distance of each other. The trade from the south must have been enormous to justify this level of state investment, and this is apparently confirmed by the growth of Egypt's major trading partner, the Kushite kingdom based on Kerma, above the Third Cataract. Egypt's southern boundary was the narrow gorge at Semna, with forts on both sides of the river to control the trading vessels coming from the south. The stelae set up at Semna, at the southern frontier, are forceful statements of the Senusret's vision of his rule which are paralleled in the many statues of the king with his distinctive facial features and stern countenance.

Amenemhat III was one of the greatest builders of the dynasty, and his pyramid at Hawara, near the entrance to the Fayum, had a temple of such scale attached to it that it entered Greek and Roman tradition as the 'Labyrinth'. Numerous inscriptions attest intensive mineral exploitation of the period: turquoise and copper in Sinai and other materials, such as amethyst, from elsewhere in Egypt and Nubia. A large number of texts carved on the rocks of the Second Cataract record the flood levels of the Nile during the reign, and reveal a series of very low floods that may have caused economic decline. The dynasty came to a close with the brief reign of Amen-emhat IV and a female ruler, Sobeknofru, perhaps his wife or daughter; presumably, circumstances appeared in which there was no direct male heir in the family. Because of its religious basis, the Egyptian monarchy was masculine, and although there were reigning women at many periods, they were all treated as pharaohs. The reign of Sobeknofru is acknowledged in the Turin Canon, and is attested by inscriptions and building. The most remarkable evidence of her reign is the fragment of a statue that shows her wearing the king's royal headcloth, the *nemes*, and a male kilt over the typically close-fitting female dress of the period, demonstrating the ways in which the Egyptians tried to assimilate the idea of the masculine kingship with a female holder of the office. This type of statue may have served as a model for the early statues of Hatshepsut in the eighteenth dynasty.

The first part of the thirteenth dynasty shows continuity in many ways, but there were many short reigns, suggested by Stephen Quirke to represent a rotation of the kingship through a number of the most powerful elite families. After a period of over a century, there was a rapid disintegration of power, in part caused by the expansion of the Kushite kingdom of Kerma. Egypt had probably supported Kerma as its main trading partner in the early Middle Kingdom, perhaps even with military support. Certainly, Kerma became increasingly powerful, and the fortresses of the Second

Cataract were attacked, looted and burnt. Statues from the temples were carried off to Kerma and help to date events quite closely. At the same time, the Asiatics who, had settled in the eastern Delta, actively encouraged by the twelfth-dynasty pharaohs, emerged as another power.

INNOVATION AND RENAISSANCE IN THE ARTS

Following the reunification of Egypt by Mentjuhotep II, there were extensive royal building projects, particularly in the Theban region. The relief sculpture from Nebhepetra Mentjuhotep II's temple at Deir el-Bahari shows an influence from the Memphite workshops, but with the attenuated figures that are typical of the Theban style of the First Intermediate Period. The king's temple-tomb at Deir el-Bahari shows a development of the Theban style of royal tomb favoured by his immediate predecessors, combined with striking architectural innovation. Although Deir el-Bahari is the best-preserved monument, fine statuary and blocks of relief decoration survive from buildings at Armant, Karnak, Medamud and Dendera. In these monuments Mentjuhotep II reinvented the cult of divine kingship, and for the first time a pharaoh is seen assuming the crowns of Amun and Min.

There was considerable architectural innovation in the monuments of the reign of Mentjuhotep III. These also have the finest quality relief sculpture, which now seems to show greater Memphite influence in the forms of the figures. This Memphite influence is also to be found in the early twelfth dynasty; indeed, the sculpture from the pyramid complexes at Lisht was directly modelled on late sixth-dynasty monuments. In the reign of Senusret II there is a change in the style of sculpture. This becomes even more apparent in the statuary of Senusret III and Amenemhat III, which have distinctive facial features combined with the traditional idealized body. The stern expression of the statues of Sensuret III has been read as an image of authoritarian kingship, reflecting the political realities of the day, or as the ruler under the burden of his office.

The twelfth-dynasty pharaohs initiated an extensive temple building programme throughout the country. Although not on the monumental scale of the New Kingdom, the surviving structures

are elegant and decorated with fine relief sculpture. The royal pyramids were mostly of brick faced with limestone and consequently
are today less impressive than those of the Old Kingdom. In ancient
times, however, the temple adjacent to the pyramid of Amenemhat
III at Hawara was considered a greater wonder than the pyramids
at Giza. At both Dashur and Lahun, jewellery belonging to royal
ladies was discovered, revealing a technical excellence and aesthetic
refinement unequalled in Egyptian history.

Throughout the Middle Kingdom there was significant royal
patronage of the cult of Osiris at Abydos, which also became a
popular pilgrimage centre. The Osirian style of burial had become
more widespread (at least among the elite) during the First Intermediate Period, and the use of 'Coffin Texts', themselves derived
from the exclusively kingly 'Pyramid Texts', combined with newer
literature, is seen as part of a process of 'democratization' of funerary
beliefs. The appropriation of exclusively royal funerary texts by the
elite is actually a process that repeats itself in later periods of
Egyptian history. With Mentjuhotep II's complex at Deir el-Bahari,
the kingship itself became closely associated with the Osirian afterlife. Although the twelfth-dynasty pharaohs returned to the Old
Kingdom form of the pyramid for their burials, the layout of corridors and chambers within them is more closely associated with the
Osirian vision of the underworld, and preludes the form of New
Kingdom tombs in the Valley of the Kings.

One important product of the Middle Kingdom is its 'literature',
surviving in a range of genres. A number of stories and other
'instructions' exist in multiple copies because they were used as
scribal exercises in the New Kingdom; clearly, the language was a
model, as well as the content.

EGYPT AND THE OUTSIDE WORLD

One of the most striking aspects of Egyptian activity in the Middle
Kingdom is the expansion into Nubia which, until the construction
of the High Dam at Aswan, had also left some of the most remarkable archaeological remains from the entire span of Egyptian history
in the great mud-brick fortresses. Although they were the only ones
that survived into modern times, the Nubian fortresses were not the

only military constructions of the period: Amenemhat I constructed a defensive network on the eastern frontier of the Delta. The exact nature of the defence – called the 'Walls of the Ruler' – is unknown, but it may have included a canal with forts.

One aspect of Egypt's activities in Nubia may have been the exploitation of the gold mines of the Wadi Allaqi. There was certainly intensive activity in the copper and turquoise mines of Sinai, and of other mineral resources, notably amethyst from the 'diorite quarries' near Toshka in Nubia and the Wadi el-Hudi near Aswan.

The trade in 'luxury' materials flourished, that from Nubia being attested by the controlling infrastructure rather than documentary sources; presumably, it comprised the usual products of the south. The timber trade with the Levantine ports continued, but numerous archaeological finds provide further detail of activity. Byblos was one of Egypt's oldest and most important trading partners, supplying cedar wood and pine, and here Pierre Montet excavated a large hoard of jewellery, along with other Egyptian objects. The jewellery, some carrying the name of Amenemhat III, has close parallels with items from the tombs of queens and princesses at Lahun. The wide range of foreign gifts is shown by the dedication excavated in the temple of Montju at Djerety (Tod). Four bronze caskets, carrying the name of Amenemhat II, contained a large number of ingots of gold and silver, with many silver vessels, probably of Aegean origin, which had been deliberately flattened, a lapis lazuli necklace and Mesopotamian seals. These may all have been a gift to the pharaoh from one of the rulers of western Asia, rather than products of individual contacts with the different regions. Further evidence for Aegean contacts comes from the small quantities of Cretan pottery that have been excavated at sites throughout Egypt, and Egyptian stone vessels and other small objects found in Crete. The contacts between Egypt and Crete may have been direct, or through the Levantine ports.

In addition to their activities in the Nile Valley, south of Egypt, the twelfth-dynasty pharaohs sent expeditions to the East African land of Punt, probably in northern Ethiopia or Eritrea. In recent years the site of the Middle Kingdom port on the Red Sea, Sawaw, has been identified at Mersa Gawasis, north of Qoseir, at the end of the Wadi Hammamat.

THE SECOND INTERMEDIATE PERIOD
(*c.* 1650–1550 BC)

For a long time, the phase between the end of the twelfth dynasty and the beginning of the eighteenth presented challenges to Egyptologists. The fragments of the Turin Canon contained numerous royal names for the period, indicating either an extremely long historical phase (as Flinders Petrie originally suggested: see Table 4.1, p. 86), or a shorter one of considerable political upheaval. On the evidence of Greek and Roman sources, and the retrospective allusions in inscriptions of the New Kingdom, it was known that Egypt had fallen under the rule of the 'Hyksos' who were clearly a people of western Asiatic origin. Not surprisingly, connections were made with the biblical story of Joseph and the Exodus. Gradually, an 'accepted' interpretation was reached, based on the available evidence, but excavation and research over the past thirty years has considerably increased our understanding of the 'Second Intermediate Period'.

The Hyksos 'problem'

The sources of the Ptolemaic and Roman Periods, such as Manetho and Josephos, call some dynasties 'Hyksos', and state that they ruled from the city of Avaris. Hyksos is clearly a Greek form of the Egyptian *heqau khasut* meaning 'rulers of foreign lands'. This term is used by some of the kings, inscribed in hieroglyphic on their monuments. The people are called 'Aamu' in Egyptian texts, which is a broad term, usually translated simply as meaning 'Asiatics'.

The discovery of objects with the names of some of the Hyksos pharaohs (e.g. Khyan) in quite distant locations, such as Knossos on Crete, Athens and Mesopotamia, led to the idea of a 'Hyksos empire'. As the Hyksos were known to have had chariots and horses (at least towards the end of the period), it was also suggested that they were of north Syrian 'Hurrian' origin and part of a wide-ranging, chariot-owning aristocracy that founded empires through the Near East (see p. 117). Early Egyptologists were also influenced by the inscription of Hatshepsut in the temple at Speos Artemidos in Middle Egypt, which narrates how Egypt fell under the control of these Asiatic peoples, and portrays their rule as a disaster in which the gods and temples were neglected. Hatshepsut's text is actually the beginning of the process of rewriting the history of the period.

Much of the earlier reconstruction of the history has been overturned by recent work, notably that of the Austrian Egyptologist Manfred Bietak and his team at Tell el-Daba in the eastern Delta. The site is certainly the ancient city of Hut-waret (*Avaris*), and the layers of settlement there have yielded a wealth of information on the complex culture of the 'Hyksos Period'. The settlement had its origin in the Middle Kingdom, and grew to a large size. Houses of the twelfth- and early thirteenth-dynasty settlement have a Syrian, rather than Egyptian, form. The next phases yielded imported objects from western Asia and Crete. Overall, the evidence suggests that Hut-waret was a major trading centre which had both Egyptian and eastern Mediterranean populations, and in its latest phase had close contacts with Cyprus.

Egypt divided

The fragmentation of Egypt seems to have followed the reign of Merneferra Ay, who is the last thirteenth-dynasty ruler with monuments in both Upper and Lower Egypt. The Middle Kingdom residence city of Itj-tawy was abandoned and a number of dynasties claimed the pharaonic style, the most important being those of Hut-waret (*Avaris*) and Thebes. In Nubia, the Kushite kingdom of Kerma took control of the forts of the Second Cataract and may have had effective rule as far north as the First Cataract.

There is now an abundance of information from the later Hyksos Period. Besides the archaeological material from the main Hyksos centre at Tell el-Daba, there is also a vast amount from the Kushite trading centre of Kerma where Charles Bonnet and a joint Swiss-Sudanese team have excavated the extensive town site. A number of significant royal and private monuments illuminate the campaigns of the Theban rulers to reunite Egypt. The most important are those of the pharaoh Kamose and the soldier Ahmose son of Ebana.

By the later years of Hyksos rule, its kings were firmly established in Lower Egypt, perhaps ruling from Memphis. The long reign of the pharaoh Apepy, at least forty years, indicates the stability of the Hyksos regime. They had control of the Nile Valley into Middle Egypt, with their southern border with the Theban kingdom in the region of Qis, to the north of Asyut. The wealth of the Hyksos kingdom was based on trade with western Asia. One of the records of the Theban king Kamose lists the commodities that were imported by the Hyksos. They include chariots and horses, timber, lapis lazuli, silver, turquoise, bronze and oil. It is also clear from the Kamose texts that the Hyksos had formal diplomatic relations with the Kushite rulers of Kerma. At Kerma itself, numbers of seals carrying the names of Hyksos kings have been discovered, and it seems clear that the exports of the Hyksos were the products of the far south. The excavated burials of the Theban rulers of this period are remarkably poor, suggesting that the Thebans had been largely cut out of the lucrative international trade.

Another significant role played by Nubia is known from cemeteries at a number of sites in Egypt. These contain the burials of Nubian soldiers, probably Medja of the Eastern Desert. They are known as 'pan grave' culture because of the shape of the graves. Some of the most significant burials are in Middle Egypt, from the region of Asyut, Deir Rifa, Mostagedda and Qau. Janine Bourriau suggests that the distinctions in the associated material from the cemeteries point to frontier garrisons on the Hyksos–Theban border, with Medja troops employed by both kingdoms.

It took the Theban rulers many years to reunite Egypt. Seqenenra Taa and Kamose led their armies south into Nubia and north into Lower Egypt. The mutilated body of Seqenenra Taa suggests that he may have been severely wounded, if not killed, in battle with the Hyksos, and although the brief reign of Kamose records significant military actions in Nubia and against Avaris itself, he too may have been killed in battle. There was a long pause before Kamose's successor, Ahmose, reopened hostilities.

THE NEW KINGDOM (c. 1550–1069 BC)

Around 1550 BC the Theban ruler Ahmose led his army north and stormed Hut-waret, drove out the Hyksos and reunited Egypt. Ahmose's success was the culmination of the campaigns and military actions of his predecessors. The Theban princes had been active on two fronts, notably in Nubia to protect their rear during the northward campaigns, and perhaps to disable the Kushites in any support of their Delta trading partners. A letter from the Hyksos ruler of Avaris to the Kushite king proposed a combined attack on the Theban kingdom, and an inscription in a tomb at Nekheb (el-Kab) records a Kushite invasion of southern Egypt. The Theban rulers first re-established control over northern Nubia as far as the Second Cataract, then they turned their attention northward. Following the reunification of Egypt they consolidated their position in Nubia, but it took a full hundred years for them to bring the Kushite kingdom to its knees, and even then it seems to have been achieved as much through diplomacy as force.

Although Ahmose appears to have been successful in crushing the Delta kingdom, there are some hints that opposition remained. An 'autobiographical' text of a military officer who served under Ahmose reports military actions against Aata, who was probably a local ruler in Nubia, and against Teti-an, who was possibly a leader of anti-Theban opposition in Middle or Lower Egypt. Ahmose's successor, Amenhotep I, may also have had to face opposition within Egypt. Both Amenhotep I and Thutmose I were involved in large-scale military actions in Nubia and in western Asia. It is generally

Figure 6.1 The pharaoh of the New Kingdom as chariot warrior: Sety I on the exterior of the Hypostyle Hall at Karnak.

assumed that Egyptian activities in western Asia were initiated to protect the northern frontier, and to establish Egypt's role in relation to the emerging powers of north Syria, most importantly the kingdom of Mitanni.

Thutmose I led the Egyptian armies across the Euphrates river into Mitanni. The range of these campaigns is extraordinary and reflects a new military system within Egypt itself. These changes included a large permanent standing army and some significant developments in technology. The most important of these was the horse-drawn chariot which was introduced into Egypt during late Hyksos times (Figure 6.1). At first both horses and chariots were rare, all acquired from Asia (probably north Syria) but the Egyptians soon developed their own form of chariot modified for use in their specific terrain, even if constructed from imported materials. By the early nineteenth dynasty, hundreds of chariots were being deployed by Ramesses II and the Hittite king at the great international conflict at Qadesh. With the introduction of the horse and chariot, a totally new type of warfare developed and along with it came a new elite ethos. The ability to read and write had always been the distinguishing feature of the Egyptian elite; to this was added the skill of using chariots.

AN AGE OF EMPIRES

The Egyptian 'New Kingdom' (c. 1550–1069 BC) is the Late Bronze Age of the Near East. It was the time of large empires: the Hittites in Anatolia, Mitanni in north Syria, and Assyria in Mesopotamia. Although there was conflict and rivalry for control of different regions and control of materials, this was also a period of intense diplomatic communication and state interdependence.

The pharaohs Ahmose, Amenhotep I and Thutmose I consolidated their dynasty's rule in Egypt, recovered Lower Nubia and exerted pressure on the Kushite kingdom. They also led their armies into western Asia, establishing a sphere of Egyptian influence over Canaan and south Syria. Egyptian expansion reached its limit in the reign of Thutmose III. At his accession, Thutmose III was a minor, and his father's chief wife, Hatshepsut, acted as regent. After a few years, Hatshepsut assumed full royal style as a pharaoh, and she reigned alongside Thutmose III until her death in year 21 or 22. During this period attention seems to have focused on Nubia, with four campaigns, one going as far as Miu in the savannah of the Sudan. The intense military activities in Asia began following Hatshepsut's death. Between years 22 and 42 Thutmose III campaigned almost every year, gaining control of the whole region as far as the Orontes river, and beyond that establishing Egypt's position in relation to the kingdom of Mitanni; the emerging Hittite kingdom in Anatolia did not yet pose a threat.

Thutmose III was, without doubt, the most active and successful of Egypt's warrior pharaohs. By the end of his reign, Egypt exerted direct control over Canaan, the coast of Lebanon and parts of north Syria. This was ruled through allies and vassal rulers, and policed with garrison forts. In Nubia, Egypt directly controlled and administered the valley as far as the Third Cataract. Beyond that, the region of the Third to Fourth Cataracts, including the rich heartland of the Kerma kingdom, was left under the direct authority of vassal rulers. Egyptian involvement here was to defend the southern frontier, and to control trade. Thutmose III was also a great builder, completing the enlargement of the Theban temples initiated by Hatshepsut, and constructing temples throughout the rest of Egypt and Nubia, all decorated with elegant relief sculpture.

From the reign of Thutmose I onwards, the Egyptians increasingly employed non-military methods to ensure their rule. They took the sons of foreign rulers for education at the Egyptian court; this was, no doubt, beneficial to both sides, the princes eventually being installed as successors to their fathers, but, in theory at least, pro-Egyptian. Their loyalty was bolstered by lavish gifts of gold and luxury materials and objects, and by military support for their regimes. By the end of the reign of Thutmose III the states, large and small, appear to have achieved such a level of interdependence that for the next hundred years conflict was limited. There were still 'rebellions' at the change of ruler, and this was a time when treaties had to be renegotiated, but there are less than a dozen significant campaigns recorded for the 75 or so years of the reigns of Amenhotep II, Thutmose IV and Amenhotep III. There is, however, a mass of diplomatic correspondence detailing the relationship between the great powers.

EFFECTS OF EMPIRE

What were the internal effects of the expansion of Egypt into Nubia and Asia? There were significant and quite rapid changes in warfare, and consequently there were changes in elite education. Literacy remained the defining characteristic of the elite, but boys were trained from an early age in the skills required for driving chariots, and particularly for chariot warfare. Even though there were vassal rulers and local elites incorporated into the rule of foreign territories, Egypt's empire must have seen an increase in the size and professionalization of the bureaucracy. The 'Foreign Office' certainly played a significant role, with the royal envoys involved in diplomatic contacts between the pharaoh and foreign rulers, both vassals and those of the other kingdoms. The extensive diplomatic correspondence preserved from Akhetaten (the 'Amarna Letters') shows that there were scribes skilled in the international language, Akkadian, and probably in other languages.

The relatively few 'autobiographical' texts that describe official careers indicate that elite education – in one of the temple or palace schools – combined literacy skills with those of chariotry. Most careers then seem to have followed a move through three stages from junior scribal positions to increasingly specialized and senior ones. Since these records generally apply to high-ranking officials, they do not reflect the careers of the majority of 'scribes' who formed the bulk of the civil service. In the tomb paintings showing the large and extended families of senior officials, such as that of the vizier Rekhmire (one of three viziers from the same family), it is notable how many carry 'lowly' titles.

Certainly, there was increasing specialization throughout the New Kingdom and, following education and, perhaps, a period serving in the chariotry, young members of the elite moved into one of the branches of the state: the priesthood, the military, the diplomatic service, the civil administration or the palace. The question then arises, was there a developing sense of 'institutions' and institutional power? Many Egyptologists have explained the 'religious reforms' of Akhenaten as a direct response to the power of the Amun priesthood. The accession of Horemheb and of the family of Sety I and Ramesses II is likewise seen as the culmination of the 'rise of the military'. The New Kingdom ends with the emergence of the independence of Upper Egypt ruled by the high priests of Amun. These interpretations of the evidence have become rather firmly embedded in Egyptology, but may be unduly influenced by Western European developments. They are important issues to consider when we try to understand how ancient Egypt functioned, and will be considered in more detail in Chapters 8 and 9.

THE ROLE OF THEBES

Earlier Egyptologists placed great emphasis on the role of Thebes in the eighteenth dynasty, generally speaking of it as the 'capital'. We recognize increasingly that the preservation of monuments in the Theban region is actually due to the town's location far from the main centres of population and power in later periods, and that this was equally true in ancient times. Thebes certainly was important and was lavishly endowed by the eighteenth-dynasty pharaohs. It was the ancestral home of the eighteenth- (but not the nineteenth- or twentieth-) dynasty royal family, and served as the burial place of the pharaohs and the most important members of the royal family into the twentieth dynasty. Its temples were enlarged and endowed under royal patronage, and Amun was elevated to be one of the state gods of Egypt. Thebes was actively promoted as a southern counterpart of the northern cities of Heliopolis and Memphis, but those cities were certainly as large and as important, if not more so.

Undoubtedly, royal patronage was a major factor in the enlargement of the Theban temples and the importance of the city. The pharaohs of the early eighteenth dynasty, notably Amenhotep I, rebuilt the temple of their town god and donated wealth from foreign campaigns to it. Hatshepsut was another key figure in the elaboration of the religious role of the city. As wife of Thutmose II, Hatshepsut held the office of God's Wife of Amun, which had considerable prestige and economic power. Thebes was no better placed to serve as the principal administrative centre than any of the other towns of Upper Egypt: Koptos and Edfu had better connections with the Eastern Desert routes and the Red Sea; Tjeny was better placed for access to the western Oases; Abedju had greater religious significance. It was the royal patronage that established Thebes's importance. Thebes was never in a position to act as Egypt's 'capital'; it was too far removed from the centres of population, and too far from the main area of Egypt's foreign interests, western Asia.

THE 'AMARNA REVOLUTION'

The peaceful years of the mid-eighteenth dynasty saw Egypt pre-eminent in the world of north-east Africa and the eastern Mediterranean. The gold and other luxury products of her African dominions maintained that position. The zenith was achieved in the reign of Amenhotep III, a period of unrivalled building and artistic production. It was also a reign that saw an attempt to re-establish the position of the pharaoh as it had been in the Old Kingdom: the living sun-god on earth. Amenhotep III's son and successor took this even further. After a few years of reign as Amenhotep IV, he assumed a new name, Akhenaten, and founded a new city in Middle Egypt, which was to replace Thebes. Called Akhetaten, 'The Horizon of the Sun-disc (Aten)', but now usually known as Amarna, the city was dominated by vast solar temples, modelled on those of Iunu (*Heliopolis*). A dramatic new artistic style was developed to portray the king, his wife Nefertiti, their children and courtiers.

Inevitably, within the context of the New Kingdom the 'Amarna' period has figured large. Lasting for only 30 years at most (embracing the last years of Amenhotep III and the reigns of Akhenaten's immediate successors), it would be easy to dismiss it as a relatively minor episode in Egypt's history; but since the West first encountered them, the bizarre art, the apparent monotheism and the savage destruction of the monuments has drawn the attention of Egyptologists. The dominant view of Egyptology in the early to mid-twentieth century emphasized the monotheistic features, drew connections with the Psalms and Judaism, and proposed a direct link with Moses. Akhenaten has been claimed, on free interpretation of the evidence, as not only a monotheist but a pacifist, a homosexual, and even a vegetarian (though he was not, as he is shown eating kebabs). The view of him as the first monotheist, with or without some of the other speculations, has been deeply influential, and has achieved a wide currency through many Egyptological works, and through numerous novels based on them. This idealized view was expressed most recently in Philip Glass's opera *Akhnaten*. It has also been significant in the development of numerous elements of Egyptology's 'fringe', notably theosophy, and the Rosicrucian church. One attraction of Akhenaten to many people, not only Egyptologists and psychologists (Freud most influentially), is the idea that we can penetrate the *personality* of the king. We cannot. The major studies of Akhenaten all shed some light on the period, but they probably tell us far more about the attitudes of Egyptology as a discipline, and of individual writers, than the psyche of Akhenaten.

At the beginning of the twenty-first century, Egyptology offers two contrasting interpretations of Akhenaten. One is a modified version of the monotheistic pharaoh, playing down some of the earlier notions of his idealism. The other projects Akhenaten as a reactionary figure, establishing a totalitarian regime focused on himself. Some Egyptologists have argued, and with some good reason, that what happened would have happened even without Akhenaten himself as the driving force. Certainly, some of the significant features of the reign can be traced back through those of Amenhotep III and Thutmose IV; they are responses to Egypt's imperial expansion in the early to mid-eighteenth dynasty. Even if much that has been written about the personality of Akhenaten is speculation and cannot be supported by cold examination of the evidence, the personality of the king must surely have been an important factor. The promotion of the solar and royal cult in the last years of Amenhotep III's reign is very different from that of Akhenaten's: a different king may have taken a different route, as Ramesses II was to do.

So how important is the reign of Akhenaten? And what does it actually tell us? The swift restoration of the state cults and the unprecedented destruction of the king's monuments show that there was some fundamental failure. Also, taking the longer view, we can see some significant changes that appear in Egypt in the 'post-Amarna' period. Perhaps the most important of these is the personal relationship between an individual and a god that becomes clear in tomb decoration. The emphasis in decoration moves away from the official and his relationship to the pharaoh, to funerary scenes and texts. However, our understanding of Akhenaten's reign is much more limited than we like to think it is: there is, so far, very little evidence from sites other than Amarna and Thebes. Egypt appears to have recovered quickly from Akhenaten's experiment, and that, perhaps, reveals the underlying strength of its system.

THE RAMESSIDES (c. 1295–1069 BC)

The accession of Horemheb as pharaoh has often been interpreted as the culmination of the 'rise of the military' and, therefore, as representing changes in Egypt throughout the eighteenth dynasty. Horemheb was certainly the leading military figure in the reign of Tutankhamun, but that does not necessarily mean that that was the reason he became pharaoh, nor does it indicate the power of the army as an institution. We do not know what factors led Horemheb to select another important military officer, Sety I, to be his ultimate successor. On Horemheb's death, Ramesses I briefly held the throne, which, in Egyptian ideology, was valuable for the dynasty, as Sety then ascended the throne as the son and rightful heir of a pharaoh. Intentional or not, Egypt needed military pharaohs, as the rapid rise of the Hittite empire (Khatti) threatened her interests in north Syria. Under its own dynamic military ruler, Suppiluliuma, the Hittite kingdom had expanded to control – directly and indirectly – much of Anatolia and was moving to gain control of the important regions of north Syria that had been controlled by Mitanni and Egypt. There were clashes between Egypt and Khatti late in the reign of Akhenaten, and in that of Tutankhamun. Sety I was active in re-establishing Egypt's position in north Syria, and the struggle for control of the region culminated in the battle of Qadesh, in year 5 of Ramesses II.

In Egypt, Sety I founded many temples and a new residence city in the eastern Delta, close to Hut-waret. This area, if not the town itself, appears to have been his own ancestral home. The new city was completed by Ramesses II and named, after him, as the 'Estate (*per*) of Ramesses-mery-Amun Great-of-Victories', more generally known as Per-Ramesses. The city was certainly very large and contained four major temple complexes; but almost nothing survives on the site as the temples were dismantled and most of the stone transferred to Djanet (*Tanis*) at the end of the twentieth dynasty. Within the city, numerous twelfth-dynasty statues were reused. They were not 'usurped', since the names of the original pharaohs remained, but those of reigning monarchs were added; this linked the living pharaoh and his city with the glorious past.

Ramesses II has long been known as 'the Great', and described as 'Egypt's greatest pharaoh' and greatest warrior. Perhaps more than with any other ruler, Egyptologists have fallen victim to the king's own propaganda, but a dispassionate reading of the evidence hardly supports his claims. The much-vaunted 'victory' at Qadesh was nothing of the sort, and Ramesses' later military activities made no lasting gains in north Syria. For the last 45 years of his reign the pharaoh did not lead further campaigns. Ramesses II's greatest legacy was as a builder and as Egypt's greatest recycler: huge numbers of statues, many from the reign of Amenhotep III, were skilfully recarved to adorn his temples. Ramesses II was possibly more successful as a theologian than a warrior, developing a version of the royal cult that was more politically and theologically astute than that attempted by Akhenaten. Where Akhenaten removed the images of the gods to direct focus onto himself and an abstract solar deity, Ramesses multiplied images, the king and gods appearing side by side. Nor did Ramesses promote only the solar cult, although that was prominent. The temples built in the later years of his reign show an increasingly complex theology.

The long reign of Ramesses II has to be set against the growth of an international crisis. The expansion of the Hittite kingdom (Khatti) and of Assyria had effectively destroyed Egypt's old rival and ally in the region, Mitanni, and forced the smaller states of north Syria into new alliances. But there were now internal problems in Khatti which loosened its control of satellites. Further south, in Palestine, there were certainly political changes, although these are unclear. By the reign of Ramesses' successor, Israel (in some form) had come into existence. To the west, attempts to control the movements of Libyans into Egypt were abandoned, and they were accommodated as troops in settlements in the eastern Delta. In Nubia there were intermittent problems with the kingdom of Irem, which probably lay on the southern border of the Egyptian dominion. The length of Ramesses II's reign was to have repercussions in Egypt itself: his twelve eldest sons died before him, and his successor was the thirteenth, Merneptah, presumably quite elderly himself.

At the beginning of the reign of Merneptah there was some recovery of Egyptian influence in Canaan, but this was followed by a major Libyan invasion in his fifth year. This is stated to have been provoked by famine in the Libyan homeland. The Libyan forces approached Memphis, but were repulsed. They were accompanied by contingents of the 'Sea Peoples' who were to reappear in the reign of Ramesses III. The 'Sea Peoples' included the Peleset (Philistines) and the Shekelesh, Shardana and Lukka, whose names clearly associate them with Sicily, Sardinia and Lycia. The 'Sea Peoples' are one of the main problems of Late Bronze Age archaeology. For over a century historians have argued that they were a mass migration of peoples that came through Anatolia and along the Levantine coast, causing destruction in numerous cities and the collapse of major states. The individual 'tribes' are certainly prominent in Egyptian records of the nineteenth and twentieth dynasties, but the older interpretation of them as one of the principal forces in the end of the Late Bronze Age is almost certainly wrong.

The two decades following the death of Merneptah witnessed dynastic crises. Sety II faced a rebellion by a rival, Amenmesses, perhaps his own son. The dynasty came to an end with the short reign of the young king Siptah and that of Sety II's widow, Tawosret. As with Sobekneferu and Hatshepsut, Tawosret assumed the style of a female pharaoh. A court official of Syrian origin, Bay, was extremely powerful in these reigns and may have attempted to seize the throne. However, a new dynasty assumed power with the brief reign of Sethnakht and the much longer one of his son, Ramesses III.

Ramesses III has generally been rather unfairly treated by Egyptologists. He is often considered to be a pale imitation of Ramesses II, and some Egyptologists have even claimed that the military victories recorded in his temple at Medinet Habu were not his, but copied from earlier temples. An alternate view calls Ramesses III 'the last great pharaoh', neatly dismissing a thousand years of pharaonic history. Ramesses III does seem to have regained control of much of Canaan, but he also faced major problems with two Libyan wars (in years 5 and 11), a battle with the 'Sea Peoples' (in year 8), and conflict in Nubia, against Irem. A long papyrus document records the trial and execution of a number of people involved in a conspiracy to murder Ramesses III and make one of his sons (by a minor wife) pharaoh. A large number of palace staff, as well as some significant officials, were implicated. As this investigation and trial was ordered by his successor, it seems likely that the plot was, in part, successful and that the king was indeed murdered.

The reigns of Ramesses III's successors are usually characterized as a period of decline dominated by economic crisis, and the rise of the power of the priesthood of Amun. This view is probably exaggerated. We actually have an unparalleled wealth of documentary evidence for the period, almost entirely from the Theban region, and little to give a good balance from elsewhere in Egypt. From official archives, the documents begin with the 'Harim Conspiracy' trial and detail looting in the royal tombs at Thebes, theft of temple grain over an extended period, and the problems that affected Thebes in the reign of Ramesses XI. Rather than being a sign of a collapsing regime, the sort of events recorded in these documents may actually reflect the 'normal' pattern of Egyptian life. The fact that all of the crimes were tried in the courts indicates that central authority was still working efficiently.

There was certainly a problem in the succession: Ramesses III's immediate successors had short reigns, and there is some evidence that Egypt may have been struck by plague. The remnants of the Asiatic empire were lost under Ramesses VI. The family connection of the last rulers is obscure, but there were some fairly long reigns. We can be certain that the empire in Nubia came to an abrupt end quite late in the reign of Ramesses XI, and the evidence suggests that Egyptian centres south of the Second Cataract were closed down and the frontier redrawn. This may have been a response to an emerging power in the south of Nubia, perhaps the kingdom of Irem.

WHAT CAUSED THE IMPERIAL COLLAPSE?

The collapse of the twentieth dynasty has been attributed to a military coup or to the power of the Amun priesthood at Thebes. Egypt is often said to have been bankrupt, an 'enfeebled old wreck' with a corrupt bureaucracy. Egypt's supplies of new gold from Nubia had certainly been exhausted by the reign of Ramesses III, but there were still considerable amounts held within the temples and in the royal tombs. There was certainly some state 'looting' of the royal burials, no doubt to bring the gold back into circulation. A crisis did occur in the reign of Ramesses XI; there was some sort of civil war and the abandonment of southern Nubia. Order was announced with the establishment of a new era named 'Wehem-mesut', 'The Repeating of Births'. But the problems that beset Egypt are part of a much broader crisis in the eastern Mediterranean that began in the reign of Ramesses II and saw the collapse of the great empires of the Late Bronze Age. There is evidence for famine in Libya and the Hittite empire, but there is nothing to suggest that there was a major climatic change at the time. Blame for the collapse of the great empires has frequently been put on invasions and mass migrations by a number of groups from outside the region, notably the 'Sea Peoples'. However, the old interpretation is probably wrong and such movements of population as there were may be a result of the crisis, rather than a cause. Whatever factors caused the 'end' of the Late Bronze Age, between 1200 and 1150 BC the empires of western Asia were replaced by a host of smaller successor kingdoms and the region passed through a period of considerable change. The new order that emerged had the trading kingdoms of Israel, Judah and Damascus at its heart, and the rising powers of Assyria in the east and Nubia in the south.

7

CONTINUITY WITH METAMORPHOSIS

Egypt 1100 BC to AD 641

Since the decipherment of hieroglyphic and Egyptology's reconstruction of its history, the history and culture of Egypt after the
New Kingdom has suffered from unfair neglect in general studies.
This is the more remarkable because many Egyptologists have
been particularly attracted to certain aspects of these periods, such
as Demotic texts. The pre-nineteenth-century European image of
Egyptian art was derived almost entirely from monuments that
were the products of the Late, Ptolemaic and Roman Periods.
In recent years, interest in Ptolemaic and Roman Egypt and their
monuments has increased enormously among Egyptologists, rather
than being the preserve of classicists, particularly papyrologists.
Popular interest has also been stimulated by the underwater discoveries in the area of Alexandria. However, the centuries from
the end of the New Kingdom to the conquest by Alexander the
Great of Macedon in 332 BC remain a period that excites little
popular interest. Why?

The reason for the lack of general interest in these later periods
stems from Egyptologists themselves. Many of the classic histories,
such as those of Breasted, Wilson and Gardiner, devote relatively
little attention to the periods, which are generally depicted as times
of 'decline'. First, Egypt came under the rule of 'foreigners': Libyans,
Kushites, Assyrians, Persians, 'Greeks' (actually Macedonians) and
Romans. Second, it suffered internal divisions and lost its empire.
Egyptologists, along with many other historians writing in the
late nineteenth to mid-twentieth centuries, equated possession of
empire with 'greatness' and loss of empire with failure (a view that

has, perhaps, not entirely disappeared). Chapter titles such as 'The Broken Reed' (John Wilson 1951) and 'Decline and eclipse during the Late Period' (Cyril Aldred 1961) epitomize their attitudes.

Clearly, the post-New Kingdom – essentially the first millennium BC, the Iron Ages of Near Eastern archaeology – is a different world from that of the Bronze Age. The collapse of the Bronze Age empires and kingdoms certainly had major repercussions throughout the region. But does the lack of an empire and rule by 'foreigners' denote an inferior state? What are the real changes in this period? Certainly, there were significant economic changes, notably the invention of coinage. But how far is the underlying social and belief system essentially the same as it had been earlier?

For Egypt, the periods from the end of the New Kingdom to the Arab conquest (AD 641) are actually the richest in terms of surviving monuments and documentary material. Many of Egypt's largest and best-preserved temples were constructed by the pharaohs of the thirtieth dynasty and their Ptolemaic and Roman successors: Behbeit el-Hagar, Dendera, Esna, Edfu, Philae and Kalabsha, to name only some of the most complete. Huge archives of papyrus documents detail the life and economy of Egypt, as well as the religious beliefs. The artistic production of the Late Period is grudgingly acknowledged as technically equal to anything produced earlier, although this is usually followed by disparaging aesthetic judgements.

So, did Egypt 'decline' during these periods? And in what ways did Egypt change and stay the same?

THE THIRD INTERMEDIATE PERIOD
(c. 1069–664 BC)

The period immediately following the New Kingdom is now usually known as the 'Third Intermediate Period'. This term became popular in the 1960s by analogy with the First and Second Intermediate Periods. It embraces those dynasties conventionally numbered 21 to 25. Previously, it had been called the Libyan and 'Ethiopian' Periods. Ethiopian (i.e. dynasty 25) was dropped as a term in the 1970s as being too easily confused with the modern state of that name and has been replaced by 'Kushite' or 'Nubian'. Some Egyptologists prefer to place dynasty 25 in the Late Period.

131

One of the key issues has been the length of the 'Third Intermediate Period'. There is an enormous amount of material surviving, but the fragmented nature of Egypt during some of the period makes reconstructing the evidence difficult. The conventional date for the end of the New Kingdom, marked by the death of Ramesses XI is around 1070 BC.

A number of Egyptologists propose reductions of the overall length of the Libyan Period, and the lowering of the reigns of certain rulers (specifically Takeloth II and Sheshonq III). In suggesting lower dates and overlapping reigns, some Egyptologists extend the rule of other pharaohs to fill the gaps that they have created, whereas others recommend an overall lowering. A number of Egyptologists have suggested that the Third Intermediate Period should be shortened by fifty or a hundred years. This would place the end of the New Kingdom between 1020 BC and 970 BC. An even more radical proposal of reducing its length by 230 years is not widely accepted by most Egyptologists, although it has some limited support from archaeologists working in other parts of the eastern Mediterranean. Such a reduction would bring the end of the New Kingdom to around 840 BC, leaving a period of only a century for the independent rule of the Libyan pharaohs. The accession date of Taharqo in 690 BC is a fixed point, and although there is uncertainty about the exact reign lengths of some of his Kushite predecessors (Shebitqo, Piye and Kashta), the Kushite invasions of Egypt must have taken place between 740 and 720 BC. Apart from the archaeological repercussions throughout the eastern Mediterranean, shortening the Libyan Period actually makes it a much more dynamic phase, and also explains the Kushite expansion far more satisfactorily than the conventional, longer chronology.

THE LIBYAN PHARAOHS

The Libyan Period falls into two parts: the earlier is a continuation of the late Ramesside Period, both artistically and politically. Although Egypt had lost much of its empire in western Asia and Nubia, it was still ruled by one king. However, the tensions apparent in Upper Egypt in the reign of Ramesses XI grew. The late Libyan Period saw the fragmentation of the country under the rule of four pharaohs and a number of Libyan Chiefs and Great Chiefs in Lower and Middle Egypt, and the territory of Thebes initially independent and later under Kushite control. The fragmentation process began in the reign of Takeloth II.

There are large amounts of archaeological and inscriptional material surviving from the Libyan Period, but there is a geographical imbalance in this. The main centres of power were in the Delta, initially Djanet (*Tanis*) and Per-Bastet (*Bubastis*), later Sau (*Sais*), with Memphis remaining significant as a royal residence and administrative centre. Excavation in all of these sites has, until recently, been restricted to the major temple areas. The tombs of some pharaohs were excavated at Djanet, but we do not have the quantities of funerary material of the period that survive in the drier conditions of the Theban region. However, the Theban evidence relates to the elite families of the city rather than to the reigning Delta pharaohs. Some changes in burial practices are also apparent in the Theban region, in part deriving from the reduced size of the royal workshops there and the concentration of activity in the north.

With the twenty-first dynasty the city of Djanet (*Tanis*, the biblical Zoan) replaced Per-Ramesses as the principal royal residence in the eastern Delta. Of the vast archaeological site, only the principal temples have been thoroughly excavated. These temples were built with stone blocks and adorned with statuary and obelisks, much of it granite taken from Per-Ramesses. Egypt was united under this dynasty, with the pharaohs ruling from Djanet (and probably Memphis) and with Thebes under the control of other members of the family in the offices of high priest and God's wife of Amun. There was, however, another emerging power: the family of the Libyan Chief Sheshonq, which probably had a power-base in the region of Per-Bastet (*Bubastis*).

The succeeding dynasties – 22 and 23 of Manetho – present a major problem to any Egyptologist trying to rationalize the material. While the names in Manetho's dynasty 22 clearly correspond to Sheshonq, Osorkon and Takeloth, the monumental evidence shows that there were more of them than Manetho lists. Manetho's dynasty 23 is difficult to tie to the archaeological and epigraphic evidence, since there are many pharaohs attested by monuments who are not named by Manetho. A recent controversy has arisen, claiming that the 'twenty-third dynasty' is a series of rulers in Thebes – but the proposer of this idea includes none of Manetho's twenty-third-dynasty kings in it. This highlights the problems of Manetho's work for periods of disunity. It is more satisfactory to list the Libyan kings in groups according to family, attested inscriptional links or known power base.

The first group is essentially the 'dynasty 22' of most Egyptologists, with some later rulers whom others ascribe to 'dynasty 23': the evidence seems to be clear that they constitute one family and line of succession. They gained control over the whole of Egypt with Sheshonq I, although his uncle, Osorkon, appears to have assumed royal style earlier. At least one marriage (probably more) tied this Libyan family to that of the twenty-first dynasty. Sheshonq I was certainly a dynamic ruler, leading his armies into Israel, where a stele fragment indicates some control over Megiddo. His successes, however, were short-lived. Close trading links with Byblos continued under his successors, Osorkon I and Osorkon II. It was in the reign of the latter, and of his successor Takeloth II, that the fragmentation of Egypt began.

The early Libyan pharaohs installed their sons as high priests of Amun at Thebes, and as high priests of Ptah at Memphis. This policy ensured dynastic control, but the marriages of these princes with the local elites was a root cause of the troubles of the later Libyan Period, when rival lines with royal descent laid claim to the kingship and priesthoods. Hints of the impending crisis appear in an inscription of Osorkon II in which the pharaoh prays for unity among his descendants. The first major conflicts are attested in the reign of Takeloth II, when his son – the crown prince and high priest of Amun, Osorkon (later Osorkon III) – faced 'rebellion' in Upper Egypt over a period of twenty-eight years. The prince, who also had the rank of Army General, violently suppressed revolts in Khemenu (*Hermopolis*) and Thebes on several occasions.

On the death of Takeloth II, the designated Crown Prince Osorkon did not immediately ascend the throne, but recognized another ruler, Sheshonq III, who had already assumed royal style. The rise of power of Sheshonq III is extremely obscure, but shortly after his reign, other rulers appeared in the Delta town of Tent-remu (*Leontopolis*), and at Nen-nesut (*Herakleopolis*) and Khemenu (*Hermopolis*) in Middle Egypt.

The other important power centre to emerge during this time was Sau (*Sais*) in the western Delta. Sau was an ancient city, but little is known of its role during much of Egyptian history as there has been relatively little excavation there. In the later Libyan Period it came under the rule of Tefnakht who carried the Libyan titles 'Great Chief of the Libu' and 'Great Chief of the Ma'. Two inscriptions show that Tefnakht was expanding his area of control from Sau over much of the western Delta in the years 36 and 38 of a pharaoh Sheshonq. The great 'Victory Inscription' of the Kushite king Piye begins with a messenger arriving in Kush to say that Tefnakht had gained the support of other Libyan rulers, captured Memphis and was marching his army south to seize the cities of Piye's allies, Peftjauawybast of Nen-nesut and Nimlot of Khemenu. Piye's army was ultimately victorious and he received the submission of all of the Libyan pharaohs and rulers, although he left them in office. Tefnakht was succeeded as ruler of Sau by Bakenranef, probably his son. By the time of Piye's death, Bakenranef had assumed kingly style and captured Memphis. Piye's successor in Kush, Shabaqo, led his army to Egypt and defeated the king (c. 710 BC); Greek tradition claims that Bakenranef was burned alive. Unlike Piye, Shabaqo and his successors ruled as pharaohs from Memphis, although many of the Libyan rulers were left in control of their princedoms. The monuments of Bakenranef ('Bocchoris' in Greek sources) are not numerous, but they are intriguing. Sau had probably established good trade links with the Phoenicians. Sau itself stood on the main Nile branch in the western Delta, and the Phoenician trading ships probably sailed along this towards Memphis, rather than directly along the coast. It is possible that the Greek trading centre of Naukratis replaced a Phoenician-Saite one.

Egypt's international position is generally regarded as weak during the later Libyan Period. It is certain that the dominant power in western Asia was the expanding empire of Assyria, and that the kingdoms of Israel, Judah and Damascus were vying for control of the trade routes. There is also a dearth of evidence from Egypt itself for major military activities in the Levant and Syria-Palestine. Egypt's internal problems may have prevented an actively expansionist policy. The only attempt to reassert Egypt's role in western Asia seems to be the campaign of Sheshonq I, which has for long been identified with the biblical account of the sack of Jerusalem by the 'Pharaoh Shishak' in about 925 BC. Whether or not Sheshonq was Shishak, Sheshonq's campaign was wide-ranging and the first major military action since the twentieth dynasty. It is recorded by the long list of captive towns presented to the god Amun in a large relief on the outside wall of the Hypostyle Hall at Karnak.

The bulk of the evidence for Egyptian activities in western Asia is economic. The location of Djanet (*Tanis*) and Sau (*Sais*) would have favoured their roles as trading cities. This was the period of Phoenician expansion around the Mediterranean and particularly along the North African coast. Egyptian material, especially faience and alabaster vessels, is found in archaeological sites of this period widely distributed around the Mediterranean, and the Phoenicians were undoubtedly the intermediaries. Assyrian and other documents show that ivory, elephant skins and other exotic products of north-east African origin were being acquired through Egypt's old trading partners of Byblos, Tyre and Sidon. One product that became especially important at this time was papyrus, which was used for written documents as Aramaic became the dominant international language. Assyrian reliefs frequently show two scribes making records of events, one writing on a clay tablet (in cuneiform) and the other on a papyrus roll (in Aramaic). Egypt had the monopoly on papyrus production (and, indeed, it may have been a royal monopoly too), most of which was manufactured in the Delta. The trading activities of the Greek and Phoenician colonies in the western Mediterranean have resulted in Egyptian objects being excavated at sites in the Aegean, Greece, Sicily, Italy (particularly Etruria), Spain and north-west Africa (notably Carthage).

Whether the rule of independent Libyan pharaohs lasted the two hundred years of conventional chronology or for a century, their legacy was considerable. There are strong indications that the artistic renaissance that came into full flower under the succeeding Kushite and Saite dynasties originated in the Delta in the later phases of Libyan rule. The cultivation and development of the Delta, particularly the eastern part, was probably largely carried out in Libyan times. The significant role played throughout the Late and Ptolemaic Periods by an hereditary military 'class', called the *machimoi* in Greek texts, is recognized as a development of a Libyan system.

Although the pharaohs adopted the Egyptian style, there were Libyan features that remained. The acceptance of other rulers of almost equal rank – the Great Chiefs and Chiefs of the tribal groups (the Meshwesh and Libu) – allowed the fragmentation of Egypt to take place, and this was to have important consequences throughout the following periods. Libyan traditions may be reflected in the changes in burial customs and certainly lie behind the lengthy genealogies that appear on monuments of the period, an inheritance from oral traditions.

THE KUSHITE PHARAOHS (c. 750–664 BC)

The rise of the kingdom of Kush is still rather obscure. In attempting to explain it, archaeologists have placed far too much emphasis on the elite cemetery of ancient Napata, at el-Kurru, close to Gebel Barkal and the Fourth Cataract, ignoring other material. The el-Kurru cemetery contained the burials of the twenty-fifth-dynasty pharaohs Kashta, Piye, Shabaqo and Shebitqo and a series of earlier graves, almost certainly of their ancestors. However, the rise of this family is probably only one factor in the emergence of a Kushite state sufficiently large and unified to be capable of conquering Egypt.

Already in the nineteenth and twentieth dynasties, the kingdom of Irem on Nubia's southern border was a periodic threat to the stability of the Egyptian empire. The precise location of Irem is still disputed, but it was probably in the Bayuda Desert or Shendi Reach of the Nile. The Egyptian abandonment of Upper Nubia in the reign of Ramesses XI might have been caused by threat, or actual invasion, from further south. For understanding the development of this new Kushite state, the length of the Libyan Period is quite important.

There are some inscriptions that indicate a Kushite kingdom contemporary with Libyan rule, perhaps based in the Dongola Reach of Upper Nubia. There is also some indication of conflict, and perhaps civil war. There was certainly a conscious modelling of the new Kushite kingship on that of Egypt, and the cult of Amun was promoted by the new rulers. Beyond that we can say little until more archaeological and inscriptional evidence is found.

By the mid-eighth century BC the Kushite army was able to capture the southern border at Aswan and gain control of Thebes and Upper Egypt. Kashta is the first Kushite king known to have been active in Egypt, and the inscriptions of his successor, Piye, indicate that the Kushites were recognized as the rulers of the whole of Upper Egypt. Piye himself had alliances with the Libyan rulers of Khemenu (*Hermopolis*) and Nen-nesut (*Herakleopolis*) in Middle Egypt, and came to their aid when Tefnakht of Sau began to expand his power southwards.

Piye's successor, Shabaqo (*c.* 710–695 BC), crushed the power of Sau temporarily and established himself as pharaoh in Memphis, although leaving the remaining Libyan dynasts in office. For the ultimate success of the dynasty this was an unwise policy, as in the subsequent reigns the self-interest of the Libyan princes aided the invasions by the Assyrian army. The Kushites did, however, re-establish Egypt as a major power in western Asia, acting as the defender of the kingdoms against Assyrian aggression. During three decades of relative peace, trade expanded enormously, and the luxury commodities of Africa were exchanged with the timber and metals supplied by the Phoenician ports. In Egypt, the Kushite pharaohs paid particular attention to Thebes and its fortunes revived, with considerable building work and artistic production. The artistic style of the Late Period developed under Kushite patronage, although its origins may be detected in the late Libyan Period. It is character-ized by what is generally termed 'Archaism', a conscious looking back and modelling on the styles of the earlier high points of Egyptian art, particularly the Old Kingdom.

Kushite rule in Egypt was brought to an end by the Assyrians and the Libyan dynasts. Chief among the latter were the princes of Sau, who allied themselves with Assyria. Over a period of fifteen years, in the latter part of the reign of Taharqo (690–664 BC) and of his successor Tanwetamani (664–656 BC), the Assyrians under Esarhaddon and Assurbanipal invaded Egypt on several occasions, defeating the Kushites and driving them from Memphis. The Kushites regained control, but the Libyan dynasts constantly changed sides. Ultimately, Tanwetamani was defeated, Thebes was sacked and the king of Sau, Psamtik I, was installed as an Assyrian vassal. Psamtik, however, learnt from Kushite mistakes and gradu-ally eliminated the other Libyan rulers, reasserting the authority of the pharaoh as the unique power.

CONTINUITY WITH METAMORPHOSIS

THE SAITE PHARAOHS (664–525 BC): ATTEMPTS AT REGAINING EMPIRE

In his long reign of 54 years, Psamtik I (664–610 BC) established a stable dynasty. Psamtik was fortunate that Assyria was preoccupied with problems both internally and throughout its empire, enabling him to reunite Egypt, completely remove the Kushites from Thebes and Upper Egypt, reduce the power of the Delta dynasts and gain influence in western Asia. Psamtik's son, Nekau II (610–595 BC), tried to build on these successes and re-establish Egypt as the major power in western Asia, but he had to confront the armies of Babylonia which had emerged as the dominant kingdom in Mesopotamia. Egypt now had to act as the defender of the last Assyrian king. Nekau led his armies to Carchemish on the Euphrates, thus matching the campaigns of Thutmose I and Thutmose III. He defeated the king of Judah en route. In the conflict with the Babylonians, however, Egypt was defeated and Nekau II's ambitions were not realized. Psamtik II (595–589 BC) had some success on his southern frontier, sending his army into Nubia. Whether this was a response to a Kushite attempt to invade Egypt is not stated in the surviving records, but the Egyptian armies, with large numbers of Greek and Carian mercenaries, advanced beyond the Third Cataract. They left inscriptions on the statues of Ramesses II at Abu Simbel and fought a battle at Pnubs; they may even have attacked Napata. Some permanent Egyptian control may have been established over the region immediately to the south of Aswan. The fortress of Dorginarti near the foot of the Second Cataract was occupied during Saite and Persian times, although it may have served to protect trade, rather than being purely defensive.

Although Nekau II and Psamtik II failed to restore the Egyptian empire, internally Egypt seems to have been prosperous. Babylonia continued to be the dominant power in the Near East, and the reigns of Wahibre (Apries, 589–570 BC) and Ahmose II (Amasis, 570–526 BC) were defensive rather than expansionist. Wahibre, along with the rulers of Judah and Phoenicia, attempted to hold off the Babylonian advance, but without success: the kingdom of Judah was crushed, Jerusalem captured and its people taken into exile. Wahibre himself was deposed in a coup that brought Ahmose II to

139

the throne. A Babylonian attempt to restore Wahibre was success-fully repulsed. The reign of Ahmose II saw Egypt looking westwards to an important new neighbour, the Greek colony of Cyrene in Libya. Ahmose entered into a political alliance with Cyrene, which was sealed by marriage, presumably with a member of the ruling house. Ahmose was also forced by events into an alliance with Babylonia. The kingdom of Persia expanded rapidly under the dynamic rule of Cyrus the Great (559–530 BC), threatening to become the major power in western Asia. Egypt, along with Babylonia and Sparta, joined an anti-Persian alliance led by Croesus, the king of Lydia. In the event, it was Lydia that fell first to Cyrus (546 BC), but a few years later the Persian ruler entered Babylon in triumph (538 BC), gaining control of its whole empire. Throughout the twenty-sixth dynasty, the pharaohs had fostered increasingly strong relationships with the Greeks, first of Asia, then of Libya. Now Ahmose looked to mainland Greece for alliances, establishing a policy that was to continue for Egyptian rulers in the two centuries following.

EGYPT AND THE ACHAEMENID EMPIRE:
525–332 BC

Despite an active foreign policy and some successes, Egypt failed to regain its empire under the Saite dynasty, and at the end it fell, like its major rival Babylonia, to the rapidly expanding empire of Persia under the Achaemenid dynasty. For nearly two hundred years, from 525 BC, Egypt was under the rule of Persia or attempting to gain, or maintain, its independence. Following the conquest by Cambyses (525 BC), Egypt was placed under the rule of a satrap (viceroy), usually a royal relative. Apart from the installation of a satrap, the Persians retained the Egyptian administrative and legal system, largely in the hands of the Egyptian elite. The official administra-tive language was Aramaic, and there was an office of translators, but otherwise Egyptian government functioned as it had done under the Saites. Garrisons were installed throughout the country, and a number of major fortresses have their origins in the Persian Period. The best documented garrison is that based on the island of Abu (*Elephantine*) at the foot of the First Cataract. This garrison included a significant number of Jewish soldiers. A large archive records the marriages and lives of these soldiers, their intermarriage with local Egyptians and their dealings with other troops from western Asia stationed at Abu and on the mainland at Syene (Aswan). One important group of letters narrates the destruction of the Jewish temple on Abu and the attempts to rebuild it.

The Persian Great Kings were usually resident in Iran or on campaign, and those who actually went to Egypt went as conquerors to regain the country after rebellions. In administrative documents and official monuments they were presented not as absentees but as continuing the tradition of the pharaohs: they adopted the full titulary and their patronage of the Egyptian cults was shown by the temples built in their names, in which they were depicted in full pharaonic style. Although Persian cultural features in Egypt are limited, some Egyptian features were incorporated into Persian architecture, and Egyptian sculptors produced statues of the kings in a mixed Egyptian-Persian style. Egyptian soldiers and resources were employed in the campaigns of Darius (490 BC) and Xerxes (480 BC) against Greece.

Egypt, like most of the satrapies of the Achaemenid Empire, took the opportunity to break away at the death of the Great King. There were always dynastic rivalries at the Persian court, and the change of rulers allowed satraps or indigenous elites the chance to bid for independence. Much of the evidence for historical events in Egypt under Achaemenid rule comes from Greek sources, in which Egypt was an important incidental to the narrative of Greek conflict with Persia. As a result, the evidence for any Egyptian opposition to Persian rule suggests that this was confined to Lower Egypt. The best documented opposition is the rebellion of Inaros (463–454 BC), largely because of the military and naval support that it received from Athens. There were other indigenous rulers, mostly in the Delta, who assumed pharaonic style, but how effective they were at establishing their authority beyond a small regional power base is impossible to know. There is no evidence of rebellion in Upper Egypt, but, given the propensity of Thebes to independence in the Libyan Period, and again in the Ptolemaic Period, it may simply be that no evidence has survived.

The first rebellion came only a few years after the Persian conquest, with the death of Cambyses in 522 BC. It was perhaps led by Pedubast III, who is attested by a number of small monuments proclaiming his pharaonic style. Darius I regained control of Egypt, but there was another rebellion at his death and the accession of Xerxes I, in 486/485 BC when Psamtik IV may have launched this unsuccessful bid for independence. It was Psamtik's son, Iretenhorru (usually known by the Greek form of his name, *Inaros*), who led a major rebellion following the death of Xerxes in 465 BC. He was supported by Amyrtaios (Egn Amenirdis) of Sau, and in 460 BC received considerable naval and military aid from Athens. The rebels gained some successes, killing the satrap in battle, but the Persians eventually besieged them and the rebellion was finally crushed in 454 BC. Despite this disaster, Athens continued to support pretenders who, in return, supplied the city with corn from Egypt. Another Psamtik and another Amyrtaios appear to have conducted a guerrilla war during the reign of Darius II. There was rebellion throughout the satrapies of the empire at the death of Darius II in 405 BC and Egypt successfully broke away from Persia under the leadership of Amyrtaios, but a number of contending dynasts appeared as rivals. Amyrtaios was overthrown in 399 BC by the prince of Djedu (*Mendes*) whose own dynasty (29) was itself ousted by the prince of Tjeb-netjer (*Sebennytos*) in 380 BC.

Although the rulers of the twenty-ninth dynasty, Nefaarud I, Hakor and Nefaarud II, all had short reigns which appear to have ended violently, their royal style shows that they were attempting to emulate the Saite twenty-sixth dynasty and reinstate a truly Egyptian kingship. Nefaarud I and Hakor are attested as patrons of cults throughout Egypt, and this continued in the period of relative stability and prosperity of their successors in the thirtieth dynasty.

The prince of Tjeb-netjer, Nakhtnebef (Nectanebo I), assumed the throne of the pharaohs in 380 BC and adopted as his throne name Kheperkare, which had also been that of the twelfth-dynasty ruler, Senusret I: he clearly had ambitions to restore Egypt's glorious past. His eighteen-year reign (380–362 BC) saw the inauguration of building works on a scale that had not been seen for centuries. He founded new temples or began to rebuild ancient ones throughout Egypt, from the Delta to Philae at the First Cataract. However, Nakhtnebef's attempt to ensure a peaceful succession failed, and his son Djedhor (Djeho, Greek *Teos*) was deposed shortly after his accession in a family coup, in which his cousin, Nakhthorheb (Nectanebo II) was installed in his place. After facing considerable opposition from other dynasts, Nakhthorheb successfully established himself as a strong ruler, and fended off the attempts of Artaxerxes III to regain control of Egypt. The thirtieth dynasty saw the restoration of the pharaonic monarchy, and a renaissance in artistic production and temple building. Relations with the Greek city states and the Greek rulers of Cyprus were stronger than ever.

The achievements of the thirtieth dynasty came to an end with the successful invasion of Persian forces under Artaxerxes III in 343–341 BC. The last decade of Persian rule ensured that all Persian rule would be vilified in Egyptian priestly tradition: the wealth of the temples was looted and it is said that the statues of their gods were removed to Persia. The four decades of rule by Egyptian pharaohs seem to have inspired strong opposition, which led to the appearance of a new pharaoh, Khabbash. Khabbash is attested with pharaonic style in the western Delta and at Memphis, where he was certainly acknowledged by the priesthood of Ptah. The date of his brief rule is uncertain, perhaps between the death of Artaxerxes III (338 BC) and accession of Darius III (336 BC). Hatred of Persia was so intense that nearly thirty years later, in 311 BC, Ptolemy I found it politic to resurrect the memory of the last indigenous ruler and to confirm the grants of land that Khabbash made to the temples in Buto.

In 332 BC Egypt fell without conflict to Alexander III of Macedon, who installed his own commanders of garrisons, visited the oracle temple of Ammon at Siwa and founded Alexandria, before continuing on his march to the heart of the Persian empire.

An extremely hostile attitude towards Persia appears in later Egyptian literature, which certainly had its origins in the last Persian rulers' despoliation of the Egyptian temples. This hostility was recognized by the early Ptolemies in their own patronage of the indigenous cults. Ptolemy I, acting as satrap for Alexander IV and Philip Arrhidaios, continued the construction of the temples begun under the thirtieth dynasty. He confirmed the land grants made by Khabbash, and his successors claimed to have brought back the statues of gods removed by the Persians. This hostility also strengthened Egyptian opposition to the Seleukid dynasty, who could be seen as the heirs to much of the Persian empire, but whose kings regularly attempted the annexation of Egypt and Egyptian territory in Palestine.

THE PTOLEMIES (332–330 BC)

Egypt under the early Ptolemies emerged as the richest and most powerful of the Hellenistic kingdoms. Ptolemy I gained control of Cyrenaica to the west and Coele-Syria (Lebanon), Cyprus and many of the islands of the Aegean, with a number of important coastal towns of Anatolia. Although the Egyptian navy lost control of the sea in the reign of Ptolemy II, possession of Cyprus and many of the Asiatic cities enabled the rulers to maintain their influence in the northern Mediterranean. Coele-Syria was a continual source of conflict between Egypt and the Seleukid kings of Syria, until it was formally ceded as the dowry of the Seleukid princess Kleopatra I on her marriage to Ptolemy V.

In Africa, Egypt gained control of the northern part of Nubia, the Dodekaschoinos. There appears to have been an increase in population in Nubia, perhaps settled from further south, which was now ruled by the kingdom of Meroe. New temples were built throughout the Dodekaschoinos and agriculture was more intensive. This prosperity was to increase in the early decades of Roman rule. Trade was no doubt a major factor. Ptolemy II sent expeditions along the Nile routes and Ptolemy III was active along the Red Sea Coast, founding or expanding the ports. The usual trade continued, but live elephants were now brought to Egypt for use in the army, to emulate, and to rival, those of the Seleukids, which came from India. Elephants were first used, with great effect, in the Egyptian victory over the forces of Antiochos III at the battle of Raphia (217 BC). By the end of the Ptolemaic era the sea routes to India and Ceylon had been opened. To the west, the Ptolemies controlled the coast and the wealthy cities of Cyrenaica, and were active in the oases.

Within Egypt, the Ptolemies were great builders of temples to the Egyptian gods, some of the largest existing, such as Edfu and Dendera, being their foundations (Figure 7.1). They intensively cultivated the Fayum region, settling veterans in new villages and towns. However, there were tensions between the Greek and Macedonian settlers and the indigenous population. This was due to a number of

Figure 7.1 The classic temple in its ultimate form: Dendera.

factors, notably the political favours given to the Greek settlements and the exclusion of Egyptians from the army. A period of peace in the reign of Ptolemy III actually led to the crisis. Ptolemy IV needed extra troops for his conflict with Antiochos III of Syria and included indigenous Egyptians for the first time. Their success at the battle of Raphia (217 BC) was followed by a rebellion of the troops on their return, and the last years of the king's reign saw a widespread 'native' revolt in Upper Egypt, with Egyptian rulers proclaimed in Thebes. This rebellion lasted for nearly twenty years (205–186 BC), but Thebes was the focus for a number of later revolts and at least one more aspiring Egyptian king.

Following the murder of Ptolemy V, his two sons, Ptolemy VI and Ptolemy (VIII) Euergetes II, and his daughter, Kleopatra II, were made joint rulers. This was to be the origin of a long and increasingly complex dynastic feud, as one brother ousted the other. The situation became worse when Ptolemy Euergetes II married his widowed sister, Kleopatra II, then rejected her in favour of her daughter, Kleopatra III, by whom he had already had a child. Dynastic war tore Egypt apart, and shortly after peace was achieved both elder parties died, leaving Kleopatra III to play similar games with her own sons and use her daughters as pawns in the politics of Seleukid Syria.

The dynastic conflicts of the Ptolemies brought increasing reliance on Roman intervention, and also a significant role played by the Alexandrian mob. The bloody and colourful dynastic quarrels have perhaps played too significant a part in narratives of the period, obscuring the fact that Egypt was still the most important kingdom of the Mediterranean world and, despite the economic crises it suffered, potentially the most wealthy. Egypt's main rival, Seleukid Syria, had torn itself to pieces, its eastern territories falling to the Parthians, the fragments of the west to Rome, and in its heart a new Jewish state had emerged under the leadership of the Maccabees and then of Herod.

The last decades of Ptolemaic rule saw an increasingly important role being played by Rome, which had already gained control of Cyrenaica. Ptolemy XII 'Auletes' ('the Flute Player') owed his throne to the Roman Senate, and the Romans became active in the dynastic crisis following his death. The events of the Roman Civil War brought Julius Caesar to Egypt, and he chose to support Kleopatra VII in her conflict with her brothers. Despite her own personal success as a ruler, when Kleopatra met Marcus Antonius ('Mark Antony') she found another Roman who would help her retain her kingdom and, perhaps, increase it. This ambition failed and, in an unpredicted reversal of fortune, Egypt fell to the Romans.

Egypt under Ptolemaic rule achieved an empire and political importance as great as that of any earlier high point in its history. If building is a sign of success, then Ptolemaic Egypt was successful, with large new temples throughout the country and the splendours of Alexandria and the other Greek cities. Agriculture was encouraged, and the Fayum region was settled and developed. Culturally, too, Egypt flourished: Greek scholarship and literature were promoted at the court, and the literature of the Egyptian religion was written on papyrus and carved on temple walls. Cross-fertilization can also be noted in literature and was probably encouraged: Ptolemy II ordered a Greek translation of the first books of the Jewish bible (the Septuagint), and there were certainly Greek translations of Egyptian texts. The Egyptian tradition of sculpture on the colossal scale was revived and, combined with Egyptian and Hellenistic architecture, created a distinctive Ptolemaic style. Despite the political advantages given to their compatriots by the Ptolemies, there were certainly many intermarriages between 'Greek' settlers and Egyptians, and something that might reasonably be called a Graeco-Egyptian middle class emerged. Hellenistic culture played an increasingly large role, perhaps to the detriment of some Egyptian tradition. The later Ptolemaic Period saw economic crises, partly as a result of the dynastic conflicts but also because of corrupt admin-istration. This had a particularly harsh effect on that significant part of the indigenous population that did not enjoy the rights of the Greeks.

ROMAN AND LATE ANTIQUE EGYPT
(30 BC–AD 642)

Egypt under Roman and Byzantine rule appears to have been rela-tively stable. No longer the seat of a monarch, it was less embroiled in the international conflicts that were characteristic of most of its history, and only the occasional bid for the imperial purple was made by its prefects or citizens. Following the Roman occupation, there was considerable activity to secure the southern frontier with the Sudanese kingdom of Meroe, and after an initial period of conflict a mutually advantageous trading relationship was established. It was only in the later periods that there were serious threats from external powers: Zenobia and her Palymerene forces brought Egypt temporarily under their control (AD 268–70); raids by the Blemmyes of the Eastern desert forced Diocletian to redraw the southern fron-tier at Aswan (c. AD 300); finally, Egypt was taken by the armies of the Sasanid Persians, before falling to the Arabs under Amr ibn al-Asi (AD 639–42).

Although under Roman rule, Egypt was treated as a personal possession of the emperor. Unlike the other provinces of the Empire, Egypt was governed by a prefect of equestrian, rather than senator-ial, rank. Beneath him was a thin level of Roman government officials, with the bulk of the administration adapted from the Ptolemaic government and employing Graeco-Egyptians. In temple decoration the emperor was depicted as all Egyptian pharaohs had been. Absent he may have been, but the pharaonic tradition continued. Egypt's wealth was the key to this situation: grain production, mineral exploitation, and foreign trade using both the Nile routes and the sea routes to India. Rome relied heavily on Egyptian grain. The ships left Egypt in May or June, taking between one and two months to reach Italy, but returning far more quickly. The Roman Period saw cultivation in some difficult terrains: in Lower Nubia, there are indications of more intensive activity than in earlier periods, probably due to the introduction of the *saqia* wheel; throughout the remote oases of the Western Desert there are Roman Period sites and the remains of irrigation systems; and the Fayum villages flourished in the first centuries of Roman rule. However, there were widespread economic difficulties, beginning in the third century.

Mineral exploitation in the deserts was not only for gold but also for decorative building material: granite from Aswan and porphyry from the Eastern Desert. Discovered in the reign of Tiberius (AD 14–37), the purple porphyry of the Mons Porphyrites (Gebel Dokhan) near the Red Sea continued to be quarried until the fifth century.

International trade was a major source of exotic and luxury goods. The Nile trade with the Sudanese kingdom of Meroe was particularly important in the first century AD, and attested by the considerable quantities of imported Roman goods found in the elite burials at Meroe and in Lower Nubia. The Red Sea trade with East Africa and with India began in the Ptolemaic Period, but became increasingly significant during the later Roman Empire. The two main ports on the Red Sea were Myos Hormos and Berenike. Myos Hormos, now certainly identified as Quseir el-Qadim at the end of the road through the Wadi Hammamat to Koptos, was developed in the early Ptolemaic Period, but Berenike, much further south, came to be the more important in the later Ptolemaic and Roman Periods. Berenike is almost on the same latitude as Aswan, and trade goods had to travel the long desert road to the Nile at either Contra-Apollonos (opposite Edfu) or Koptos (350 kilometres (218 miles) away). Navigational problems in the northern part of the Red Sea actually made this a more viable route than sailing to the Gulf of Suez.

For over two centuries Alexandria remained the most important city of the eastern Mediterranean, before political circumstances gave that position to Antioch in Syria. Throughout the Roman Period there were increasing problems with the Alexandrian mob, and factional warfare was frequently sparked off by minor incidents. There was a huge Jewish community in Alexandria and, at times, considerable anti-Jewish feeling, notably at the time of the wide-spread 'Jewish revolt' (AD 115–17) in the reign of Trajan. Later, when Christianity was the main religion, the riots were provoked by sometimes quite obscure theological debates. Alexandria itself was the centre of the 'Arian heresy' which threatened church unity in the fourth century, and the orthodox Patriarchs imposed by Constantinople were usually greeted with riots.

One of the most important aspects of Roman Egypt is its religious development. Temples to the Egyptian gods continued to be built in the names of the emperors; some works begun by the Ptolemies (such as Dendera, Esna, Kom Ombo and Philae) were completed, but there were also new foundations, particularly in the villages of the Fayum and Oases, and in Lower Nubia. In the Ptolemaic Period some of the Egyptian cults had spread throughout the Hellenistic world. Notable among these were the related cults of Serapis and Isis which had become 'mystery' cults requiring initiation. Egyptian religion in the Roman Period absorbed many influences from other parts of the Empire and beyond, notably Persia, resulting in what is usually called 'Gnosticism'. The region of *Panopolis* (Akhmim) and Thebes appears to have played a particularly important role in these developments. Christianity, too, came to Egypt very early in the first century AD and developed in a distinctive way, absorbing many aspects of the indigenous religion. One of the most important aspects of Egyptian Christianity was monasticism. Developed by St Paul and St Anthony, and owing much to a form of non-Christian monastic practice, monasticism became a popular way of life in the fourth century. It was also to have an economic effect as increasing numbers abandoned the land and towns.

The undoubted problems of Egypt in the Roman Period have their origins in the Ptolemaic system. The majority of the indigenous population was forbidden the rights and privileges of the new settlers, and this led to resentment, breaking out in civil disturbances. But Roman Egypt did prosper in many ways and its legacy

149

is in the religious and cultural life that continued to metamorphose, absorbing Hellenistic, Roman and Persian elements, and the new Jewish sect of Christianity. In numerous ways Roman Egypt was strikingly different from the Egypt of the first pharaohs, but in many ways it was very much the same.

8

RULERS AND
RULED

The monuments of ancient Egypt present the image of an un-changing society. The scenes of 'daily life', particularly agricultural life, are essentially the same in Old Kingdom mastabas, Middle and New Kingdom rock-cut chapels and the early-Ptolemaic tomb of Petosiris at Tuna el-Gebel. Costumes may change slightly, as may the domesticated animals and birds, and there may be some tech-nological differences, but the image remains essentially the same, with the tomb owner overseeing the work on his estates and scribes assessing the revenues. In some ways this does present a version of Egypt, certainly as the elite wished it to be seen, but all societies do change, even if reluctantly. The problem for us is assessing significant changes over the millennia.

From the Predynastic Period onwards, Egyptian society was strati-fied. In the Old Kingdom the elite was certainly very small in number and in percentage of the population. By the New Kingdom society was much more complex, and it has been suggested that there were three main divisions: the royal family, the most important officials and some of the 'provincial nobility', forming an 'upper class'; lesser bureaucrats and priests, wealthy farmers, artisans and military officers forming a 'middle class'; and minor officials and priests, tenant-farmers, soldiers and peasants forming the 'lower class'. This is a rather Western division of society and ignores one of the key factors, the restriction of literacy and education.

So how should we divide Egyptian society? Or perhaps we should ask, how would the Egyptians have divided it? At the top was a small elite class comprising the royal wives and royal children, all officials (administrative, priestly, and military) and most 'scribes', with their families. The men of this class were able to read and write. The skilled artisans formed a specialized group that was closely controlled by the chief institutions of the state. The majority of the population were the agricultural workers, with domestic servants and slaves, most soldiers and industrial workers.

All of these people were subjects of the ruler, the pharaoh, who was the link between the human and divine worlds.

THE PHARAOH

The king – 'pharaoh' (from *per-aa* 'the Great House', i.e. palace) – is central to Egyptian religion and life. There has in recent years been a tendency for archaeologists to try to concentrate on 'ordinary' people, and on 'social history' rather than chronicles of kings and narratives of events; but we cannot understand Egypt without understanding what the kingship was about.

As with any monarchy, the role of the pharaoh changed throughout the course of Egyptian history, as the political and social circumstances dictated. Much of the Egyptological literature focuses on the king's administrative and warrior roles, treating the pharaoh like any Western ruler, with religious activities and policies generally regarded as important, but not his *raison d'être*. We often place more emphasis on the king's building activities than on his cultic role. The exception, of course, is Akhenaten, discussions of whom emphasize the religious policies. But, from the beginning of Egyptian history the pharaoh's prime function was as a priest, performing the cult for the gods, and acting as the intermediary between heaven and earth. This is the role that is most frequently depicted, even for the 'warrior pharaohs'. Rather than looking at early modern European monarchies for analogies, we should really be looking elsewhere. The medieval and Renaissance popes are the closest that a European monarchy provides, and from elsewhere, the Chinese emperors, and perhaps the inka, provide some useful parallels. Some earlier writers, such as Henri Frankfort and Charles Seligman, looked closer to Egypt, drawing analogies with other East African monarchies, which they 'understood' through anthropology.

The pharaoh was a ruler engaged with day-to-day administrative and 'political' affairs, but that was within, and never without, the religious context. The pharaoh probably led a highly ritualized life.

THE SYMBOLS OF KINGSHIP

Royal iconography is the most complex of any in Egyptian art. Indeed, the 'canonical' mode of depicting the human form was created specifically for the royal image. We can understand the significance of many particular items of the regalia and attributes of the pharaoh, but attempts to establish rules for their usage in scenes have generally failed. For example, although the Blue Crown (*khep-resh*) was dubbed the 'war helmet' by earlier Egyptologists, it is not the only crown that can worn by the pharaoh when he is depicted as a warrior: he may be shown wearing any of the crowns – Red, White, or a variety of plumed crowns that clearly have no practical function. Similarly, he can wear a range of different crowns when performing the rite of offering incense, or any of the food- and libation-offering rituals. The Red and White Crowns representing Lower and Upper Egypt can be used significantly in decorative schemes, on the north and south sides of the temple axis, but usage of other crowns generally defies analysis. However, evidence for the alteration and recutting of reliefs shows that the choices were not random, and that specific regalia were appropriate in certain places.

In addition to the crowns, there were other emblems that were frequently carried. Of these the most frequent were the 'crook' (*heqa*) and the 'flail' (*nekhakha*). The mace was both a weapon and an object used in ritual. A range of other staffs and sceptres had specific meaning and functions. All of these objects were imbued with divine power (*heqa*) like the person of the king himself.

The earliest name by which the pharaoh was known was one that identified him as the living manifestation of the god Horus. This name is also known as the *serekh*-name because it is written inside a sign representing the palace enclosure, with the palace façade at the bottom and the falcon on top. The name is closely identified with the royal *ka* (see below). The earliest pharaohs had Horus names that generally implied violence or control: Narmer ('the mean cat-fish'), 'Scorpion', Djet ('the cobra'), De[we]n ('the [head]cutter').

Gradually, other names were added during the Old Kingdom until there was a full complement of five. The 'Nebty' ('Two Ladies') name indicated that the pharaoh was protected by the goddesses Nekhbet and Wadjyt, the patronesses of Upper and Lower Egypt and of the two crowns. The goddesses themselves could appear on the pharaoh's forehead as the vulture and cobra (the 'uraeus'), although a single uraeus is more frequently shown. The other early name was 'Golden Horus' (or 'Horus of Gold'). Although both the Nebty name and the 'Golden Horus' name were established for the pharaoh at his accession, they were not rigidly fixed and could be varied according to circumstances.

Written with the 'heraldic' hieroglyphic signs of the bee and the sedge plant, the title *nesu bity* is usually rendered 'King of Upper and Lower Egypt' and was written within a cartouche. This name was adopted by the king at his coronation and was the principal one used during his reign and after his death. It is referred to as the 'throne name' and invariably includes the name of the god Ra.

The title 'Son of Ra' appears in the later Old Kingdom, and some Egyptologists suggest that it implies a diminution in the status of pharaoh at the time: no longer the living sun-god on earth, but his son. Written in a cartouche, this was the king's birth name and is the one used by Egyptologists to designate a pharaoh (e.g. Amenhotep III, Tutankhamun, Ramesses II).

In addition to these names, other titles and epithets were frequently used, preceding the cartouche names. *Neb-tawy* 'Lord of the Two Lands' (or 'Lord of the Two Shores') and *Neb-khau* 'Lord of Appearances' (or 'Lord of Diadems') are the two most frequent. The second title is difficult to render, as the word '*khau*' has a range of related meanings. It derives from *kha* 'to arise in glory' and is written with the hieroglyph of a hill with the rays of the sun rising. It is therefore used for the royal accession, coronation, crowns and appearance (either on the dais or in the 'window'), which should be like the sun in full splendour. *Neb-ir-khet* is usually rendered 'Lord of action' but by some as 'Master of the cult', referring to the king's priestly function. *Netjer-nefer* 'the Perfect God' (in older books 'the Good God') seems to imply the king's position as a junior sun-god. In the New Kingdom a large number of other titles and epithets were created to reflect the status of pharaoh as the pre-eminent ruler among the Great Kings: 'King of Kings', 'Ruler of the Rulers' and 'Lion of the Rulers'. From the later eighteenth dynasty the words *per-aa* 'pharaoh' and *heqa* 'the ruler' are frequently used in texts.

These titles emphasize the religious aspects of the kingship, and the names used, particularly in the variable Golden Horus and Nebty names, inform us about the duties and role of the pharaoh. They

Figure 8.1 Ramesses III performs religious rites (*see also* p. 164) which culminate in the announcement of his universal rulership. Medinet Habu, twentieth dynasty.

might allude to the king's role as universal conqueror and subduer of foreign lands, but more frequently they extol his virtues as the creator of laws, as the bringer of peace and prosperity to Egypt, and as the one who builds the temples for the gods and fashions their images.

KNOWLEDGE AND POWER

Egyptian elite society was about the control of knowledge. To know is to be able to control, and the pharaoh's divine power was based upon his knowledge of the gods, their secret names and their actions. An important text known as the *Treatise on the King as Sun-Priest* details this aspect of the pharaoh's role. The following series of statements tells us the sort of information that the king knows:

> He [the king] knows their [the gods] appearance and incarnations
> He knows the place where they stand
> He knows the words spoken by [*god X*]
> He knows how Ra is born and his metamorphoses in the flood, etc.

Among many other things, this text tells us that the king knows 'that secret speech which the Eastern Souls speak', but it gives no indication of what the content of that speech is, nor does it identify the 'souls'. But who the souls are and what they say is not what matters: what matters is that the king *knows* who they are and what they speak, and others do not. Ideally, the pharaoh was the unique possessor of such knowledge, but clearly he could not be everywhere at once to perform the cult. Therefore, others had to be able to share the knowledge in order to act on the pharaoh's behalf. On their monuments, members of the elite might indicate that they were privy to secret or restricted knowledge, but they do not reveal what that knowledge was.

One issue that has divided Egyptologists in the past, and to some extent still does, is that of royal divinity. Many Egyptologists argue that, except perhaps in the earliest periods, the king was not considered to be a living god on earth. The king was a possessor of divine power, he acted like the gods and on behalf of them, but there were limits to his divinity. However, on his death he acquired complete divinity and could then be worshipped.

Even if he was destined from birth to become pharaoh and was educated for that office, it was only during the coronation, with the acquisition of the royal insignia and the process of 'unification with the royal *ka*', that the king gained divine power and was able and fit to rule. The royal *ka* represented the divine aspect and continuing office of kingship, and each individual king was the living possessor of it. Each pharaoh was thus part of a continuous sequence stretching back through the earliest recorded Egyptian history to the gods themselves. The royal *ka* was the divine force which descended upon the king at his coronation. The concept has parallels with aspects of medieval European kingship and the rites of coronation that bestowed that power. In retrospect it could be claimed that the *ka* had not descended on certain proscribed rulers such as Hatshepsut, and Akhenaten. The concept of the royal *ka* also had practical implications for the kingship, since only one person could be the possessor of it at any one time.

In temple scenes the royal *ka* is frequently seen accompanying the king, and is specifically associated with the god Horus and with the king's Horus name. When we talk about the worship of the king, royal divinity and deification, it is usually the royal *ka* which is the recipient of the cult and worship. Statues of kings that served as intermediaries with the gods were frequently described as images of the royal *ka*.

THE PHARAOH AS RULER

The pharaoh was responsible for law, and this too had its divine aspect since he acted as judge like the sun-god Ra-Harakhty. Indeed, Iunu (*Heliopolis*) was the principal seat of law in Egypt, as it was of the solar cult. The 'Edict of Horemheb' (late dynasty 18) deals with numerous very specific concerns that must have been placed before the pharaoh and which received legislation. The dispensation of justice was carried out through the chief officers of state, notably the Viziers, although other officials could be directly appointed by the pharaoh to hear trials. In the case of palace conspiracies, as in those against Pepy I and Ramesses III, trials might be held secretly and judged by delegated palace officials. The trials associated with robberies of royal tombs in the Valley of the Kings were heard by the high priest of Amun and other Theban officials. Punishment for all crimes was harsh: execution, mutilation, impalation, enforced suicide and internal exile are all documented.

The local courts (called *qenbet*) comprised royal appointees and local officials (such as the mayors and priests), with the inevitable host of scribes keeping record. Two main courts (the Great *Qenbet*) were based at Iunu and its southern counterpart, Thebes. From the late New Kingdom onwards the power of the *qenbets* declined, probably due to historical and political factors, and oracles were increasingly used to resolve disputes, until the whole legal system was revised under the Saite pharaohs. Inevitably, there are numerous records of collusion, bribery and corruption.

The pharaoh was the controller of Egypt's wealth. This aspect of the kingship must be closely associated with its origins. If, as seems likely, one element in the early kingship derives from a 'cattle culture', then wealth would have been in cattle. The control of the agricultural surplus and the control of trade would have developed in the sedentary societies of the Predynastic Period. Many features of the king's role as administrator derive directly from the control

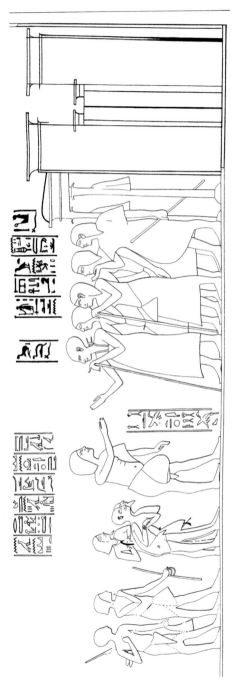

Figure 8.2 Egyptian officials at work: the Chief of Police in the city of Akhetaten, Mahu, brings three captured felons to the Vizier: Tomb of Mahu, el-Amarna, reign of Akhenaten (after N. de G. Davies, *Rock Tombs of el Amarna IV*, London, 1906, Plate XXVI).

of agriculture: the construction and maintenance of canals and dykes, land reclamation, taxation, storage against times of famine and low Nile floods.

Although it can be documented at all periods, the control of wealth is particularly clear in the evidence of the later eighteenth dynasty. The scenes and inscriptions relating to 'reward' detail the ways in which wealth could be acquired. The pharaoh controlled foreign trade, which was, essentially, gifts of raw and manufactured materials passing between rulers. In Egypt these were redistributed as gifts and rewards to officials, supplementing the produce of their estates. The scenes of reward pay particular attention to precious metals such as gold. It is clear that the items given were very carefully accounted for and were no doubt allocated on a very strict system. Equally, the 'Amarna Letters' detailing gift exchange between rulers include the number and type of precious stones in necklaces with their weight and the weight of gold and silver used. Inevitably, the evidence emphasizes particularly valuable raw commodities such as gold, ebony, ivory, incense and animal skins through Nubia and timber (cedar and pine), copper and lapis lazuli from Asia. But manufactures were equally significant in real terms. Furniture was made from ebony, ivory and Asiatic woods. Weaponry – the international arms trade – was particularly important in the New Kingdom, and chariots, horses, shields, bows, arrows, spears, armour and troops were exchanged between rulers. Detailed evidence from administrative texts for the Nubian trade includes lots of rather more mundane products such as dates, date paste, palm leaves, baskets and fans, along with various minerals and pigments.

The palace also controlled a range of other valuable commodities through its own workshops. Among the most important was linen, particularly *byssos*, the finest quality of 'royal' linen. This was exported to towns such as Tyre, where it was dyed with 'purple' from the local murex shellfish, and then turned into garments. Another important manufacture was papyrus, although it is uncertain whether this was always a royal monopoly. In the first millennium BC this became an especially important export as Egypt was the only producer, and the spread of Aramaic as an international language required papyrus instead of clay tablets. Papyrus continued to be exported in huge quantities until about AD 1000.

One of the commonest and most potent images of the pharaoh is the warrior. So he is depicted on monuments from the Predynastic Period to the Roman Period. However, most of these images of the pharaoh as conqueror are symbolic, rather than specific records of military action. War may have brought about the unified state, and force – or the threat of force – remained a central element in its continuity. Evidence from the Old Kingdom suggests that the pharaoh sent, rather than led, his army on campaign. Pharaohs of the Middle Kingdom may have taken a more active role, but even in Nubia, where the campaigns are quite well documented, the lead was often taken by other officials, notably the vizier. It is only in the New Kingdom that the pharaoh is frequently depicted and described as an active warrior. This is surely linked to the changes in military technology at that time. The introduction of the horse and chariot revolutionized warfare. A new elite chariotry corps was created, and the pharaoh could appear in appropriately divine form at the head of his army, in his gilded chariot. Certainly, the difference is clear in the scenes of battle that appear. The traditional image of the warrior pharaoh is that of the isolated ruler smiting his enemies with a club. In the battle scenes of the New Kingdom the colossal image of the pharaoh can dominate a mêlée in which his soldiers and enemy forces clash. He can strike dramatic and athletic poses, drawing his bow, or wielding the curved *khepesh* sword above his head; he charges through the fallen enemy, one foot on the axle of the chariot, as he leans out and seizes their ruler.

The narratives of military action also allow the king's divine role to dominate. In the council of war the generals propose one method of attack which is dismissed by the pharaoh, who offers his own, usually bolder, plan and which is always successful; this demonstrates his divine wisdom, his percipience (*sia*).

FAMILY AND SUCCESSION

Ideally, a pharaoh should be the son of his predecessor; hence, any children of the eldest twelve sons of Ramesses II, who had all predeceased him, were overlooked in favour of the living thirteenth son, Merneptah. At some periods Crown Princes were appointed, certainly in the reigns of Sety I, Ramesses II and Merneptah, and in the Libyan Period. Another means of securing the succession was co-regency. This contradicted the ideology by which there was only one Horus king, and was probably used only under unusual circumstances. Some Egyptologists have argued that co-regencies were a feature of the twelfth dynasty, but the interpretation of the evidence is still disputed.

The failure of dynastic lines inevitably caused problems. The Egyptian kingship was masculine and was meant to pass in succession from father to son. This ideological base meant that there was no concept of a ruling queen; when historical factors meant that the heir to the throne was a woman, as happened on a number of occasions, the Egyptians accommodated this as best they could. Unfortunately, little is known of the early female rulers Mer-Nit and Nitoqert. Sobeknofru at the end of the twelfth dynasty is better attested, and was recognized in official records. She, like Hatshepsut in the eighteenth dynasty, was originally associated with a male ruler. The imagery of Sobeknofru as king combined male attributes, such as the *nemes* (headcloth) and the kilt, with female dress. Depictions of Hatshepsut began with a similar combination of attributes, but these were later dropped, and Hatshepsut was finally depicted as fully male, both physically and in costume. Nefertiti, too, may have reigned as king alongside Akhenaten, and for a short period following his death (as Smenkhkara). Tawosret at the close of the nineteenth dynasty was depicted wearing the king's crowns and male costume of the nineteenth dynasty, a long pleated robe but with female physique. All of these women ruled as 'pharaohs', not queens. The titles they were given were easily modified by adding the female ending so that they could become 'the female Horus' and 'daughter of Ra'. For Hatshepsut, the usual eighteenth-dynasty style 'Horus mighty bull' (*Hor Ka-nakht*) was cleverly realigned as 'Horus powerful of *kas*' (*Useret-kau*), exploiting both the identical sounds of the words for 'bull' and 'soul' and the association with the royal *ka*.

Sometimes the succession passed to a new family through the female line; this appears to have happened several times during the Old Kingdom, and perhaps in the early eighteenth dynasty with the accession of Thutmose I. The death of Tutankhamun marked the end of the direct line of Amenhotep III, and the immediate successor Ay *may* have seized the kingship in place of Horemheb whose numerous titles suggest that he was destined for the office. Horemheb's origins are unknown, and his own record of his

161

accession ascribes it to divine intervention. Horemheb had no children and appointed as his successor Ramesses I, possibly associating him as co-ruler at the very end of the reign. Clearly, Horemheb was looking to the future and at Ramesses' son, Sety. When Sety I did ascend the throne, it was as a king's son and legitimate heir, and without recourse to miracles of divine intervention. The role of the elite at these times of dynastic change was no doubt immense and must at times have led to open conflict. Potential sources of conflict were the families of the king's mother and the king's wives, particularly the chief wife.

We do not know how the pharaoh's chief wife, the 'Great Royal Wife', was chosen. A prince was probably married at about 16, and if the eldest son, he was potentially the next pharaoh, even if not designated as Crown Prince. There is a likelihood of fierce competition among the elite as to whose candidate would become Great Royal Wife, and no doubt tensions with the family of the King's mother or existing Great Royal Wife. It is possible that the title was given to the first wife to give birth to a son. Custom may have varied at different periods. The desire of wives, particularly 'minor' wives, to place their sons on the throne certainly led to attempted coups (the 'harim conspiracies' of an earlier generation of Egyptologists). For obvious reasons, little information survives on these attempted coups, but the one against Ramesses III is well documented, and shows that the wife implicated had mustered some considerable, and powerful, allies within the palace and branches of the government.

Pharaohs had several wives, even if not the vast 'harims' of orientalist fantasy. There is, however, remarkably incomplete knowledge of their families and what happened to them. The best documented is certainly the family of Ramesses II, and he was unusual in having processions of all his sons and daughters depicted in temples.

The visibility of royal relatives varies at different periods. In the Old Kingdom relationship to the royal house was not hidden; indeed, many of the chief officials were brothers or cousins of the king. In the eighteenth dynasty, sons of a reigning king appear but generally disappear at the accession of their brother; presumably, many of them were absorbed into the elite. Similarly with royal daughters, in the Old Kingdom we know of kings' daughters who became wives of officials, but this is less clearly documented in the

New Kingdom (with one or two notable exceptions). Numerous marriage alliances were arranged between the Libyan pharaohs and the elite, a policy continued by the Kushites.

Kings did marry their sisters, but this was neither required, nor a regular occurrence. It was certainly not, as Gaston Maspero proposed, the means of legitimization throughout the eighteenth dynasty. Maspero misinterpreted the evidence available; unfortunately, his idea gained currency through repetition and has been extremely influential.

WHAT WAS IT LIKE TO BE A PHARAOH?

The king probably led a highly ritualized life. We have evidence only of the great national festivals in which he performed a leading role. Doubtless, every day he had to enact rites for the gods. His public appearances would have been theatrical. Again, the evidence is mostly of New Kingdom date, and there were innovations at that time, such as the Window of Appearances. This is best documented from Akhenaten's city of Akhetaten (Amarna) and is frequently depicted in tomb scenes showing the reward of officials. The elevated window was in the façade of a palace attached to the temple complex. A columned porch gave shade to the important dignitaries admitted to the royal presence, while other onlookers, such as foreign diplomats, stood in the open courtyard beyond. The panels of the window were opened to reveal the pharaoh, his wife and his family. Similar windows can be seen attached to the palaces of temples at Thebes. Within the palace itself a similar revelation of the king took place. Doors were opened to reveal the king, seated on the dais, to the officials. The ultimate example is the 'Palace of Merneptah' at Memphis, which is designed as a temple. In all of these we see the king revealed as a divine statue would be within the sanctuary of a temple.

At Akhetaten, Akhenaten and his family drove in state along the main road to perform duties in the temples and palaces of the central city. On other occasions the king was carried in the palanquin, an elaborate structure with sides in the form of lions, carrying a throne with sphinxes, protected by two goddesses. The same type of throne is used for carrying divine statues in procession, and the distinction could not have been great: in one instance, Ramesses III is shown being carried in this throne at the festival of Min, preceded by a priest burning incense as if he was a divine image too, which, in effect, he was.

Depictions of public appearance are limited to the celebration of religious festivals and the 'jubilee', but the king was in constant progress, performing his religious and civil duties. For the majority of the population of Egypt the distant appearance of their sovereign surrounded by gold, colour, and splendour would have been like the appearance of a god on earth.

The ritual texts that survive reveal the lengthy rites which the pharaoh had to endure. Following cleansing and anointing he had numerous amulets tied to his person, then the appropriate costumes and regalia, each put on with the appropriate prayers, anointing and censing. There is a remarkable similarity between the way the king is treated and the rites attending divine statues in the daily temple ritual. No doubt the purpose was similar: to ensure that the royal *ka* descended upon the living ruler, imbuing him with the power to perform his royal duties.

Despite the divine associations of the kingship, there was, of course, a potential for conflict within the palace. The political realities were the pharaoh's abilities to do what he wanted, to control his officials, and to control the power of the elite. Within his immediate family circle, too, there was always a possibility of conflict, particularly as the pharaoh aged and his sons reached maturity. Although the direct evidence is limited to an instance in the sixth dynasty, the death of Amenemhat I and the 'Harim Conspiracy' that may have resulted in the death of Ramesses III, there was doubtless much more dynastic conflict. The well-documented conflicts and murders in the Ptolemaic royal house may actually be more typical of 'normal' palace life. Such conflicts are well known in other ancient monarchies – Persia and Assyria particularly – and with such high stakes it is not surprising. In Assyria some kings took violent steps to ensure their positions, on accession murdering all of their brothers and their brothers' sons.

THE ELITE

The Egyptian elite and their families formed a very small percentage of the entire population, but it is largely through them – through their monuments and their writings – that we know about ancient Egypt. They shared a common education and through that a common ideology and culture. To be a member of the predominantly male, ruling elite, literacy was the essential factor. This required many years of schooling, and we may be certain that birth was the key to gaining education, and that the elite was largely self-perpetuating.

The most detailed account of time spent in education and different posts is that given by Bakenkhons, who lived in the reigns of Sety I and Ramesses II. Bakenkhons spent four years at school, followed by eleven in the 'stable' of Sety I. Bakenkhons probably started school at about the age of four, and those early years would have been spent on reading and writing. In the stable he would have continued his education and learnt how to drive a chariot and use a bow. This may have culminated in a period of 'national service' in the chariotry corps. Bakenkhons then joined the clergy of Amun at Thebes, his way no doubt made easier by the fact that his father was already a priest there (rising to be Second Prophet of Amun). After four years as 'pure' (*wab*) priest, the lowest rank, Bakenkhons became a prophet, and after a further twelve years, he was appointed to one of most important offices, Third Prophet of Amun, eventually rising to Second Prophet and finally First Prophet ('High Priest').

A contemporary of Bakenkhons, Setau, has also left an outline of his career, but without information on the number of years spent in each post. Although Setau does not name his father, he enjoyed a palace education, and no doubt came from a prominent family. After schooling, Setau joined the office of the vizier as a civil servant. He clearly showed great administrative skills, as he was appointed Chief Steward of Amun at Thebes. This was one the most powerful offices in Egypt, controlling the vast estates and revenues of the Amun temple throughout the country. Assuming that he had reached the pinnacle of his career, Setau had his tomb at Thebes and some of his funerary objects decorated using this title. But he was then promoted even further, to become viceroy of Nubia, where he served Ramesses II. Both Setau and Bakenkhons lived at the height of the New Kingdom, when chariotry was an essential element of elite education; schooling in the Old and Middle Kingdoms would have been slightly different.

The number of major offices was extremely small, and the ruling elite itself would have numbered only a few hundred. There were larger numbers of 'minor' office holders and civil servants ('scribes'), and it was this sector that grew in number in the Middle and New Kingdoms. With their families, the ruling class was probably a mere 2–3 per cent of the population.

At the heart were those who had direct access to the pharaoh. These, of course, included the royal relatives: families of the royal wives, and the king's mother. As in many other monarchies, the court officials were holders of great power, and those who granted, slowed or denied access to the pharaoh were the most powerful. Particularly close to the king were the royal stewards. Their wealth and influence is clear in that they owned some of the largest private tombs in Egypt, but they were also the officials most likely to fall from favour (witnessed by the savage destruction of their tombs).

Officials who worked in other branches of the administration might be brought more directly into the royal circle through the ranks of royal scribe, fan bearer on the right hand of the king, royal acquaintance or king's son. The importance of these royal connections is clear from the tomb painting showing the funeral procession of the Upper Egyptian vizier, Ramose, who served Amenhotep III. The procession is headed by the king's representatives: the Viceroy of Kush, who was both an Upper Egyptian official and a royal one (ranking as a 'king's son'); he is followed by the First Royal Herald, the Great Overseer of the Treasury, the Second Royal Herald, the Great Royal Acquaintances, and then the 'Great ones of the City (Thebes)'. Many of these court officials would have been brought up with the king and educated with him in the palace school, hence the positions of trust. A significant number of major office holders in the New Kingdom were the sons of 'royal nurses' or of women with the title 'royal ornament'. Royal stewards and butlers were sent on a range of official duties, and were prominent in the investigations of the 'harim' trials of Pepy I and Ramesses III.

In the Old Kingdom there were relatively few key offices of state that were held as long-term appointments, officials appear to have been delegated for specific purposes, such as overseeing the quarrying of stone, leading military campaigns or trading expeditions, all combined with periods of temple service. This changed later and there was an increase in professionalization in the New

Kingdom, as the complexities of each branch of government required specialization. Nevertheless, literacy remained essential, with the addition of skills in chariotry and horsemanship. Schools may have been more widespread and allowed for the much larger number of scribes; this in itself may been seen as opening the elite a little. But there were still very few major offices of state – less than fifty – and the information that we have shows that major office holders, such as the Vizier of Upper Egypt, might have brothers who were 'only' scribes. Clearly, personal ability, as well as family influence, played an important role in advancement.

There was a potential conflict of interests between the crown and the elite, and also between the court and the 'provinces'. This stemmed from the royal control of access to positions of power and the ideal of hereditary office. In the late Old Kingdom the nomarchs appear to have increased their local power, reflected in the events of the First Intermediate Period. When Egypt was reunited and centralized in the Middle Kingdom, the royal response was to weaken the power of the nomarchs and to restructure the administration, absorbing their families into the wider bureaucracy. In the New Kingdom the expansion of Egypt's borders must have seen an increase in the size of the elite itself, probably leading to some of the changes in the role of pharaoh. However, the number of key offices did not increase vastly, even if 'junior' positions did. Elite families still had their local power bases and occasionally there are indications that pharaohs tried to control this by installing their own nominees.

In the Libyan Period an almost feudal system emerged. The pharaohs allied themselves by marriage with powerful local elites, but office became effectively hereditary within families, and it is clear that claims could be made for offices held by the father's or mother's family. With families controlling office and the land that was attached to that office, allied with weaker direct control by the pharaoh, something approaching the feudal was arising. There is evidence that when the Kushites (and later the Saites) gained control of the Theban region, they reallocated some offices. Such tension must have been an ongoing problem that pharaohs had to control.

Despite the personal and family self-interest of the elites that might have been a cause of conflict, the interests of the pharaoh and elite were essentially the same – the control of knowledge and the control of wealth – hence the concentration of resources on elite projects. This is of enormous importance when we are trying to generalize about what people thought in ancient Egypt. The percentage of the population who left any information was extremely small; the potential for leaving any record of dissent was even smaller.

AN EGYPTIAN MIDDLE CLASS?

So was there a 'middle class' in dynastic Egypt? Many Egyptologists think that we can start talking about a middle class during the New Kingdom. The idea that it was possible to rise to high rank from 'humble' origins is also quite widely accepted. This is based, very largely, on evidence from the reign of Akhenaten in the tombs at Akhetaten, but it is equally common in earlier New Kingdom autobiographical inscriptions. The Amarna tombs, more than any other group, emphasize the pharaoh and ignore heredity. Officials repeatedly attribute their success to Akhenaten and greet him with the phrase 'you appoint from the lowest orders'. So Egyptologists said that Akhenaten really did appoint 'new men': but where would he have found literate and qualified men except among the elite? This again reflects the 'myth' of pharaoh and the elite: whatever political realities and conflicts underlie the relationship, the elite acknowledged that all of their power derived from the pharaoh. Frequently, officials are reticent about identifying any office that their fathers may have held. Many of the highest officials, if they do name their fathers, called them *sab*, literally 'judge'. Egyptologists have often taken this to indicate that they were of 'modest' background; yet instances can be cited where we know who these men actually were, and they usually turn out to be immensely important office holders. Officials attribute their promotion to the king; they also emphasize their own abilities and virtues, all at the expense of the advantages of heredity.

Of course, with a limited number of major offices available, ability must have played some role and cannot be totally rejected as a factor. We find families, such as that of Rekhmire, in which the office of vizier was held for three generations and in which some members are described 'simply' as 'scribe'. Even if, as seems likely within the context of small villages, promising boys were taught to write, the likelihood of them achieving high office must have been remote. Access to writing and education must have been jealously controlled by the elite.

The problem, as highlighted at the beginning of this chapter, is a tendency to divide society according to a rather Western notion of hierarchy, when the division was actually more fundamental – the literate and non-literate. As literacy gave access to knowledge and knowledge to power, social mobility must have been restricted. Within monetary economies, trade and industry have been important in social mobility because the acquisition of wealth has enabled people to break into the system. So who, if anybody, in ancient Egypt was in a position to do this?

In the New Kingdom, one way of acquiring wealth and status was through military service. The soldier Ahmose, son of Ebana, active in the wars against the Hyksos in the early eighteenth dynasty, was rewarded for deeds of valour on the battlefield with gold, captives given to him as slaves and land. At the same period, Neshi was also given land that was held by his descendants to the reign of Ramesses II (see Chapter 9). He presumably also received gold and slaves. Ahmose, son of Ebana, came from Nekheb (el-Kab) in Upper Egypt and his tomb was constructed for him by his grandson, who was mayor of the town. It seems possible that Ahmose was the founder of the family's advancement, with private land ensuring an income and wealth in terms of gold and slaves. Ahmose may have been able to get his sons educated in the local temple school, opening the way to their social advancement. Grants of land were made to veterans, the best documented being foreign soldiers such as the Shardana and the Libyans, who were integrated during the nineteenth and twentieth dynasties. As with the Nubian soldiers of the First Intermediate Period recorded by inscriptions at Gebelein, they must have received rewards for valour and also land, allowing them an entry to other aspects of elite society.

Other people who may have been able to gain wealth were 'merchants'. The conduct and role of private trade in the Egyptian economy is very unclear, but there is evidence for 'merchants' in the New Kingdom. They appear to have been attached to temples, and may therefore have been from elite families.

While it might be inappropriate to talk about a 'middle class', we can define an 'urban' 'class in the middle'. This would have included the holders of numerous minor administrative offices, priesthoods and scribal positions. Probably many of the skilled sculptors and artisans could be added, along with members of the military who had acquired wealth. But, while some of these people may have been moving up the social scale, or breaking into the system, we should not forget that most of them would be from elite backgrounds in the broadest sense. They would have been educated within the system and they may have been scions of families that held key offices. As the hereditary claims to offices increased in the late New Kingdom and Libyan Period, this sector of society must have become more clearly defined. The lengthy genealogies of the late Libyan and Saite Periods reveal the existence of families who held the same 'minor' priesthoods and administrative offices for generations. But even if the bureaucracy did increase significantly in numbers during the years of Egyptian imperial expansion, it still remained only a very small percentage of the total population.

THE MAJORITY

The evidence for discussing the bulk of Egypt's population is extremely limited. First, the descriptions of jobs or depictions of non-elite work are composed by or for members of the elite; there are no personal records from the non-elite. The school texts known to Egyptologists as the *Satire on the Trades* extol the merits of education and the scribal position to the detriment of every other occupation. They point out the physical labour involved, the long hours, the smells and the small reward. In tomb scenes the owner surveys the agricultural idyll from his chair, or stool, often beneath a sunshade. Scenes of production in temple workshops give little indication of the physical labours involved. Here, the 'satire' is a little more honest: all of the many unpleasant, backbreaking aspects of labour – the effort of pumping bellows to heat a furnace to smelt metals; the labour of using a bow drill on small beads; the stench of the tannery; the heat of the potters' and bread ovens; the work of chipping sharp pieces of granite off colossal statues – are sanitized to emphasize the end-product (wealth for the temples, the pharaoh and the elite) and the advantages of being the one who oversees this work, rather than the ones who do it.

In terms of archaeological evidence, too, we lack a very personal contact with the majority. Non-elite cemeteries are relatively rare. Most studies of 'ordinary' people in ancient Egypt concentrate on the abundant wealth of material from the 'workmen's villages' at Deir el-Medina, Kahun and Giza. Deir el-Medina is certainly the richest site for evidence about a community in the New Kingdom, and it does give us a chance to penetrate 'real lives'. But we should not forget that these villagers were a relatively privileged group, as the quantity of written material shows.

The majority of the population was occupied with agricultural activities which had their own specific seasonal tasks. These included the digging and clearing of canals, the sowing and reaping of crops, threshing and winnowing. In addition to wheat and barley, fodder for animals and flax for linen, there were vegetable crops and fruit trees to tend. Significant numbers of workers would have been taken as *corvée* labour for state projects. It has long been assumed, on the testament of Greek writers, that much of the work on state projects was carried out in the inundation season. However, this would not have been a good time for quarrying in the desert, and inscriptional evidence suggests that work there took place at other times of year. The inundation may have been a good time to transport large blocks of cut stone, with water covering more land, but this could equally present problems of shallow water and the increased speed of the current. There were exemptions for certain groups, such as temple workers, from draft into the *corvée*, and the description *neferu* suggests that it was usually young men who were taken. The major projects for *corvée* labour were agricultural: the clearing of canals and maintenance of dykes. The role of the *corvée* in the construction of the pyramids and temples (long assumed) is less clear.

The produce from the agricultural estates was brought to the 'urban' centres where much of the processing was carried out. In the New Kingdom, the temples – and probably the palaces – were the centres of production. Presumably, and again the evidence is rather scanty, the houses of members of the elite were also mini production centres for some manufactures. The spinning of thread and weaving of linen was certainly carried out in private houses and palaces as well as in the temples. Women, including elite women, played a major role in its production, although men are also shown both spinning and weaving. Butchery was a feature of all temples, particularly at festivals, but it is also shown as part of the life on the elite estates. The processing of the by-products, such as hides, glue and sinew, could have been carried out as large- or small-scale operations. Indeed, evidence shows that production was generally carried out in small workshops, and that instead of larger factories and workshops, the small ones were duplicated. This is shown particularly clearly in the evidence for bread production at Amarna, where the small-scale bakeries are repeated, rather than redesigned as larger units with greater capacity. A similar small-scale production seems to apply to workshops, and scenes of those show the manufacture of a wide range of products – statuary, stone vessels, jewellery and furniture – rather than separate specialized workshops. Some production, such as metal casting, pottery, faience and glazed wares, would have required small and specialized industrial centres.

Egypt did not have large-scale agricultural slave labour, and the majority of agricultural workers in Egypt might best be described as 'serfs', tied to the land and the land-owning institutions. There were slaves in Egypt, most acquired as captives in war by the Egyptians themselves, or captives sent as 'gift' by foreign rulers. Most slaves in Egypt appear to have been employed in domestic (in the broadest sense) service. Some certainly wielded power, especially if they were employed by the palace.

GODDESSES, QUEENS, MUSICIANS, WEAVERS, GLEANERS: WOMEN IN EGYPTIAN SOCIETY

In tomb and temple scenes women occupy a prominent position, yet there were restrictions throughout the Dynastic Period on the roles that they could actively play in society. Women were not given access to the administrative offices, but they could hold a small number of religious offices that had considerable economic and political power. The most significant of these, the position of God's wife of Amun, developed in the early eighteenth dynasty, became extremely important during the later Libyan and Kushite periods. This office was held by royal women, kings' wives or daughters. Other religious positions were held by the wives of members of the elite, and in some cases related to their husbands' positions. For example, the chief of the *hener* ('harim' or 'musical troupe') of a god was usually the wife of the high priest, or another leading official of the temple. Elite women were often 'chantresses' and sistrum players, and are shown in some scenes performing on the great festival days. The status of other musicians is less clear. They play a range of sophisticated instruments: harps, lyres, flutes, 'oboes' and a variety of percussion instruments, usually accompanying singers, and occasionally dancers.

The biggest question surrounding elite women is whether they were literate. There are archives of documents from all periods that show women deputizing for absent husbands, receiving and replying to letters. But this did not necessarily require the women to be literate if there were scribes or literate sons to read and take dictation (bearing in mind issues of trust). In most societies where there are attempts to restrict literacy, some women succeed. It is quite possible that women who performed major religious duties (such as the royal women and God's wife) may have needed to be able to read.

One of the main industries that involved women, probably including royal and elite women, was the manufacture of textiles. Many tomb scenes show women spinning and weaving. Women do not appear to have been involved in many of the agricultural activities in the fields, although they may be shown harvesting flax and following male reapers collecting grain. They are more frequently involved in the processing, such as winnowing and grinding grain, preparing bread and beer. However, there may be particular reasons (e.g. religious) for not showing women performing certain activities. Women were responsible for the running of the house, and for the family. They had considerable economic rights and are known, through a few depictions and through documents, to have supplemented their husbands' wages through exchange of produce, either manufactured or surplus foodstuffs.

As with many aspects of Egyptian society, there were changes in the Ptolemaic and Roman Periods with the introduction of Greek cities and settlers, and a different economic system.

9

TOWN AND COUNTRY
IN ANCIENT EGYPT

THE LAND

Re-creating the ancient Egyptian landscape is quite difficult: ancient Egypt may have looked very much like rural Egypt today or as it does in the 'orientalist' paintings of the nineteenth century, but that is difficult to prove. There are very few 'landscape scenes' in tombs or temples, and the depictions of agricultural life and the desert are schematic and dictated by the function of the scene. The annual deposits of silt and the constant cultivation of the land conceal from us many ancient features, such as irrigation canals, dykes and small settlements.

To understand how land was divided and cultivated, we have to examine a fairly limited range of documents from different periods. The most detailed sources are from the Ptolemaic and Roman Periods, and these do give considerable information on the owner-ship, use and position of fields in relation to settlements. Documents from earlier periods are generally less informative, at least in this type of detail. For the later New Kingdom, the best source is the 'Wilbour Papyrus'. This was bought by the Brooklyn Museum as a memorial to one of its benefactors, the American businessman and collector Charles Edwin Wilbour. Dated to year 4 of the reign of Ramesses V, it is 10 metres (33 feet) long, with 127 'pages' totalling 5,200 lines. Large as it is, it is only a part of an even larger group of documents (the others now lost) which measured and assessed fields. The Wilbour Papyrus covers an area of northern Middle Egypt at the entrance to the Fayum, ranging some 150 kilometres (90 miles) from Shedyt (*Krokodilopolis*: Medinet el-Faiyum) southwards towards el-Minya. From the text we have learnt an enormous amount about the land holdings of the major temples of Thebes, Iunu and Memphis, and about smaller, local temples, divine and royal statues, rented land and the *khato*-lands of the pharaoh (a special part of the royal domain, about which we are still a little unclear). However, it is also certain that the Wilbour Papyrus does not cover *all* of the land in this part of Egypt. Nor does it detail the size, shape and use of the fields. It is always dangerous to make generalizations from one source, but the papyrus is the only one that gives us such detailed information about land holdings.

The Wilbour Papyrus indicates that the people renting land were, in order: stable-master (198); soldier (153); lady (131); priest (112); small farmer (109); herdsman (102); Shardana (68), and scribe (30). The Shardana were one of the groups which appear as the 'Sea Peoples' in the nineteenth and twentieth dynasties, but were also widely used as mercenaries. They may have come from Sardinia. As veterans, they were settled in this part of Egypt, just as Libyan soldiers were settled around Per-Bastet in the eastern Delta.

One of the surprises of the Wilbour Papyrus is the large number of 'ladies' (the third largest group); and this is further indication of the ability of women to act economically on their own behalf in Egypt. Many of these parcels of land would, of course, have been worked by others on behalf of the land holders who would have received a proportion of the produce: the purpose of the papyrus was to assess what proportion was to be paid as income to the land-holding institution.

The Wilbour Papyrus highlights the complexities of land ownership in late New Kingdom Egypt. Most land was owned by the pharaoh, either directly or through the state institutions and temples. This was then rented to officials or attached to offices to provide the income. However, we do have evidence of land which was granted by the pharaoh to individuals, usually as a reward for military action.

One highly informative inscription records the legal battle over some land in the region of Memphis. The text is carved in the tomb of a man named Mose who lived in the early nineteenth dynasty. The dispute arose over land that had been given by the pharaoh Ahmose to a ship's captain, Neshi, as a reward (probably for actions in the Hyksos wars) at the beginning of the eighteenth dynasty.

The land then passed to Neshi's descendants. Trouble began in the reign of Horemheb and went as far as the Great Court in Heliopolis where the Vizier sat in judgment. Until this time the land had been held as one unit by all of the descendants, but the court now decided to divide it into six parcels. Objections were raised by some of the litigants and the case dragged on beyond year 18 of Ramesses II (so for at least 35 years and perhaps 40 years or more), revealing forgery, collusion and corruption, before being settled. This estate was not large and the family not particularly influential. The text does reveal, however, the complexity of land holding and also that this family was able to prove that it had cultivated the land and paid tax on it for over two hundred years, and to prove their descent from the original grantee.

Joint family ownership of privately held land was doubtless common. There were very few top jobs, and the biggest earner in the family would probably have been responsible for supporting many collateral relatives. The situation is reminiscent of the ownership of date trees in Nubia into modern times, where a tree could be owned by a large number of descendants of the original owner (planter), each of whom received a proportion of the produce; and, of course, individuals could have part-ownership of many trees. This system of multiple ownership is also documented by the papyri of the Ptolemaic and Roman Periods from the Fayum and the region of Pathyris (Gebelein) in Upper Egypt. There are detailed records of ownership and sales of property over extended periods, and these show that one individual might have shares in many small fields. Part-ownership of a quarter or an eighth of a field is not unusual; but the other owners of the shares and whole fields are usually relatives, suggesting partition of fields following the death of a parent. Presumably, in many of these cases it was the produce that was divided proportionately. The documents describe the fields by reference to the owners of fields that surround them and to other features such as canals, the desert, date groves and roads. They allow us to sketch, in a schematic way, the cultivation surrounding the villages. We can assume that the fields were rectangular, with low dykes around them to retain the water when they were flooded.

Egypt was a bureaucrat's dream: a country divided into a patchwork of small fields owned by a huge number of different individuals and institutions. It is not surprising that tomb scenes show armies

of scribes measuring fields and recording, in triplicate, the numbers
of cattle and geese, and the quantities of grain.

TOWNS AND VILLAGES

Although we talk about 'towns' and 'cities' in ancient Egypt, they
were actually very different from our modern understanding of those
terms in many ways. Our image of the ancient 'towns' and 'cities'
is coloured by the expansive remains of religious buildings and the
cemeteries, but also by what we expect a town to be like. There are
surprisingly few settlement sites that have been well preserved and
excavated, and we have relatively little surviving evidence for
'typical' residential and industrial areas. The reason for this is rather
obvious: the ancient Egyptians constructed most of their buildings
from unbaked mud-brick. They intended these buildings to be
renewed and replaced regularly. Many ancient sites have been badly
damaged, if not completely destroyed, because ancient mud-brick
makes good fertilizer, just as old stone from temples made either
good building material or excellent lime. The works of nineteenth-
century European travellers are full of stories of how temples,
even whole cities (such as *Antinoöpolis* in Middle Egypt) vanished
into the lime-kilns, and how major mud-brick ruins were dis-
appearing. Some archaeologists even encouraged the destruction of
'late' (i.e. Ptolemaic, Roman and medieval) levels because they
were interested in the earlier periods only. Fortunately, most early
archaeology in settlement mounds focused on the temple sites and
was oriented towards the excavation of sculpture (particularly statuary) and inscriptions. As a result, the settlement and industrial
areas were left largely undisturbed, and those that have survived are
now yielding important evidence. The past thirty years have seen
considerably more urban archaeology, and increasingly scientific
excavation, such as that pioneered by Barry Kemp and his teams at
Amarna, with remarkable results.

Some earlier archaeologists did excavate settlement sites, notably
at Kahun, Amarna, Sesebi and Deir el-Medina. These sites are often
regarded as untypical of Egyptian towns; but is that really the case?
In examining the evidence from archaeology and other ancient
sources, it soon becomes clear that urban settlements in Egypt were
very different from those in some other parts of the ancient world,

and certainly from what we mean by 'town' or 'city'. The term 'capital city', particularly, is one that it is difficult to justify for ancient Egypt. It was often used in the older literature for Memphis in the Old Kingdom and Thebes in the New Kingdom.

The evidence for reconstructing what an Egyptian town was like is actually remarkably limited. There are very few depictions that may be considered 'townscape' in Egyptian art. Ironically, the largest number of scenes of buildings and town life are in the tombs at Amarna (Akhetaten), which is also the town best known archaeologically but generally thought of as 'atypical'.

Although many relatively small areas of domestic and industrial building have been excavated throughout Egypt, and for different periods, the sites most frequently used to discuss 'urbanization' and planning are those that have been almost completely excavated: Kahun, Amarna, Sesebi and Deir el-Medina.

Tell el-Amarna (now usually referred to as 'Amarna'), the ancient Akhetaten, is immensely important to the study of urban settlement in Egypt. Flinders Petrie made the first excavations in 1891–2, followed by major digs until 1936. A team led by Barry Kemp has worked at the site since 1977. Akhetaten was a royal residence city with temples, palaces, residential and administrative buildings, yet it was occupied for a very limited period during the reign of Akhenaten (1352–1336 BC). While it has been regarded as atypical, it does contain all of the major features of a town in Egypt. Because of its short occupation period its remains are generally well preserved. Much of the stonework from the temples was removed and recycled by Ramesses II, but sufficient remains to give the plans and general appearance of the major structures. More importantly, extensive mud-brick ruins allow the layout of the residential and administrative buildings to be surveyed in detail.

It is the unusual historical and religious circumstances that led to the building of Akhetaten that also make it atypical. The site chosen was in Middle Egypt, with the town itself built on the east bank of the river in a natural semi-circular bay in the hills that had not been occupied by any earlier settlement. There is a very narrow cultivable strip of land on the east bank, but the west bank is one of the broadest regions of agricultural land in Egypt. The territory given to Akhetaten was delimited by boundary stelae, which record the king's choice of the site and the foundation of the city.

There were guard posts controlling access to the urban area. At the very north end of the site was the North Riverside Palace, which is mostly unexcavated. It was a large fortified enclosure which lay alongside the river and doubtless had its own harbours and quays. Close by lay the North 'suburb' with other palaces. From the Riverside Palace a Royal Road ran to the Central City. This was perfectly straight for much of its length and was used when the king made his ceremonial appearance accompanied by the army and the officials.

In the Central City were the main temple precincts, small palace complexes, administrative buildings and residential quarters. A large religious complex, the Maru-Aten, lay at the south end of the site, connected to the Central City by a continuation of the Royal Road, and there were other smaller religious areas between the town and the encircling cliffs. A complex of roadways, generally straight, connected different elements of the city together. Cultivation along the river bank has obliterated areas where quays and harbours in the Central City might have been located, but the scenes in the tombs show that they lay close to the main buildings.

The residential quarters show a mixture of centralized planning and 'organic' growth. Official residence compounds are generally laid out on a grid system, but often with space around that became filled with other houses. The official houses seem to have carefully allocated space according to rank. Each stood within a high-walled compound with only one main access. The house stood at the centre of the compound surrounded by beehive-shaped granaries, stables and other storage facilities, servants' quarters and a garden. The access is not in a direct line, either from the entrance gate to the house, or from the house entrance to the main reception hall; there are many turns in the route. The main audience hall of the house was where some of the official's business would have been conducted; tomb scenes at Thebes and Amarna show us houses with officials at work. At Amarna, the house of the sculptor Dhutmose had workshops adjacent to the residential compound.

At Amarna, the private quarters of the house are situated around the main audience hall and there may have been upper storeys to some of the houses. The main room, being at the centre of the house, was lit with high clerestory windows. All of the officials were paid in kind through their estates, which lay in the rich agricultural land on the west bank of the river. The produce was brought and kept in the granaries and storerooms adjacent to the house. From there it was presumably redistributed to those for whom the official was directly responsible. This appears to be reflected in the layout of the town. The major villa compounds were placed fairly regularly, but around them there grew up a network of smaller houses – presumably those of the dependants.

Part of the function of the ceremonial centre of the city was the public 'reward' of officials. This is one of the major features of tomb decoration at Amarna (although known from Thebes and Memphis as well). 'Reward' was used to distribute all of the 'luxury' commodities directly controlled by the palace. This included, most significantly, gold, but also ivory, ebony, semi-precious stones and similar types of goods. There are still some difficult outstanding questions about the functioning of the economy in Egypt, but we can make a generalization that an official's basic rations were provided by his estates; the luxuries came as 'gift' and 'reward' from the king. However, when an official was rewarded, this benefited all of his dependants as well. In reward scenes we find scribes writing (usually in triplicate) the exact amount of each 'gift'; reward was carefully calculated according to rank. Although the focus in reward scenes is on gold, this was not the largest gift made: we see furniture, made in the royal workshops from imported royal monopolies like cedar, ivory and ebony, being carried out from side doors, large numbers of amphorae containing wine and beer, to be enjoyed by the whole entourage, and other foodstuffs, perhaps imported produce such as olive oil.

Due to the nature of Akhenaten's solar cult, the religious centre of Akhetaten differs from other New Kingdom towns for which we have evidence (such as Thebes). At Akhetaten the festival processions of divine statues between temples were probably replaced by the royal procession from the palace to the Central City, and to the Maru-Aten, a religious complex in the south of the city. The distribution of cult centres and burial places raises another important issue about Egyptian towns: their sacred landscapes, a feature which has been increasingly studied in recent years.

Exactly contemporary with Akhetaten is the town site of Sesebi in southern Nubia. Sesebi was a planned settlement, but on a much smaller scale. Within an enclosure wall, the town is divided into two roughly equal parts, one containing temple structures and storage, the other residential quarters. The houses are planned with a strict hierarchy of space: the largest are detached buildings, although without the gardens and compounds found at Akhetaten; the other houses are terraced, with two distinct types. The differences between Akhetaten and Sesebi reflect the very different functions of the two settlements: one a major royal residence, cult and administrative centre, the other a colonial administrative centre without a royal residence.

Unlike most other surviving planned settlements, Akhetaten is not enclosed by city walls, but the river and the surrounding line of cliffs with their limited, and strictly controlled, access served that function. Akhetaten is also somewhat freer in its planning than Sesebi and the twelfth-dynasty settlement at Kahun.

'Kahun' was the name given by Flinders Petrie to the ancient settlement site of Hetep-Senusret, which he excavated in 1889. The site lies close to the pyramid of Senusret II at el-Lahun, near the entrance to the Fayum, and is often described as a 'workers' village'. It has been assumed that it was constructed for the workers who built the pyramid and the 'priests' that served the king's mortuary cult. It seems more likely that it served as a major elite residential and administrative centre during this reign. The town was enclosed and hierarchically planned. Only a part of the site survived at the time of its excavation and its full extent remains unknown. The houses are of two strikingly different types. There are a small number of extremely large houses (perhaps eleven), each with up to seventy rooms. They were almost identical in plan, with garden court, granaries and storage rooms, and residential accommodation. As at Amarna, these are self-contained and very private dwellings, with long corridors and complex plans, and only one entrance from the street. Indeed, the streets of Kahun must have been rather forbidding. The majority of houses are small terraced blocks, without large storage facilities. It is likely that the smaller houses were dependent on the large ones for supplies of rations. The total population is rather difficult to estimate, and a range from 3,000 to 9,000 is suggested using different criteria.

The village site at Deir el-Medina, on the west bank at Luxor, also shows official planning and allocation of space. The village is only one element in the city of Thebes, although because of the wealth of surviving material, it is often discussed in isolation, as a complete entity. The comparable village at Akhetaten, also separated from the main part of the city, is even more rigidly planned, with 73 identical houses.

Centralized planning of settlements was clearly an ideal for the Egyptian state, but it is difficult to know exactly how widespread it was. The fortresses in Nubia are good examples of official building and the use of a grid plan inside irregular enclosures. Planned settlements are known from the Old to later New Kingdoms: however, we have much less evidence from the Libyan and Late periods. It seems likely that planned settlement was particularly associated with royal activities, whether royal administrative and residential complexes within Egypt or military and 'colonial' administrative centres in the empire. We might expect the appropriate parts of the nome capitals, major religious centres and major residence cities to be similarly rigidly planned, but with a far more 'organic' settlement around them.

Although there is rich archaeological evidence from the settlement sites that have been excavated, it is extremely difficult to detail changes to towns over time. It has been assumed that a planned settlement might over time be largely rebuilt with a more 'organic' development. This seems to have happened at Sesebi in Nubia, where there is some evidence of later rebuilding. This reflects the change in the nature of the settlement, which ceased to be the administrative centre for southern Nubia in the early nineteenth dynasty, and probably became a farming village. There was modification of houses at Kahun, too. Recent surveys and excavations at some sites in the Delta have, remarkably, identified Early Dynastic settlements, suggesting that the official centres of towns moved around over time.

One important factor is that all Egyptian houses were built of sun-dried mud-brick and could be renewed and rebuilt relatively easily. As we know very well from the *tells* of western Asia, the ground level rose over time due to the accumulations of debris and rubbish. This resulted in adjacent houses sometimes being on different levels. As the ground level rose, the lower rooms became basements and ultimately were used just for rubbish, as new floors were added above. Although the towns grew higher, the planned areas, such as the temple, remained the same, and if they were rebuilt, it was generally at the same level, so even in ancient times many of the towns would have been raised above the central temple precinct. Excavations at Khemenu (*Hermopolis*) in Middle Egypt show that by the Late Period the town was higher than the temple and processional ways.

In trying to reconstruct what Egyptian towns were like during the Dynastic Period, we can supplement what the archaeology tells us with broader considerations. First, what are the elements of an 'urban' settlement? Clearly, there were some changes over the course of Egyptian history, but in the pre-Ptolemaic town the focus would have been the religious buildings. From the Middle Kingdom onwards these were the increasingly large temple complexes. Most towns would have had a small palace adjacent to the temple for royal visits. There must have been administrative buildings for the town and a *nome*, or surrounding region, perhaps focused on the palace. There were residential areas, probably hierarchically organized. By the New Kingdom the main storage buildings, and manufacturing and industrial areas were attached to the temples. Throughout the valley the cemeteries for the towns were situated in the cliffs or desert areas nearby.

Egyptian settlements were largely elite residential and adminis-trative centres rather than homes of the workers of the surrounding agricultural land. The population was thus largely the administrators and priests (hardly distinct) and their families, and the artisans and other workers employed by the institutions. There were harbours and boatyards, as most traffic went by river. The main towns and cities, such as Thebes and Memphis, would have acquired other popula-tions, such as foreign traders and garrisons of troops.

Clearly, the functions performed by towns were another important factor in their populations and layout. Towns which had a strategic position, such as Abu-Syene (Aswan), would have had large garrisons and fortresses. Serving as the base for military and trading expeditions into Nubia and for local granite quarrying, Abu-Syene was certainly fortified and had a large port and, presumably, ship and barge build-ing yards with other necessary facilities, such as the manufacture of rope and sailcloth. Towns such as Abedju (Abydos), which had a par-ticularly important religious significance, would perhaps have had to deal with large numbers of pilgrims for the major festivals.

Egyptian towns were not occupied by the mass of the agricul-tural workers; we assume that they lived in smaller villages and scattered settlement throughout the agricultural land. In most pre-industrial societies only 5–8 per cent of the total population lived within urban settlements. Although extremely difficult to calculate, the population of ancient Egypt is estimated at 1.2 million in the Old Kingdom, increasing to 2.1 million during New Kingdom and 3.2 million for the Ptolemaic–Roman Periods. This would mean that between 60,000 and 96,000 people in the Old Kingdom and between 105,000 and 168,000 people in the New Kingdom were living in Egypt's towns.

Most urban centres would have been quite modest in scale and there were probably very few large ones. Barry Kemp estimated the population of Akhetaten (Amarna) at 20,000–30,000, and that the agricultural land owned by the city could probably support a population of around 45,000. However, other Egyptologists have estimated that it had between 50,000 and 100,000 residents, but this is probably too large. The New Kingdom populations of Thebes and Memphis have been estimated at perhaps 20,000–40,000.

Certainly, the economic and social structure of Egypt meant that the towns lacked a number of the principal features of most ancient and medieval settlements, features that we regard as typical, if not defining elements, of towns and cities. First, they had no large, centrally planned markets with stalls and shops comparable with the Greek agora or Roman forum. Private barter and exchange is known to have existed, and there is one (only one) tomb scene showing sailors exchanging goods at small riverside booths. The lack of an agora or forum space does not just reflect the economic differences but the social ones too. There was no large meeting place as the focus of the community. In Greek and Roman towns, the agora or forum was the centre of the legal and political life of the town: the Egyptian system did not allow for this. There were no public theatres, another important aspect of Greek and Roman towns, nor were there public bathhouses. It could perhaps be argued that the apparent lack of markets is not evidence that there were no markets, but that they were outside state control and hence do not feature in official records. This is possible, but given the Egyptian state's urge to control, and to levy taxes at every opportunity, it seems unlikely.

The evidence reveals an urban settlement that is very different from the kind that developed in the Greek and Roman Periods (and was introduced into Egypt by the Ptolemies). The evidence seems to indicate towns that avoided large public open spaces, except when they were attached to temples. The main ceremonial routes were also religious. Security was important. All major buildings and complexes had high defensive walls, and garrisons controlled the access to towns. These emphasize the settlements as centres of wealth, not just in terms of gold and similar materials but also in agricultural wealth. The towns, specifically the temples, were the banks of ancient Egypt, where the state's wealth, in all its forms, was stored and used to pay the population.

HOUSES

As with temples and other major buildings, the evidence for palaces and houses indicates that they were often enclosed within compounds. Their layouts imply privacy and seclusion, with strictly controlled access.

We have evidence for state-planned houses from a number of sites. At Akhetaten (Amarna), where the evidence is good, Barry Kemp observed that there were eight basic house types forming three 'classes'. The largest houses were only 7–9 per cent of the total, with the intermediate forming 34–37 per cent and the smallest 54–59 per cent. Sesebi and Kahun show similar hierarchical planning. Most houses in enclosed planned settlements were terraced. At Kahun, even the largest houses were terraced. Akhetaten is a notable exception, and at Sesebi a few large houses were detached, although because of the lack of space, they did not have gardens and enclosure walls.

Depictions of houses are quite rare and frequently rather schematic. Most date from the New Kingdom. Often the house is reduced to a white square with door and windows indicated. Usually the house stands on a low platform with steps, suggesting a measure to prevent flooding by the inundation. Although they are quite rare, most images of houses in tomb paintings or papyri imply a detached residence within a compound, very much in line with archaeological evidence from Akhetaten. This perhaps contradicts our assumption that houses in cities such as Thebes and Memphis were multi-storey and less 'villa-like'.

The exteriors of houses were rather blank, perhaps whitewashed. Some depictions show houses white, but others are pink, suggesting

Figure 9.1 A simple depiction of a house with *mulqufs* to catch the cool breeze and ventilate the interior: Thebes, Tomb of Nebamun, eighteenth dynasty (after N. de G. Davies, 'The Town House in Ancient Egypt', 246, Figure 10).

unpainted mud-brick. The entrance gates to the compound and the main door of elite houses were often of finely dressed stone, inscribed with the names and titles of the owner. Inside, the walls and floors were plastered and painted. The flooring was probably frequently renewed: one of the palaces at Akhetaten seems to have something like sixteen levels of plaster flooring for an occupation of probably little more than a decade. Some floors were elaborately painted. Walls were probably left white with a colourful dado frieze and another just below the ceiling. These friezes can be quite abstract, but are generally made up of protective emblems such as the *ankh* (life) or *sa* (protection) signs. The main room of a house was usually near the centre, and was higher than those around, lit by clerestory windows. One pillar or, in a large room, four pillars of wood or stone would support the ceiling. They usually had stone bases and carved floral capitals. There were shrines, usually of the 'false-door' type, built against the walls of the main rooms. Ceiling patterns are well known from tomb decoration, and are again frequently elaborate geometric designs including many protective emblems. Rush matting (perhaps coloured) would have been laid on the floor (perhaps carpets in elite houses). Most of the furniture would have been made from reeds and wicker: surviving wickerwork is of very fine quality. Wood was rare, and high-quality timber had to be imported, so chairs in cedar or ebony could only be acquired as 'gift' from the king, who controlled foreign trade. This style of furniture was often imitated by painting poorer-quality timber black and white for 'ebony' and 'ivory', and yellowish for 'cedar'.

Cleanliness was important, particularly for the elite, and shower rooms survive in some of the palace complexes. Razors were of

Figure 9.2 A house within a compound surrounded by trees; the windows allow the depiction to be read as a two-storey house: Thebes, nineteenth dynasty (after N. de G. Davies, 'The Town House in Ancient Egypt', 243, Figure 7).

copper, bronze or flint (a common material and doubtless extensively used for tools into the latest periods). Lavatory seats are known (a comfortable stone one was found at Akhetaten); a large pottery vessel served as the pan. When full, it would have been thrown on the local rubbish tip.

Applying the knowledge that we gain of settlement to the main centres, such as Thebes and Memphis, is extremely difficult. It has been assumed that houses in those cities would have been multi-storey, rather than the villa layout typical of Akhetaten. However, we should be wary of making assumptions when we have so few houses surviving. Undoubtedly, there was less land available in the big towns, but houses would have been regularly rebuilt. The elite were probably able to construct such villa-type houses in areas of Thebes and Memphis, surrounded by their own enclosures and with large storage areas for foodstuffs, stables for the horses and chariots, gardens and separate servants' quarters. There is also evidence that such types of house were built in or near the larger 'provincial' centres for both the local officials and others who had ancestral ties to a town. These 'villa' compounds are the type most commonly depicted.

One Theban tomb has a scene showing what appears to be a multi-storey house, of the type assumed to be more usual in the larger towns. In the semi-basement men and women are shown spinning and working at looms and grinding corn. The main reception rooms appear to be on the first floor (a staircase is shown). The main room has windows high in the walls and a column supporting the ceiling, and a shrine on the wall. The upper floor has other rooms and we see the official carrying out his duties and with his scribes to hand. A stairway leads to the roof, where the cooking is taking place; there are also grain bins here. But it is possible that some of the elements of this house should be read laterally, as if they were at ground level (logically, the kitchen and storage bins).

We learn much about the adaptation of houses in the northern part of Thebes from papyrus documents of the early Ptolemaic Period (c. 324–240 BC). From these we find that a family house could be divided between the heirs, with divisions of the courtyard areas and new doors creating two properties. In succeeding generations these new houses had additions built and were given as marriage settlement, used as security on loans and rented out. In one instance the loan could not be repaid and the house was taken to settle the debt.

So, from a house occupied by a single nuclear family, the property became a block of five flats in multiple occupation, with only part still owned by descendants of the original owner. Another example from the same part of Thebes and the same period reveals the complexities of bequest following the death of the house owner, and the subsequent division of a house, further complicated by the fact that both partners had married more than once. It also indicates the intermarriage between close neighbours (who might be cousins anyway) and has parallels in modern Egyptian and many other villages. How far these documents reflect what happened in earlier periods is very difficult to know: the economic world of the early Ptolemaic Period is very different from that of the Old to New Kingdoms, although a sophisticated private non-monetary economy certainly functioned then.

We still have remarkably little evidence for agricultural villages. They were probably built on *geziras*, areas of higher ground, throughout the flood plain. There are many large agricultural villages of Ptolemaic and Roman date in the Fayum. They contain all of the elements we would expect, but this type of village cannot be projected back into the Dynastic Period. One small village has been excavated, within the confines of the temple enclosure at Medinet Habu, on the west bank at Thebes. The village developed during the Libyan Period, and its streets and houses were not formally planned, with narrow twisting streets and blind alleys. This village was one part of the city of Thebes, but may reflect the 'organic' growth of many settlements in Egypt.

Another aspect of settlement about which we have little evidence is the 'country house' of the elite. In one of the most important scribal teaching texts a pupil describes the villa that he has built for his teacher. It is a rural idyll, surrounded by its fields and fishponds, with an abundance of animals and trees. We might assume, given Egypt's climate and the nature of the land ownership, that the elite had villas away from the urban centres. However, we have very little evidence from 'texts' and none from archaeology.

LINKING TOWN AND COUNTRY:
THE ECONOMY

Scenes in tombs at Thebes and Amarna are a primary source of information on the role of the temples as production and storage centres.

Documents such as the Wilbour Papyrus give much more detail on the land holdings of temples and the way in which their land was used. A mass of records from the village of Deir el-Medina allows us an insight as to how the economy actually functioned (and how it occasionally did not).

The following description of the economy really applies only to the New Kingdom (dynasties 18–20), when the temples were the dominant economic centres. In the Old and Middle Kingdoms the economy functioned in a similar way, but we have much less evidence; during that time the royal pyramids were probably the major landholders. In the post-New Kingdom Period the basis of the economic system probably remained the same into the Late Period, although the authority of the pharaoh declined and the local elite families probably had more direct control of regional resources, as had happened during the First and Second Intermediate Periods. There are large numbers of legal and economic documents surviving from the twenty-fifth and twenty-sixth dynasties from the Theban region. Many relate to sales of land, and women figure prominently in the transactions. Coinage was not introduced until the time of the Persians (dynasty 27) and did not become common until the Ptolemaic Period.

The importance of the temples within the New Kingdom economy is clearly shown by an inscription at Nauri in southern Nubia. This details the wide range of economic interests of one temple, probably that built by Sety I at Sesebi. The inscription tells us that the temple owned bird-trapping and fishing rights, fish pools, cattle, asses, dogs and goats; the agricultural employees mentioned are bee-keepers, gardeners and vintners. Other employees were involved in gold washing (the temple was situated in a gold-producing region). The temple also possessed its own fleet and was involved in foreign trade, bringing gold, ivory, animal tails and leopard skins. This document shows the ways in which a relatively minor 'provincial' temple was used as the focus of the agricultural and industrial life of a district. Although not mentioned in the text, the temple would have had its own workshops for the production of sculpture, pottery, and perhaps faience and gold work. There would have been beer and wine production, bakeries and butchers' yards with their by-products such as fat and leather. Fish and poultry were preserved by drying and salting. This particular temple appears to have been administratively attached to the temple of Sety I in

Abedju (Abydos), and some of the products, particularly of the long-distance trade, would have been paid to it.

During the New Kingdom the temples became the main centres for storing the nation's wealth (Figure 9.3). The texts known as the 'Annals of Thutmose III' record that king's military campaigns in Asia and also list some of the booty and 'tribute' paid to the temple of Amun at Karnak during the king's reign. This tells us that in four years of his reign (years 34, 38, 41 and 42) the temple received 8,616 *deben* of gold from Lower Nubia and 708 *deben* from Upper Nubia. One *deben* weighed about 91 grammes, giving an average

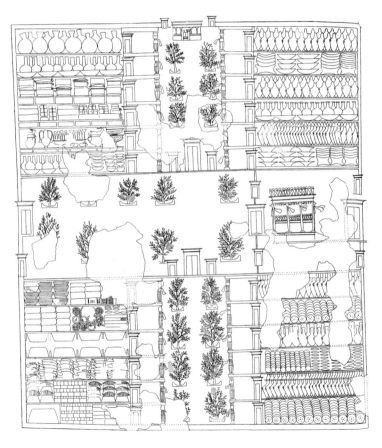

Figure 9.3 Temple magazines in Akhetaten: the arrangement of gateways shows the limits of access (after N. de G. Davies, *Rock Tombs of el Amarna II*, London, 1903, Plate **XXXI**).

yearly production of around 248 kilogrammes for Lower and 15 kilogrammes for Upper Nubia. However, Upper Nubia provided far more cattle than Lower Nubia. The inscriptions tell us that by the end of his reign Thutmose III had given to the temple at Karnak over 152,107 *deben* in nuggets or rings along with objects and other smaller specified amounts totalling in excess of 15,000 kilogrammes (i.e. 14.76 tons). Other materials, such as ivory and ebony, are not quantified. All of this 'tribute', 'tax' or 'booty' went into the magazines to be turned into objects for temple use or for distribution to the elite as 'reward' and 'gift'. So the temples became the great manufacturing centres, but always under royal control. Unfortunately, we do not have any details of how large the donations to the temples in Memphis and Heliopolis were. Scenes in tombs at Amarna show temple magazines with large quantities of agricultural produce and manufactures (Figure 9.3). The magazines contain amphorae of different shapes (perhaps containing wine, beer and olive oil), 'hides' of copper, metal vessels, chests (perhaps containing jewellery and precious materials), elaborate metal vessels, bread and cakes, and preserved fish.

The majority of the population was employed by the state, whether attached to the palace, the temples, one of the main administrative departments or the army. Put simply, every office (e.g. high priest of Amun, vizier) had estates attached to it, from which the official, his family and dependants drew their basic income in foodstuffs. As a specific and well-documented example, we can take the artisans who lived in the village of Deir el-Medina, on the west bank at Luxor. They were employees of the pharaoh, responsible for cutting and decorating the royal and elite tombs. The evidence from the village archives shows that, during the later New Kingdom, they were paid by the temple of Ramesses II (Ramesseum) and then by the temple of Ramesses III (Medinet Habu). They received their income as foodstuffs, most importantly the grain to make bread and brew beer. In addition, they could receive linen (most of which was manufactured in the temple workshops) and garments. Additional rations were given on festival days, at the accession of pharaoh and other similar occasions. On such occasions, the Deir el-Medina villagers received several cattle, and bread and cakes from the temple offerings, along with fruits and other items. One significant fact here is that although the workers were directly employed by the palace, they were paid by a temple, which was itself attached to the domain of Amun at Thebes. Exactly how the two institutions resolved this is a little uncertain.

An inscription of the priestess Nitoqert, later 'God's wife of Amun', provides a good example of how an income was paid to an official from scattered estates. When, in 656 BC, the young princess Nitoqert was sent to Thebes to begin her religious duties, her father Psamtik I gave her revenues from numerous estates and arranged for certain officials in Thebes to supply other goods. Nitoqert received fields totalling 1,400 *arouras* in the Delta and 1,900 *arouras* in northern Upper Egypt (all in the region north of Nen-nesut (*Herakleopolis*)): a total of 3,300 *arouras* (2,230 acres). In addition, she received daily bread rations from temples in Sau (*Sais*), Djanet (*Tanis*), Per-Bastet (*Bubastis*) and other Delta cities and from Nen-nesut. These totalled 2,100 *deben* (191.10 kilos or 421.37 pounds): a lot of bread, which, after its long journey south, would have been rather stale! No doubt there was a solution: perhaps the bread was paid by the temples as part of the wages of Nitoqert's agricultural workers in their vicinity; or a deal was done with the temple of Amun at Thebes, so that it supplied the bread in exchange for the other temples supplying the corresponding amounts to its employees in the north; or perhaps the daily bread ration was converted into a corresponding amount of grain to be distributed to Nitoqert's workers in the north or shipped to Thebes. In addition to the bread, Nitoqert received 11 *hin* (= 5.54 litres or 9.75 pints) of milk per day (supplied by Theban officials); two and one-sixth cakes and two and two-thirds bundles of 'herbs' (again supplied by Thebans). She received 3 *khar* (218 litres) of emmer wheat every day, paid by the king through the temple of Re-Atum at Iunu. A group of Theban officials (each official a specified amount) was made to supply her with a total of 3 oxen, 5 geese, 35 cakes, 20 *heben* of beer, 20 bundles of herbs and the yield of a 100-*aroura* (67.6 acre) field every month. At the date of this decree, Nitoqert was probably under ten years of age; she lived for a further fifty. On her eventual accession as God's wife of Amun, she inherited the considerable estates of that office.

We cannot assess exactly what percentage of the total land was owned by the state institutions and how much was held privately. A number of records show how privately owned land was given to religious institutions. One of the best examples is from Nubia in the reign of Ramesses VI, where Pennut, the governor of Wawat (Lower Nubia), endowed a statue of the king in the temple of Horus Lord of Miam, the major administrative town in Lower Nubia. The donation is recorded in Pennut's tomb at Miam, where a copy of the legal text details the fields which Pennut donated from his own property. Their positions are described and the owners of the neighbouring fields named; so we know that some belonged to other cult images, notably a statue of Queen Nefertari, wife of Ramesses II, also in the temple at Miam. It also indicates that here in Nubia, where the cultivation was much more limited than in Egypt, the fields were mainly strips running from the river to the desert edge. Pennut's donations were scattered over quite a wide area. In return for the statue, Pennut was rewarded by the king with silver bowls and other gifts. And, more importantly, he became the priest of the statue, in which office his heirs would succeed him. What Pennut effectively did was to make his land inalienable (i.e. it could not be taken away from the statue or temple) and reduce its tax liability, yet keep control of it and its produce by becoming priest and therefore enjoy most of the revenue.

BUYING AND SELLING

The basic unit of weight, and of value, was the copper *deben* (*c.* 91 grammes). Although there was no monetary economy, metal (usually copper) values were used as an ideal and conversion, so all items are given their value in copper. For example, in the nineteenth dynasty an ox (depending on condition) was valued at 100–120 *deben* of copper, which was equal to 1 *deben* of gold. In the twentieth dynasty there is good evidence for rising prices and an increase in the value of some metals.

How the system worked is well illustrated by a transaction at Deir el-Medina recorded on an ostracon (flake of limestone or piece of broken pottery). In exchange for a coffin valued at 25.5 *deben* the seller received: two pieces of copper, one weighing 8.5 *deben* and the other 5 *deben*; one pig valued at 5 *deben*; one goat valued at 3 *deben*; a second goat valued at 2 *deben*; two logs of sycamore wood at 2 *deben*; total 25.5 *deben*.

This is relatively straightforward, but things could be more complex since the exchange could include labour or even items acquired from relatives or friends in settlement of previous transactions, or as a prospective loan to be exchanged for goods or services at some other time.

TAX, TRIBUTE, REWARD AND GIFT

Pharaoh controlled foreign trade and, of course, the workshops attached to temples and palaces. At all times, foreign trade was of immense importance to the pharaohs. It supplied them with important materials that Egypt lacked, most notably good-quality timber such as pine and cedar. It supplied 'luxuries': ivory, ebony, precious stones for sculpture (diorite) and jewellery (lapis lazuli), metals (copper and bronze), animal skins and agricultural products such as wine and olive oil. But how, without a monetary economy, did 'trade' function? As with so many aspects of pre-Ptolemaic Egypt, our evidence is most detailed from the New Kingdom. Similar systems no doubt functioned in the Old and Middle Kingdoms.

In the New Kingdom, a main source of precious and exotic substances was 'tax' and 'tribute'. Tax was levied on territories and institutions directly controlled by the Egyptians, both in Egypt and their empire. Tribute came from those regions on the Egyptian borders that fell within its sphere of influence but were not directly governed. Tribute was paid by the rulers, and the Egyptian term probably covers a range of different economic categories, but certainly includes 'gift exchange' between them and the pharaoh.

One of the most important sources for understanding how gift exchange worked is the archive known as the 'Amarna Letters'. These letters were written in Akkadian, the diplomatic language of the day, on clay tablets found at Akhetaten (Amarna). They include copies of letters between Amenhotep III, Akhenaten and a number of rulers of states in western Asia, the most powerful being Mitanni. The letters cover a wide range of subjects, but it is clear that 'gifts' were sent with every letter exchanged, and a 'gift' of equal value was expected in return. When Tushratta, king of Mitanni, wrote to Amenhotep III, he sent:

One chariot, two horses, one male attendant, one female attendant from the booty of the land of Khatti. As greeting gift: five chariots, five teams of horses. As greeting gift to Kelu-Heba, my sister: one set of gold toggle-pins, one set gold earrings, one gold *mashkhu*-ring and a scent container full of sweet oil.

> (EA 17, lines 36–45: for full text see
> W. Moran, *The Amarna Letters*, 1992: 41–2)

Kelu-Heba was Tushratta's sister and one of Amenhotep III's wives. 'Gift' was also sent when a king built a new temple or palace. There was a corresponding gift exchange between other members of the royal family and court. The evidence from the Hittite capital includes preserved letters from the reign of Ramesses II, and it is clear from them that not only were the kings in communication, but the chief wife of each ruler wrote to the other, as did the crown princes and viziers.

One of the lengthiest of the surviving letters from the Amarna archive details the enormous dowry that Tushratta of Mittani sent to Egypt when he gave his daughter, Tadu-Heba, to be Amenhotep III's wife. The dowry included not only jewellery and items for the princess herself and gifts for the pharaoh, but large quantities of military equipment. What is significant is the detail, as for example, in the following items:

One chariot: 320 *shekels* of gold used in its overlay etc.; one whip of *pishaish*, overlaid with gold and set with *hulalu* stone: five *shekels* of gold used; one *maninnu* necklace, cut from 35 lapis stones, 35 *khiliba* stones, in the centre a *khulalu* stone mounted on gold with a reddish tinge; one *zallulu*, its *rettu* overlaid with *khiliba* stone and lapis, its handle, the figure of a woman, of alabaster, the inlay lapis.

> (Abbreviated from EA 22: for full text see
> W. Moran, *The Amarna Letters*, 1992: 51–61)

Although some of the terms are obscure to us, these examples show how precisely the gifts were documented: each is described with the different materials used in its component parts. Also, the precise numbers of beads are noted and the weights of gold used. This served two functions: there would be no chance of pilfering en route; and, perhaps more important, such precision was necessary so that items of equal value could be returned. This 'gift exchange' was effectively trade between the rulers, but with social implications.

The 'Amarna Letters' with other New Kingdom sources show the vast quantities of precious objects and materials that were being traded around the eastern Mediterranean, from Greece and Crete in the west to Mesopotamia in the east and Nubia in the south. But, with this wealth controlled by the pharaoh, how did officials and even lower ranks acquire precious metals and other raw materials, and the products of international trade? It was through 'reward'.

In 'rewarding' his officials the pharaoh distributed the wealth that he controlled through Egyptian society. But, at the same time, the reward ceremonies focused attention on the officials who were favoured, ensured their loyalty and also emphasized the power of the king. The economic aspect was important, but all the social aspects were of equal significance. We have many examples of reward scenes, and these make it clear that, although gold and jewellery were focused upon as the principal items, furniture (made of imported woods), linen and foodstuffs (including wine from the royal or temple vineyards) were also given. Doubtless, the official then redistributed some of his 'rewards' to his own family and subordinates.

Reward took place when an official was appointed or elevated in office, at the accession of a new pharaoh, and on various royal occasions such as the jubilee festival. We also have good evidence that the appointment of a new official saw reward spread to others with whom he dealt; one inscription records that, after his appointment, the new Viceroy of Nubia went on his first tour of inspection during which he rewarded all of the mayors of Nubia. In other words, when an official was installed, his subordinates and many of those with whom he would have to work could expect to receive gifts from the pharaoh through the official, helping to establish the social obligations between them.

For nearly three millennia Egypt developed a complex economic system that tied the land and the 'urban' centres together, and engaged in far-ranging commodity exchange, but all without the

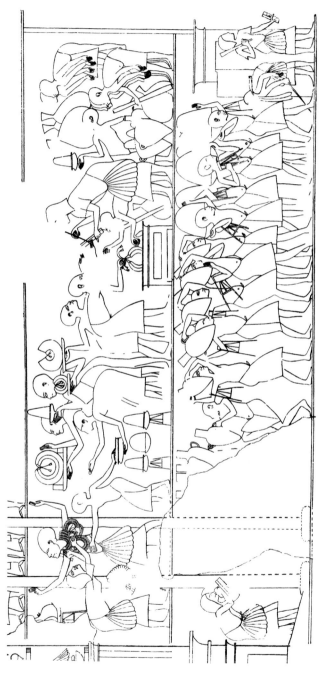

Figure 9.4 A reward scene: in the upper register, the official Parennefer is decorated with gold collars in front of the Window of Appearances; scribes keep a record of the gifts as they are put into caskets. In the lower register, servants carry away amphorae containing wine, and perhaps oil and foodstuffs; the quantities are recorded by scribes (after N. de G. Davies, *Rock Tombs of el Amarna VI*, London, 1908, Plate IV).

monetary economy that we know. Even without that monetary economy, there were fluctuations in the value of different commodities, notably grain and metals, and there were complex methods of private exchange. The state required the service of its people, but it also provided, physically and spiritually, by making the religious institutions central.

10

THE CULTURE OF
ANCIENT EGYPT

RELIGION AND THE GODS

For centuries, visitors to Egypt have been awed by the massive temples, mainly of New Kingdom or Ptolemaic–Roman date, the hundreds of tomb chapels and, of course, the pyramids. They all reflect aspects of ancient Egypt's religious life. Museums are filled with small bronze and 'faience' statues of deities with animal and bird heads, and some with more complex and bizarre combinations (Figure 10.1). Coffins and mummies, those most distinctive features of Egyptian culture, excite public interest, and suggest a society obsessed with death. Religion pervades our images of ancient Egypt. But, for all of the wealth of evidence, we are still remarkably ill-informed about religion in a number of important historical phases, and about the religious lives of the mass of the population. We can list hundreds of different gods and their forms, and we can narrate 'myths', mainly about the creation, but this does not really penetrate what the Egyptians actually believed in. Trying to come to terms with the names and forms of the many individual deities actually blocks attempts at understanding the broader issues.

The chief deity of each nome, whether male or female, was in some way a creator god. Many of them had a solar aspect, either originally or acquired later: for example, locally important deities, such as Herishef (at Nen-nesut), Khnum (at Esna, and at the First Cataract) and Sobek (in the Fayum, and Upper Egypt), were all creator gods who were later merged with the sun-god Ra.

Early Egyptologists explained the origins of Egyptian religion as they did the formation of the state, viewing the numerous creator

Figure 10.1 Figure of the god Horus in the temple at Kom Ombo (reign of Tiberius): the figure is in typical Egyptian style with falcon head and human body, wearing the double crown; the face originally had inlaid elements, perhaps in glass.

gods and triads found throughout Egypt as remnants of a tribal state, which was preserved in the later nomes. This is almost certainly a simplification, if not completely wrong. Indeed, the evidence seems to indicate that the 'triads' of gods are a later rationalization, possibly of New Kingdom date. As with so many other aspects of ancient Egypt, the evidence is extremely rich, but also remarkably patchy.

The prominence of gods, and the scale of their temples, was not necessarily due to their popularity or their religious functions, although those were significant factors in the worship of Osiris. Some deities, such as the serpent goddess Meretseger, had a very localized popularity (in her case, at Thebes). Some gods gained national importance because of royal patronage of their cults. The cult of the sun-god Ra of Iunu was promoted by the pharaohs of the Old Kingdom, notably those of the fifth dynasty, and that of Amun of Thebes by the pharaohs of dynasties 11, 12 and 18. In the late eighteenth dynasty Tutankhamun created a state triad of Ra-Harakhty, Amun-Ra and the Memphite god Ptah.

Does the available evidence enable us to build a picture of religious belief and practices that were common to all strata of society? Some Egyptologists doubt that Egyptian religion was homogeneous. They argue that the evidence that we have is primarily high status (and this includes the 'workers' of Deir el-Medina), and may not reflect the religious practices of the majority. Most Egyptologists, however, assume that the preserved (i.e. elite) records do represent a guide to religion for the whole of society.

Even if we agree that the evidence can be used for the whole of ancient Egyptian society, we have to remember that we lack enormous amounts of information. First, there is remarkably little material that allows us to explain the development of religion in the Predynastic Period, particularly the naming and depiction of gods. Early Egyptologists made much of the 'fetishes' on standards that later appear as emblems of the nomes. Whether these emblems are divine or royal symbols is still unclear. There is very little evidence for cult temples from the Old Kingdom, or for temples other than those attached to pyramids. From the Middle Kingdom there is extensive evidence for royal patronage of cults throughout Egypt. Notably well preserved are monuments raised to Amun and Montju in the Theban region, and to Osiris at Abedju (Abydos). Many temples and considerable documentary evidence for destroyed build-ings survive from the New Kingdom and later periods. But even so, there are biases in our knowledge: because of the preservation of its monuments, a tremendous emphasis has been placed on the import-ance of the cult of Amun and the role of Thebes in the New Kingdom (see Chapter 6). Without doubt, the temple of Amun was one of the chief landholders in Egypt and recipient of enormous wealth from military campaigns, taxes, foreign trade and royal patronage, but the temples at Memphis and Iunu were probably equally wealthy. The problem is that so little survives physically of the northern temples, and there is correspondingly little documen-tary material.

PYRAMIDS, TEMPLES AND STATE RELIGION

In the Old and Middle Kingdoms the main resources of the state were directed to the construction of the royal burial place, usually a pyramid, and its adjacent temple complex. The pyramids were the principal land holders in Egypt, as temples were in the New Kingdom. These pyramid complexes had strong solar associations: they had east–west orientation; the Giza and Abu Roash pyramids are clearly located in relation to the solar temples at Iunu (*Heliopolis*); and the Abusir pyramids had their own solar sanctuaries nearby. A series of smaller pyramids without burial chambers or temples was built between Sila (Faiyum) and Abu (Elephantine) in the late third or early fourth dynasty. These appear to have been centres for the royal cult and are therefore early examples of '*ka*-chapels' which are documented from the sixth dynasty onwards.

The royal cult is one of the most important aspects of Egyptian state religion until the end of the New Kingdom. Although we talk about 'cult' temples of gods, they always have a prominent place for the cult of the ruling pharaoh. This may be a small '*ka*-chapel', or, in the New Kingdom, an entire temple. These temples, called 'Houses of Millions of Years' included those that were for the king's funerary rites and mortuary cult at Thebes, but they were also built at other important places throughout Egypt. Indeed, the surviving temples of the New Kingdom are mainly those focused on the royal cult. Even the 'great temple of Amun' at Karnak had very strong royal associations in the eighteenth dynasty. The large cult temples devoted to the gods are a feature of the Late and Ptolemaic–Roman Periods, when the royal cult was a less dominant aspect of state religion. It is easier to chart changes and developments in the royal cult in the New Kingdom, than it is to comment on the roles and cults of most deities. By the late eighteenth and the nineteenth dynasties the royal cult was essentially about the worship of the state itself, represented by the person of the pharaoh. As with all aspects of Egyptian state religion, there were important political influences, and the changing role of the pharaoh in the post-New Kingdom is paralleled by the increasing importance of the gods.

The design and form of the later temples also reveals the central importance of the royal cult. The 'classic form' of the temple developed during the eighteenth dynasty and is traced through changes in the design of royal temples, mainly at Thebes (Figure 10.2). The surviving cult temples of the period do not show the same plan, although, as always, we do have to be wary of the limits of our evidence. The 'classic form' was followed, with some developments, in all of the major works of the last thousand years of Egyptian religious building. From the beginning of the New Kingdom onwards, temples replaced the royal burial place as the focus of state building projects.

Figure 10.2 The temple of Ramesses III at Medinet Habu (Thebes, west bank).

The 'classic form' of temple has a massive entrance gateway flanked by two towers (the pylon). These towers represent the hills of the horizon between which the sun rises. They usually carry scenes of the pharaoh smiting enemies in the presence of the chief deities of the temple, thus subduing chaotic forces so that the interior could be calm and stable. Many pylons have recesses for flag poles, and temples dedicated to solar deities may have a pair of obelisks flanking the gate. The main gate between the towers, made of wood plated with metal and covered with depictions of the gods, was used only for festival processions. Access to the temple for the majority was through a side gate. The gates opened on to a large courtyard, often with a colonnade. This was the most public part of the temple, and access to the interior was restricted by initiation. Beyond the court, a series of halls with service rooms to the side led to the main offering hall and sanctuaries for the divine statues. Approaching these, the floor level rose and the ceiling level was lowered. The sanctuary was the highest point, representing the first land to emerge from the flood waters at the moment of creation. Throughout the temple, walls, columns and ceilings were decorated with imagery of the primeval swamp. This plan could be enlarged or reduced in scale according to the wealth, patronage and importance of the shrine. A small village temple might be built almost entirely of plastered mud-brick and be reduced to a court with chapel and offering room.

The large temples stood within an enclosure surrounded by massive mud-brick walls. The enclosure could contain a wide range of religious, administrative, storage and craft zones. In the New Kingdom the agricultural wealth of the temple's estates was stored in the granaries and used for paying its staff and dependants. Houses for the priests when on duty, schools and, perhaps most important, the administrative offices and archives of the temple formed the non-religious area within the precinct. Butchers' halls were within the precinct, in some temples directly attached to the cult building. Surviving evidence for bakeries shows that in some places they were situated just outside the precinct, although they were supplied with grain from its stores. The temple area was thus one of the busiest parts of any 'urban' settlement and the employer of a large proportion of the urban population.

At the centre of this activity was the temple itself. Here a routine of services ensured the well-being of the deities, who, in return, guaranteed the order of the universe. The rites were certainly performed in the morning and evening, and perhaps at other times of day in simpler form. In these rites, accompanied by music, the divine statues were washed, purified with incense and clothed. The incense rite was one of the most important parts of the ritual, and made the statue a suitable place for the divine spirit to occupy. Then the offerings were made. These rites were essentially private, performed by the priests on behalf of the king.

A public appearance of the god took place on festival days, and there appears to have been an increase in the importance of processional festivals in the New Kingdom. This resulted in new temple forms and religious landscapes, with ceremonial routes connecting temples. At Thebes, for which we have most archaeological and textual evidence, there were processions at the end of every Egyptian week (ten days) when the statue of Amun was taken to Djeme (Medinet Habu) and back to Luxor (or Karnak). There were two major festivals during the year. In the Great Feast of the Valley, Amun sailed from Karnak across the river to the temples at Deir el-Bahari where he stayed overnight. In this festival the people of Thebes went to their family tomb chapels and celebrated rites of rebirth. The Great Feast of Opet was one occasion when the pharaoh went to the city, some even choosing it as a time for their coronation. At Opet, the statues of Amun, his consort Mut and their child Khonsu travelled from Karnak to the temple of Luxor to celebrate his marriage. During the New Kingdom pharaohs added extra days to the festival, so that by the twentieth dynasty it lasted for 27 days.

These festival processions became times when people could present petitions to the god. It is, however, significant that the divine statue remained unseen, sealed within the veiled shrine on the sacred processional bark. Throughout the New Kingdom, the visible images of the god that adorned the great gates of the temple, and the prow and stern of the sacred bark, themselves became the focus of worship. In Amun's case, this 'aegis' took the form of the ram's head, crowned, and with the broad collar beneath.

PRIVATE RELIGION IN ANCIENT EGYPT

Egyptian religious practice was conducted on several levels. There was the official, state religion which concentrated on the royal cult and the gods that were closely associated with the kingship. Local religion, in nome and town, focused on the performance of rites within the temple, but with public display of the gods in processional festivals. Here, the main shrines were those of the presiding local deities, with royal *ka*-chapels attached. The rites associated with 'popular religion' were conducted in the house and on certain occasions in the family tomb. These rites were daily events or for specific rites of passage. An individual could thus participate in religious acts on a number of levels: as part of collective community acts, such as festivals; collective family acts, both on a daily basis, and to mark significant points in the lives of family members; and alone in personal acts.

The overwhelming emphasis in temple scenes is on the state, the pharaoh, the maintenance of cosmic order (*maet*) by the king and the gods, and power. How the majority practised religion and what they believed is much more difficult to determine. We now acknowledge that religious rites of some sort would have accompanied important points of transition during life: birth, puberty and assumption of an adult role (including circumcision), marriage, parenthood and death. The rites surrounding death are well documented, but the others remain rather vague. One earlier Egyptologist assumed that marriage was solemnized by the couple going to the local temple, rather like a marriage in church, but the only evidence we have for marriages relates to civil contracts. Yet it would be surprising if there were no religious rites accompanying marriage, even if, as is more likely, they were celebrated in the home rather than temple.

The Egyptian world was a dangerous and unpredictable place. The appeasing, or warding off, of dangerous wild animals such as snakes, scorpions, crocodiles and hippopotami is attested in documents and by the use of amulets. There were numerous other dangers, notably to women in pregnancy and childbirth. Many children were stillborn or died shortly after birth, and many women (perhaps a majority) died in childbirth. There were certainly rituals surrounding childbirth and the mother was secluded for a time surrounding the birth.

In order to combat these dangers the Egyptians used a variety of techniques, which we generally refer to as 'magic'. Within the Egyptian contexts, magic was an essential part of religious and medical practice. Magic usually required written spells and formulae, and the evidence indicates that in many cases it was performed by the lector priest, or one of the other specialized priests, and was therefore closely related to formal religion.

One of the most dangerous times was night when people were asleep, and the act of going to bed seems to have involved spells to ward off dangers such as snakes and scorpions, spirits and ghosts. The curved wands of hippo ivory, which can be seen in many museum collections, were perhaps used to protect the bed. Many of them have incised images of the threatening creatures and protecting images of the god Bes. Spells refer to rearing uraei made of clay, with candles in their mouths, which were placed at the cardinal points of the bedroom to spit fire at any dangers. Examples of this type have been found in excavations. The implication is that religion, and religious acts of all sorts, were an essential part of the daily routine.

Excavated remains of houses show that there were false-door shrines and offering places for the practice of religion within the house. Offerings and prayers were probably made in the morning and evening, and perhaps before meals. The focus of these would have been local gods, deities that were particularly associated with protecting the house, such as Bes and Taweret, and perhaps other gods favoured by the family.

Graffiti and prayers carved on cliffs and places within the landscape indicate that they were associated with a particular deity or purpose. At Thebes, the serpent goddess Meretseger presided over the mountain that dominated the western bank, and was particularly revered by the villagers of Deir el-Medina, who lived and worked in its shadow. At several places in Middle and Upper Egypt there are temples that controlled the point of transition between the agricultural land and the wild desert beyond; their deities had ambivalent natures, and their wild aspects needed to be pacified. At Aswan, the 'Rock of Offerings' marks the point where the desert road to Nubia leaves sight of the river valley, and it was an appropriate place for those setting out on the long and dangerous journey to stop and pray.

Although there was a distinction between the organized cult practices of the temples and personal acts of devotion, there were, inevitably, times and places where the two blurred, for example, when votive offerings were presented to a deity. Although the offering was itself an expression of personal faith, the act would usually have taken place in a chapel or temple that was controlled by 'official' practices, as Egyptologist Geraldine Pinch has shown. Many of the votive gifts would have been manufactured in temple workshops and sold at the temples. The process of offering would have required temple personnel to perform rites to link the object with the donor, and to make prayers of sanctification and dedication, to place the objects in the appropriate parts of the temple and, later, to clear them away. There may have been controls on when such votives could be presented, such as festival days of the deity.

FOCUSES OF PERSONAL DEVOTION

Many discussions of private religion, whether associated with women and childbirth or the home, emphasize the presiding deities as 'lesser' gods or 'demons' and 'genies'. They cite Taweret and Bes, the various manifestations of Hathor (such as the seven Hathors who assist at labour), Meskhenet, goddess of the birthing stool, and Heqet, the frog-headed midwife. Again, as with so many aspects of Egyptology, we have to consider not only our sources of evidence, but also the timescale and the changes it brought. Much of our evidence for private religious practice comes from New Kingdom sources, and there were many changes in the post-New Kingdom, in which these 'household' gods were syncretized with other gods, especially the 'state' gods, and became more prominent in cult temples.

Local gods (town or nome gods) were an appropriate focus of devotion. In Egypt, most names were theophoric (god plus epithet), such as Sit-Amun ('daughter of Amun'), Ptah-hotep ('Ptah is satisfied'), or Montju-hir-wenemy-ef ('Monthu is upon his right side'), and they often included the name of the local town god. The 'wisdom' literature of the Middle Kingdom encourages people to worship their local gods, and monuments from the later New Kingdom express gratitude to local gods for their protection. The stela of

Pentaweret, who came from Asyut, thanks the local nome god, Wepwawet, for his salvation. Much later, the high official Sema-tawy-tefnakht, who lived through the second Persian invasion of Egypt and that of Alexander the Great (i.e. between 360 and 330 BC), donated a monument to his local deity, Herishef, the ram-headed god of Nen-nesut (*Herakleopolis*), with a hymn in praise of Herishef, equating him with the great solar god Ra. Sema-tawy-tefnakht attributed his own safety during the battles between the Persians and Alexander to his local god.

When he was at Baki, in Nubia, in the reign of Ramesses XI, the scribe of the royal necropolis, Dhutmose, prayed to his own local god, Amun, as well as to the gods of Baki, for his safe return. Dhutmose also wrote to his family at Thebes telling them to make regular water offerings to Amun. These simple offerings were to reinforce and perpetuate Dhutmose's own prayers, but, being made in the god's home town, Dhutmose perhaps thought they stood more chance of being heard than in the remote deserts of Nubia (this 'hellhole' as he described it).

In the later New Kingdom, names began to express new concepts of the relationship between individual and god. Names including the verb *shed*, 'to rescue' or 'save', are found for the first time (Shed-su-Hor, Shed-su-Amun), along with the appearance of a divinity actually named Shed, representing the concept of salvation. Shed has associations with Horus, and particularly the child Horus, and the king. *Shay*, 'fate', also makes an appearance. Whether the expression of these ideas reflects a major change in Egyptian religious ideas or whether it is a matter of expressing for the first time a feature that has always been there is a debatable issue.

Egyptian religion did have a concept of evil (*isfet*), which is characterized as the inverse of Maet, and overlaps with the idea of disorder. But there are very few expressions of scepticism in the entire corpus of Egyptian texts. One of the few is a New Kingdom text that doubts the value of making provision for the afterlife since 'there is no one who has come back from there'. A similar view is expressed in 'The dispute of a man with his *ba*', preserved on a papyrus of the twelfth dynasty, now in the Berlin Museum. Otherwise, whatever doubts any Egyptian may have had went unexpressed until the Roman Period.

FUNERARY RELIGION

Mummification and method of burial distinguished the Egyptians from other peoples in the ancient world, and it is one of the features of Egyptian culture that most excites popular attention today. The preservation of tombs, chapels and bodies has led to the image of a society that was obsessed with death and that devoted its wealth and attention to it (Figure 10.3). Certainly, the practice of mummification and burial changed significantly at different periods. For example, major shifts came in the later New Kingdom and the period immediately following. First, known primarily from the Theban region, there was a change in tomb decoration after the 'Amarna Period', with more emphasis on religious scenes than the 'scenes of daily life' and those of the official's relationship with the pharaoh that typify earlier eighteenth-dynasty tombs. The second major change came in the Libyan Period, when tombs ceased to be carved for a period, and collective burials were made in older tombs and in temple precincts. These bodies were no longer accompanied by an array of personal objects but were provided with specifically funerary materials: coffins covered with religious texts, shabti figures, amulets and funerary papyri. However, it has to be noted that the evidence is again predominantly Theban, and may have been influenced by the fact that the city was no longer the royal burial place and not a focus of major royal building activities. It may therefore have lacked the large workforce required to construct the tombs typical of the New Kingdom. When Thebes was again a major centre of royal patronage under the Kushite pharaohs (dynasty 25), large tombs reappeared. Similar changes dictated by economic conditions as much as religious change might be noted at other periods.

The purpose of the careful preservation of the body was to provide a place for the soul to return to. The rituals of opening the eyes, nose and mouth were to enable the deceased to see, breathe and speak, and to partake of the offerings made to it. Effectively, the mummy became the equivalent of a statue, and statues (or two-dimensional depictions) could serve to replace the body should it be destroyed. But the body was only one of the components of a person. The Egyptians thought of each person as five non-physical elements. The *ka*-spirit (vital life-force) was created at the same time as the body, and they were reunited at death. It was the *ka* that inhabited

Figure 10.3 The restored pyramid on the tomb of Sennedjem at Deir el-Medina (nineteenth dynasty): the doorway gives access to the chapel and stairway to the tomb chambers; the niche contained a statue of the deceased worshipping the rising sun.

the body or statues to receive the offerings. The *ba* was associated with the individual's personality: from the New Kingdom onwards it is usually shown as a human-headed bird, sometimes hovering over the mummified body. The *ba* was able to leave the mummy and the tomb, visiting places it had enjoyed while alive, but returning to be reunited with the mummy at night. The *akh* ('effective-spirit'), associated with luminous power, was the transfigured deceased who could move and function through the proper offerings and knowledge of the appropriate spells. The shadow was another integral element, but one of the most important aspects of a person was the name (*ren*). It was the name, rather than the physical features, that identified a statue or two-dimensional image, thereby making it recognizable to the soul. To destroy a person, the eyes, nose and mouth of their image would be cut through so that they could not see, breathe or eat, and their names were erased. These actions prevented the soul from finding the image and thereby from participating in the offerings.

Following death, the dead passed through a number of transformations before joining Osiris or Ra, becoming a swallow, a falcon, snake, crocodile, heron or lotus. These and other transformations, and the acquisition of attributes and powers, are detailed in the collection of 192 spells generally referred to as the *Book of the Dead*. Some chapters were ancient and have their origins in the 'Coffin Texts' of the Middle Kingdom; others were added in the New Kingdom. The corpus includes aspects of the Osirian afterlife (such as the judgement of the deceased) and the solar afterlife, reflected in the Egyptian title of the work, *The Book of Going Forth by Day*.

ART AND ARCHITECTURE

The Egyptian style is distinctive and displays a remarkable continuity over the enormous span of time from when it was developed, in the later Predynastic Period, to the Roman Period. The style is essentially the same whether using two- or three-dimensional representation and irrespective of medium – wood, metal, stone or glazed material. There were changes at different periods, and in the Ptolemaic and Roman Periods the formal Egyptian style was used on many official monuments, while alongside it a style developed combining Egyptian and Hellenistic elements. Another factor that influenced continuity was the use and adaptation of the models of the past (a process that is generally termed 'archaism'). But in looking back to the past, the Egyptian artist was rarely a stale copyist: the past served to stimulate new movements, and elements of the past were absorbed and adapted to new circumstances and purposes. It was royal and religious functions of art that first created the official style, and also dictated its continuity.

The ways of depicting people and things, as well as the rather limited range of scenes that it was deemed acceptable to show, derive from what Egyptologist John Baines has termed 'decorum'. The style was almost certainly created to distinguish the figure of the god king, and the human form is therefore shown in an idealized way, rather than naturalistically. The figure in relief and painting combines a series of separate views of the body in profile (or sections through the body). Certain elements, such as the eye, are shown as if viewed full on, although placed in a face that is in profile; the eye must be whole and complete if it is to function when the image is animated through ritual.

A 'canon of proportion' was developed for creating these figures, with the figure divided into three equal parts, at the knee, buttock and hairline. This proportion was later refined on a grid system, 18 squares high. It is the subtle variations to these proportions (such as the position of the middle, or top, of the knee at the top of the sixth square) as well as more significant modifications (most notably the introduction of the 'Saite Canon', which used 21 squares for the height of the figure) that contribute to periodic variations in style.

As with so many aspects of Egyptian society, what was first the preserve of the king was later adopted by the elite. So in private tomb decoration from the Old Kingdom onwards, there was a hier- archy of scale in depiction. The king or the tomb owner, and those closest to them, were depicted formally and were the largest figures. Agricultural labourers, dancers and others of lower social status could be depicted in actions and postures that decorum denied to the principal figures. Similarly, with the ordering of space, important figures overlap only under exceptional circumstances. So kings and their consorts may be standing or seated side by side, but each is depicted entirely separately. The exception is, inevitably, in the reign of Akhenaten, when some scenes depict the king and

Nefertiti standing or seated in 'real space', and moving in ways that defy conventional royal representations.

Scenes were ordered within clearly defined space, dictated by the architectural setting and framed above by the hieroglyph for the sky. The scenes are often divided into registers, which are not to be read as foreground to background, but may combine, as in agricultural scenes, different seasons of the year: so, for example, the tomb owner may be placed viewing the entire year's activities from ploughing to harvest and threshing. Different viewpoints are combined in one scene, or even in one object to make it more intelligible.

Egyptian art has a remarkably limited range of subjects: in tombs from the Old Kingdom to the end of the eighteenth dynasty the majority of scenes were those of 'daily life'. These actually show the activities of the official's estate, with scenes of arable farming and stock rearing, and the presentation of all types of domestic animals and birds that will supply the offerings for the afterlife. There may also be scenes of workshops (usually temple or palace), and of feasting. Occasionally, the house and garden of the official may be shown in a rather schematic way, but there are no townscapes or naturalistic landscapes. Scenes of hunting in the desert are quite common, but present the landscape in a stylized way. In the troubled times of the First Intermediate Period, tombs at Beni Hasan include scenes of military training and battle, which are extremely rare in tombs of other periods. In the eighteenth dynasty, scenes showing the relationship of the official to the ruler become frequent, and the pharaoh himself can be depicted, with the official and a range of scenes showing his duties. This reaches a peak in the reign of Akhenaten, when the tombs at Akhetaten focus almost entirely on the king and his activities. The scenes now include depictions of the temples and palaces of the city, although there is nothing comparable to, for example, Minoan townscapes. Following the 'Amarna' interlude, the emphasis is much more on religious scenes and episodes from the *Book of the Dead*, and of the family celebrating religious feasts, although the duties of the official are still depicted. In the Theban tombs of the Late Period, the decoration is almost entirely derived from religious texts, some previously a royal preserve. Scenes of 'daily life' are much rarer in tombs of the later periods.

Of course, there were changes and innovations in scene content. Some were made in response to religious and royal activities: processions of divine barks, the Opet and Valley Feasts at Thebes and the 'reforms' of Akhenaten all added to, or altered, temple decoration. Artists accompanied expeditions abroad, both military and commercial, recording elements of the landscape, animals and people encountered. The most celebrated surviving example is the expedition sent by Hatshepsut to Punt.

Perhaps the most significant non-religious changes were due to the introduction of the chariot in the early eighteenth dynasty. In tomb scenes the chariot appeared in the desert hunt and scenes of the duties of the official, and along with it came the motif of the bored charioteer. Most radically, the chariot changed depictions of warfare. Very few scenes of royal military activities survive from the Old and Middle Kingdoms, but fragments of relief sculpture indicate that they were a genre, probably of the royal temples attached to the pyramids. Whether the ruler was ever depicted in these scenes is unknown. Elsewhere, he is most usually shown as a single heroic figure smiting one or more kneeling enemies, or in the form of the triumphant sphinx crushing them under foot. With the introduction of the chariot a whole new type of military scene was developed. Unfortunately, no complete examples survive from the early eighteenth dynasty; remarkably, there are no scenes of the extensive campaigns of Thutmose III that consolidated the Egyptian empire. The earliest surviving examples of a king in battle are on the panels of the chariot of Thutmose IV, and a painted chest from the tomb of Tutankhamun; ironically, neither king is known to have taken part in a major military action. In these scenes and those of the same type that were carved on temple walls, a large figure of the king alone in his chariot dominates a mêlée of much smaller figures of Egyptian and enemy soldiers. The Egyptian style was an expression of order, but the artists seem to have relished depicting the confusion and chaos of battle. In the battle scenes of the early nineteenth dynasty, huge images of the pharaohs Sety I and Ramesses II dominate the action as they strike dramatic and heroic postures, firing their bows, or leaning from their chariots to slay foreign rulers. These scenes also introduce elements of landscape and narrative. However, even when such local features are included, and the events located in a specific time and place, there is a combination of the observed and the hiero-glyphic shorthand.

This combination of careful observation and hieroglyphic gener-alization in Egyptian depictions can pose problems to Western viewers. First, despite extremely detailed rendering of feather colours and patterns of bird, for example of ducks and geese, these do not always conform to specific species in our taxonomy. Certainly, there are very fine depictions that can be identified as specific types, such the white-fronted goose, the bean goose, the red-breasted goose or the pintail duck, but most scenes show birds that are rather more generalized in their physical forms and feathering detail. When such depictions carry captions, as in the scenes showing them as products of the elite estate, it becomes clear that the Egyptians cate-gorized birds in a very different way from us: 'species', in our sense, was unimportant and subordinate to function. One species of fowl may appear in different groups according to whether it was a bird for offering, one fattened for the table, or one for some other purpose (not always clear to us). We distinguish ducks and geese, but the Egyptians may not have. They perhaps placed more emphasis on the difference between domesticated fowl and the wild marshland birds, which could represent evil and chaotic forces.

The detail and apparent accuracy of fur, feathers and scales in depictions of the natural world is beguiling in another way. Close inspection of some scenes of hunting and fishing show that, far from the initial impression of 'naturalism' and 'realism', the birds and other creatures are usually depicted in a purely hieroglyphical manner: the wings of flying birds, particularly, are rarely attached to the body 'correctly'. However accurate the depiction of living creatures, they are often depicted against a 'natural' world that is essentially hieroglyphic: the papyrus swamp is either an elegant stylized surface or reduced to an equally stylized clump; the birds, fishes and lotus are placed flat on the surface of a lined and patterned strip that signifies the water. There are no attempts to reproduce the effects of light, no shadows, reflection or iridescence.

This difference of Egyptian perception also affects colour. The Egyptians had a very limited number of words for colour categories, and these embrace a wide range of tones, hues and shades. Modern Western artists' colours are usually named after the pigments or materials they are made of – raw umber, burnt umber, chrome yellow. Egyptian colour terms are much more inclusive, and cover a wide range of related ideas that are not colour specific. So *kem*, the word that includes 'black', also embraces the sense of dark (in contrast to bright), and *hedj* can be a term for silver, white and things that are bright. *Desher*, generally translated as 'red', embraces a wide spectrum, including brown, but is also used in contrast to *kem* and *hedj*. The closest to our own usage of a colour for wider meanings is *wadj*, which can be the colour green, but signifies things that are fresh (including meat) and healthy. Some colour terms relate specifically to minerals: *kheshed*, lapis lazuli, is also used for 'blue', *nub* is gold, and *mefkat* turquoise. In the case of that popular glazed material generally called Egyptian 'faience', although it was frequently blue, turquoise or green, its colour was not necessarily its most important feature. The Egyptian name is *tjehenet*, signifying anything that glitters, relating the material to solar and lunar light. For these reasons we may find objects painted colours that seem to us to be 'incorrect' or unnatural.

Most Egyptian 'art', whether painting, relief sculpture, statuary or the productions of the 'minor arts', were within an architectural context. Remarkably, there were more radical developments in the architectural setting than in the images that adorned it. In the Old and Middle Kingdoms, the royal pyramid complex was the focus of state building projects, and in the New Kingdom and later, the focus was the temple. In both pyramid complex and temple, there were reign-by-reign changes and adaptations until a 'classic' form was arrived at. There were presumably cultic reasons for these constantly modified plans, and, perhaps, historically specific factors.

LITERATURE AND MUSIC

Our knowledge of the Egyptian language is dependent entirely on elite sources. During Egyptian history the language changed through five forms, termed by Egyptologists Old, Middle and Late Egyptian, Demotic and Coptic, and its writers employed four scripts. Hieroglyphic was the earliest script used, and it continued to be used for religious and royal monuments to the Roman Period. Hieratic, using a highly simplified form of hieroglyphic, was developed quite early and used for bureaucratic and religious documents, continuing to be used up to the Ptolemaic Period. From around 700 BC Demotic was both the language and script used for all types of document, although hieroglyphic and hieratic were still used for royal and religious texts. Coptic was the language of Late Antique (Byzantine) Egypt, its script using signs from Demotic and Greek. The most important foreign languages were Akkadian and Aramaic, used as diplomatic languages in the New Kingdom and the first millennium BC respectively, and Greek, which was one of the official languages of the Ptolemaic and Roman Periods.

Many of the basic genres of literature are attested by the end of the Old Kingdom. In addition to the accounts and administrative documents which must have formed the bulk of written material, royal annalistic texts, private inscriptions detailing the careers of members of the elite, religious texts, hymns, songs and poetry are all preserved. Most of the non-bureaucratic texts that survive from this period are carved on stone, although papyrus and other materials must have been widely used. Occasionally, copies of letters were inscribed in stone (as in that from Pepy II to his official Harkhuf). Some 'wisdom literature' (instructions) is ascribed to authors who lived under the Old Kingdom, but it is unclear whether they really were written then. From the Middle Kingdom narrative literature, private letters, wisdom literature and teaching texts (which include copying some of the other categories) survive. All of these genres continue into the Late and Ptolemaic–Roman Periods.

Some texts show that there was rhythmical, and perhaps metrical, writing, but as our understanding of how Egyptian sounded is limited, it is impossible to reproduce it in translation. Some genres, such as hymns and religious invocations, were, no doubt, chanted, perhaps with a musical accompaniment. The narrative literature itself has a range of parallels in other genres. For example, the *Tale of Sinuhe* has been compared with official tomb biography, but includes a letter, song and prayer. The story known as the *Eloquent Peasant* has a relationship with the instructions. The *Story of Wenamun* is set at a specific historical moment (the reign of Ramesses XI), as is the *Capture of Joppa* (the campaigns of Thutmose III), and both may have been based on official reports or real events. No doubt much of the narrative literature has its roots in an oral tradition. Again, this emphasizes the elite nature of our sources: we have no means of knowing what the non-elite oral tradition contained.

Related to literature, but even more difficult to understand, is music. There are numerous depictions of musicians from all periods, and a wide range of instruments is attested by tomb and temple scenes and archaeological survivals. There is also evidence for Nubian musicians (usually associated with the army) and 'Syrian' musicians (in a court context). However, no music was written down and it is very difficult to assess what it would have sounded like. In temples, the daily office was presumably chanted by the priests; perhaps the music of the Coptic church owes something to this tradition. Instrumental music also played a part in daily rituals, but may have been additional to the liturgy, rather than accompanying it. The main instruments in a religious context were the harp and the sistrum, the sacred 'rattle' that replicated the sound of the papyrus being shaken to calm the violent cow goddess, Hathor.

It has been assumed that early music was essentially monodic, although evidence contemporary with the eighteenth dynasty from Ugarit on the Syrian coast suggests that some harmony was employed. Evidence from the Ptolemaic Period is better, as some of the earliest papyri with musical notation survive (although even they do not give much indication of length of note or rhythm) using the Greek system, and perhaps deriving from Greek musical tradition. For all that the Egyptians left us in their visual records, we cannot hear them.

CULTURAL CONTINUITY AND CULTURAL CHANGE

The culture of Egypt during the enormous span of history from the late Predynastic Period to the Islamic conquest displays a remarkable continuity. The problem for archaeologists and art historians is trying to assess to what extent that continuity is superficial. The continuity in many of the visual arts is obvious, and most clearly seen in formal temple decoration. The images of gods and pharaohs in Ptolemaic and Roman temples follow the conventions established in the depictions of the earliest rulers such as 'Scorpion' and Narmer. But tomb and coffin decoration of the Roman Period show a distinctive combination of Egyptian style and images with features that are characteristic of the Hellenistic–Roman culture of other parts of the eastern Mediterranean. Throughout the Dynastic Period, there was a constant remodelling of official production, looking back to the past ('archaism'). This dominance of official production no doubt masks considerable changes, some of which are occasionally revealed in other types of material.

Some other cultural changes can be noted. The introduction of horse and chariot had a considerable impact on warfare and consequently on 'imperial' expansion and administration. There appear to have been major legal reforms in the Saite period, although the impact of these is difficult to assess. Otherwise, as in any society, changes were occasionally sudden, more often gradual, but at different rates in different spheres. The agricultural basis changed hardly at all from the earliest to modern times; the introduction of the *shaduf* and later the *saqia*-wheel, eased irrigation, but the flooding of the Nile and basin irrigation remained the key factors. Even major religious changes, such as the arrival of Christianity, allowed significant elements to be absorbed and adapted. Although the arrival of Islam marks a major turning point in Egyptian religious and political history, there are numerous aspects of Egypt's culture that have continued. Ancient Egypt did not cease to exist at the end of the twentieth dynasty, or with the Persian, Macedonian or Roman conquests; there is much in modern Egypt that is, like its people, directly descended from the Pharaonic past.

Appendix

KING LIST

The dates here are, for the most part, those generally accepted in recent literature (e.g. Shaw 2000). Occasionally, as with Dynasties '22' and '23', I have chosen to depart from this scheme.

The list includes only those rulers mentioned in the text and others who left major monuments or about whose reigns something is known. Only the most significant Roman rulers are listed.

PALAEOLITHIC PERIOD *c.* 700,000–7000 BP

Epipalaeolithic *c.* 10,000–7000 BP

NEOLITHIC PERIOD *c.* 8800–4700 BC

PREDYNASTIC PERIOD *c.* 5300–3000 BC

Lower Egypt
Maadi-Buto Cultural Complex *c.* 4000–3200 BC

Middle Egypt
Badarian Culture *c.* 4400–4000 BC

Upper Egypt
Naqada I (Amratian) *c.* 4000–3500 BC
Naqada II (Gerzean) *c.* 3500–3200 BC

All Egypt
Naqada III/'Dynasty 0' *c.* 3200–3000 BC
Narmer (=? Meni)

EARLY DYNASTIC PERIOD c. 3000–2686 BC

Dynasty 1 c. 3000–2890 BC
Aha (=? Meni)
Djer
Djet
De(we)n
Mernit (female pharaoh)
Anedjib
Semerkhet
Qaa

Dynasty 2 c. 2890–2686 BC
Hetepsekhemy
Nynetjer
Peribsen
Khasekhemwy

OLD KINGDOM c. 2686–2125 BC

Dynasty 3 c. 2686–2613 BC
Netjekhet (Djoser)
Sekhemkhet
Huni

Dynasty 4 c. 2613–2494 BC
Sneferu c. 2613–2589
Khufu c. 2589–2566
Djedefra c. 2566–2558
Khaefra c. 2558–2532
Menkaura c. 2532–2503
Shepsekaf c. 2503–2498

Dynasty 5 c. 2494–2345 BC
Userkaf
Sahura
Neferirkara
Shepseskara
Raneferef
Neuserra

Menkauhor
Djedkara
Unas

Dynasty 6 c. 2345–2181 BC
Teti *c.* 2345–2323
Pepy I *c.* 2321–2287
Merenra *c.* 2287–2278
Pepy II *c.* 2278–2184
Nitoqert (female pharaoh) *c.* 2184–2181

Dynasties 7 and 8 c. 2181–2160 BC
Numerous pharaohs recorded, ruling from Memphis.

FIRST INTERMEDIATE PERIOD *c.* 2160–2025 BC

Dynasties 9 and 10 c. 2160–2025 BC
The 'House of Khety' ruling from Nen-nesut (Herakleopolis)

Dynasty 11 c. 2125–2025
Local rulers of Thebes
Intef I
Intef II (Wahankh)

MIDDLE KINGDOM *c.* 2025–1650 BC

Dynasty 11 (all of Egypt) c. 2025–1985 BC
Mentjuhotep II (Nebhepetra) *c.* 2055–2004
Mentjuhotep III (Sankhkara) *c.* 2004–1992
Mentjuhotep IV (Nebtawyra) *c.* 1992–1985

Dynasty 12 c. 1985–1773 BC
Amenemhat I *c.* 1985–1956
Senusret I *c.* 1956–1911
Amenemhat II *c.* 1911–1877
Senusret II *c.* 1877–1870
Senusret III *c.* 1870–1831
Amenemhat III *c.* 1831–1786
Amenemhat IV *c.* 1786–1777
Sobeknofru (female pharaoh) *c.* 1777–1773

Dynasty 13 c. 1773–after 1650 BC
Sobekhotep III
Merneferra Ay

Dynasty 14 is ephemeral

SECOND INTERMEDIATE PERIOD
c. 1650–1550 BC

Dynasty 15 ('Hyksos') c. 1650–1550 BC
Ruling from Hut-waret (Avaris) and Memphis
Khyan *c.* 1600
Apepy *c.* 1555
Khamudi

Dynasty 16 c. 1650–1580 BC
Ruling from Thebes

Dynasty 17 c. 1580–1550 BC
Ruling from Thebes
Taa Seqenenra *c.* 1560
Kamose *c.* 1555–1550

NEW KINGDOM *c.* 1550–1069 BC

Dynasty 18 c. 1550–1295 BC
Ahmose *c.* 1550–1525
Amenhotep I *c.* 1525–1504
Thutmose I *c.* 1504–1492
Thutmose II *c.* 1492–1479
Thutmose III *c.* 1479–1425
Hatshepsut (female pharaoh) *c.* 1473–1458
Amenhotep II *c.* 1427–1400
Thutmose IV *c.* 1400–1390
Amenhotep III *c.* 1390–1352
Amenhotep IV – Akhenaten *c.* 1352–1336
Neferneferuaten Smenkhkara (female pharaoh, Nefertiti)
    c. 1338–1336
Tutankhamun *c.* 1336–1327
Ay *c.* 1327–1323
Horemheb *c.* 1323–1295

Dynasty 19 c. 1295–1186 BC
Ramesses I *c.* 1295–1294
Sety I *c.* 1294–1279
Ramesses II *c.* 1279–1213
Merneptah *c.* 1213–1203
Amenemesses *c.* 1203–1200?
Sety II *c.* 1203/1200–1194
Siptah *c.* 1194–1188
Tawosret (female pharaoh) *c.* 1188–1186

Dynasty 20 c. 1186–1069 BC
Sethnakht *c.* 1186–1184
Ramesses III *c.* 1184–1153
Ramesses IV *c.* 1153–1147
Ramesses V *c.* 1147–1143
Ramesses VI *c.* 1143–1136
Ramesses VII *c.* 1136–1129
Ramesses VIII *c.* 1129–1126
Ramesses IX *c.* 1126–1108
Ramesses X *c.* 1108–1099
Ramesses XI *c.* 1099–1069

THIRD INTERMEDIATE PERIOD *c.* 1069–664 BC

Dynasty 21 c. 1069–945 BC (conventional)
Nesubanebdjed ('Smendes')
Pasebakhaenniut ('Psusennes')
Osorkon ('Osochor')
Siamun

The Libyan Pharaohs
Dynasties '22' and '23' c. 945–710 BC (conventional)
Sheshonq I
Osorkon I
Osorkon II
Takeloth II
Sheshonq III
Osorkon III; Nimlot (in Khemenu); Peftjauawybast (in
    Nen-nesut); Iuput (in Tent-remu)
Takeloth III

Dynasty 24 c. 730–710 BC
Both pharaohs in Sau, expanding their control to Memphis
Tefnakht, contempoary of Piye c. 730–716
Bakenranef ('Bocchoris') c. 716–710

Dynasty 25 c. 740–656 BC
(in Kush and Upper Egypt)
Kashta c. 740–735
Piye c. 735–710
(all of Egypt)
Shabaqo c. 710–695
Shebitqo c. 695–690
Taharqo 690–664
Tanwetamani 664–656 (in Egypt)

LATE DYNASTIC PERIOD 664–332 BC

Dynasty 26 664–525 BC
Psamtik I 664–610
Nekau II 610–595
Psamtik II 595–589
Wahibra ('Apries') 589–570
Ahmose ('Amasis') 570–526
Psamtik III 526–525

Dynasty 27 (First Persian Period) 525–404 BC
Cambyses 525–522
Darius I 522–486
Xerxes I 486–465
Artaxerxes I 465–424
Darius II 424–405
Artaxerxes II 405–359 (405–404 in Egypt)

Dynasty 28 404–399 BC
Amyrtaios 404–399

Dynasty 29 399–380 BC
Nefaarud I ('Nepherites I') 399–393
Hakor ('Achoris') 393–380
Nefaarud II ('Nepherites II') c. 380

Dynasty 30 380–343 BC
Nakhtnebef ('Nectanebo I') 380–362
Djedhor ('Teos', 'Tachos') 362–360
Nakhthorheb ('Nectanebo II') 360–343

Second Persian Period ('Dynasty 31') 343–332 BC
Artaxerxes III 343–338
Arses 338–336
Khabbash (Egyptian pharaoh) *c.* 340/336
Darius III 336–332

HELLENISTIC PERIOD 332–330 BC

Macedonian Dynasty 332–305 BC
Alexander 'the Great' (III of Macedon) 332–323
Philip Arrhidaios 323–317
Alexander IV 323–310
Ptolemy (satrap) 323–305

Ptolemaic Dynasty 305–30 BC
Ptolemy I Soter 305–285
Ptolemy II Philadelphos 285–246
Ptolemy III Euergetes I 246–221
Ptolemy IV Philopator 221–205
Ptolemy V Epiphanes 205–180
Ptolemy VI Philometor 180–145
Ptolemy VIII Euergetes II 170–116
Ptolemy IX Soter II 116–107
Ptolemy X Alexander I
Ptolemy XI Alexander II
Ptolemy XII Neos Dionysos ('Auletes')
Kleopatra VII
Ptolemy XIII
Ptolemy XIV
Ptolemy XV Kaisarion

ROMAN PERIOD 30 BC–AD 395

Augustus 30 BC–AD 14
Tiberius AD 14–37

Caius (Caligula) AD 37–41
Claudius AD 41–54
Nero AD 54–68
Vespasian AD 69–79
Domitian AD 81–96
Trajan AD 98–117
Hadrian AD 117–138
Antoninus Pius AD 138–161
Marcus Aurelius AD 161–180
Septimius Severus AD 193–211
Marcus Aurelius Antoninus ('Caracalla') AD 211–217
Marcus Aurelius Antoninus ('Elagabalus') AD 218–222
Aurelian AD 270–275
Diocletian AD 284–305
Constantine I AD 306–337
Maxentius AD 307–312
Julian AD 360–363
Theodosius AD 379–395

LATE ANTIQUE PERIOD AD 395–642

Justinian I AD 527–565
Phocas AD 602–610
Heraclius AD 610–642

Arab conquest 639–642

NOTES ON THE TEXT

Numerous different forms of names have been used for people and places. Current fashion generally prefers to use a name that is derived from a rendering of the hieroglyphic, in preference to the Greek or Latinized-Greek forms used by earlier generations. Where alternative names are given, the following abbreviations are used to indicate their equivalent:

Egn   Egyptian
Gk   Greek
L.   Latin
Ar.   Arabic

FURTHER READING

There are numerous good recent books on Egypt. The selection here is confined to authoritative works, most in English, all of which have their own guidance to more specialized literature.

1 DEFINING ANCIENT EGYPT

For the debate around imperialism and the development of academic Egyptology see:

Bernal, Martin, 1987, *Black Athena: The Afroasiatic Roots of Classical Civilization. Volume 1: The Fabrication of Ancient Greece 1785–1985*. London: Free Association Books.
Jeffreys, David (ed.), 2003, *Views of Ancient Egypt since Napoleon Bonaparte: Imperialism, Colonialism and Modern Appropriations*. London: UCL Press.
Reid, D., 2002, *Whose Pharaohs? Archaeology, Museums and Egyptian National Identity from Napoleon to World War 1*. Berkeley, CA: University of California Press.

A whole range of perspectives of how Egypt has been perceived and used can be found in the series *Encounters with Ancient Egypt*:

Humbert, Jean-Marcel and Clifford Price (eds), 2003, *Imhotep Today: Egyptianizing Architecture*. London: UCL Press.
MacDonald, Sally and Michael Rice (eds), 2003, *Consuming Ancient Egypt*. London: UCL Press (specifically the chapter by Lynn Picknett and Clive Prince, 'Alternative Egypts': 175–93).
Matthews, Roger and Cornelia Roemer (eds), 2003, *Ancient Perspectives on Egypt*. London: UCL Press.
Ucko, Peter and Timothy Champion (eds), 2003, *The Wisdom of Egypt: Changing Visions Through the Ages*. London: UCL Press.

For Egypt and Africa:

O'Connor, David, 1993, *Ancient Nubia, Egypt's Rival in Africa*. Philadelphia, PA: University Museum of Archaeology and Anthropology.
O'Connor, David and Andrew Reid (eds), 2003, *Ancient Egypt in Africa*. London: UCL Press.

On Egyptian ethnicity:

Baines, John, 1996, 'Contextualizing Egyptian Representations of Society and Ethnicity', in J. S. Cooper and G. M. Schwartz (eds), *The Study of the Ancient Near East in the Twenty-First Century: The William Foxwell Albright Centennial Conference*. Winona Lake, IN: 339–84.

2 THE EGYPTIAN WORLD

Baines, John and Jaromir Malek, 1980, *The Atlas of Ancient Egypt*. Oxford: Phaidon.
Manley, Bill, 1996, *The Penguin Historical Atlas of Ancient Egypt*. London: Penguin.
Butzer, Karl W., 1976, *Early Hydraulic Civilization in Egypt: A Study in Cultural Ecology*. Chicago: University of Chicago Press.
Butzer, Karl W., 1998, 'Late Quaternary Problems of the Egyptian Nile: Stratigraphy, Environments, Prehistory', *Paleorient* 23: 151–73.

3 ESOTERIC KNOWLEDGE AND ORIENTAL MYSTERY

The tradition of Egypt in the West, its legacy and its influence on the development of Egyptology are all considered in:

Hornung, Eric (trans. D. Lorton), 2001, *The Secret Lore of Egypt: Its Impact on the West*. New York: Cornell University Press.

4 CONSTRUCTING THE EGYPTIAN PAST

For the texts of Manetho's *Aigyptiaka* see:

Waddell, W. G., 1940, *Manetho*, Cambridge, MA.: Loeb Classical Library.

and now:

Verbrugghe, G. P. and J. M. Wickersham, 2000, *Berossos and Manetho, Introduced and Translated: Native Traditions in Ancient Mesopotamia and Egypt*. Ann Arbor, MI: University of Michigan Press.

For the Egyptian sources see:

Redford, Donald, 1986, *Pharaonic King-Lists, Annals & Daybooks. A Contribution to the Study of the Egyptian Sense of History*. Mississauga, Ontario: Benben Publications.

The Turin Canon of Kings:

Malek, Jaromir, 1982, 'The Original Version of the Royal Canon of Turin', *Journal of Egyptian Archaeology* 68: 93–106.

The Palermo Stone:

Wilkinson, Toby A. H., 2000, *Royal Annals of Ancient Egypt. The Palermo Stone and its Associated Fragments*. London: Kegan Paul International.

The Amarna Letters:

Moran, William L., 1992, *The Amarna Letters*. Baltimore, MD: The Johns Hopkins University Press.

For Egypt's view of its past see:

Tait, John (ed.), 2003, *'Never Had the Like Occurred': Egypt's View of its Past*. London: UCL Press.

On Arabic sources see:

El Daly, Okasha, 2003, 'Ancient Egypt in Medieval Arabic writings', in Peter Ucko and Timothy Champion (eds), *The Wisdom of Egypt: Changing Visions Through the Ages*. London: UCL Press: 39–63.

Explaining the evidence and the archaeological problems, and challenging the accepted chronology:

James, Peter J. (ed.), 1991, *Centuries of Darkness*. London: Jonathan Cape.

The most recent history of Egypt is:

Shaw, Ian (ed.), 2000, *Oxford History of Ancient Egypt*. Oxford: Oxford University Press (with chapters by a range of specialists).

For Egypt in the context of the ancient Near East:

Kuhrt, Amélie, 1995, *The Ancient Near East*. London: Routledge.
Redford, Donald, 1992, *Egypt, Canaan, and Israel in Ancient Times*. Princeton, NJ: Princeton University Press.

5 ORIGINS AND FIRST FLOWERING

There have been a number of good recent studies of Egypt during the Prehistoric, Predynastic and Early Dynastic Periods, discussing the emergence of the state:

Midant-Reynes, Béatrix, 2000, *The Prehistory of Egypt from the first Egyptians to the first Pharaohs*. Oxford: Blackwell.
Wilkinson, Toby A. H., 1999, *Early Dynastic Egypt*. London: Routledge.
Wilkinson, Toby A. H., 2003, *Genesis of the Pharaohs*. London: Thames & Hudson.

Good studies of the Old Kingdom:

Andreu, Guillemette, 1997, *Egypt in the Age of the Pyramids*. London: John Murray.
Malek, Jaromir, 1986, *In the Shadow of the Pyramids. Egypt during the Old Kingdom*. Cairo: The American University in Cairo Press.

The most recent authoritative pyramid studies are:

Lehner, Mark, 1997, *The Complete Pyramids*. London: Thames & Hudson.
Verner, Miroslav, 1997, *The Pyramids: Their Archaeology and History*. London: Atlantic Books.

A climatic explanation for the end of the Old Kingdom was argued by:

Bell, Barbara, 1971, 'The Dark Ages in History I: The First Dark Age in Egypt', *American Journal of Archaeology* 75: 1–26.

But rejected by:

Butzer, Karl W., 1997, 'Sociopolitical Disunity in the Near East c 2200 B.C.E.: Scenarios from Palestine and Egypt', in H. N. Dalfes (ed.), *Third Millennium B.C. Climate Change and Old World Collapse*. Berlin: Springer: 245–96.

6 IMPERIAL EGYPT

Recent works on the Middle Kingdom include:

Delia, Robert, 1980, *A Study of the Reign of Senusert III*, Ann Arbor, MI: University Microfilms International.
Leprohon, Ronald, 1980, *The Reign of Amenemhat I*, Ottawa: National Library of Canada.
Obsomer, Claude, 1995, *Sésostris Ier, étude chronologique et historique du règne*. Brussels.

Quirke, Stephen, 1990, *The Administration of Egypt in the Late Middle Kingdom*. New Malden: SIA.
Quirke, Stephen, 1991, *Middle Kingdom Studies*. New Malden: SIA.

The Second Intermediate Period:

von Beckerath, Jurgen, 1965, *Untersuchungen zur politischen Geschichte der zweiten Zwischenzeit in Ägypten*. Glückstadt: J. J. Augustin.
Ryholt, K. S. B., 1998, *The Political Situation in Egypt during the Second Intermediate Period*. Copenhagen: CNI.

For the Hyksos:

Bietak, Manfred, 1991, 'Egypt and Canaan during the Middle Bronze Age', *BASOR (Bulletin of the American Schools of Oriental Research)* 281: 27–72
Oren, Eliezer, (ed.), 1997, The *Hyksos: New Historical and Archaeological Perspectives*. Philadelphia: University of Philadelphia Press.

Surprisingly, there is no single volume on the New Kingdom in English. Among the most important recent studies:

Bryan, Betsy M., 1991, *The Reign of Thutmose IV*. Baltimore, MD: The Johns Hopkins University Press.
Cline, Eric H. and David O'Connor, 1998, *Amenhotep III: Perspectives on his Reign*. Ann Arbor, MI: University of Michigan Press.
Kozloff, Arielle and Betsy Bryan, 1990, *Egypt's Dazzling Sun: Amenhotep III and his World*. Cleveland, OH: University of Ohio Press.

The most authoritative recent study of the historical and archaeological evidence relating to Akhenaten is:

Reeves, Nicholas, 2001, *Akhenaten: Egypt's False Prophet*. London: Thames & Hudson.

For a stimulating analysis of the ways in which Akhenaten has been used and abused in the West:

Montserrat, Dominic, 2000, *Akhenaten, History, Fantasy and Ancient Egypt*. London: Routledge.

For Egypt and Hittites:

Murnane, William J., 1990, *The Road to Kadesh: A Historical Interpretation of the Battle Reliefs of King Sety I at Karnak*. Chicago: Oriental Institute of Chicago Press.

The Egyptian Empire in Asia:

Cohen, Raymond and Raymond Westbrook (eds), 2000, *Amarna Diplomacy. The Beginnings of International Diplomacy.* Baltimore, MD: The Johns Hopkins University Press.

Higginbotham, C. R., 2000, *Egyptianization and Elite Emulation in Ramesside Palestine: Governance and Accommodation in the Imperial Periphery.* Leiden: E. J. Brill.

Liverani, Mario, 2001, *International Relations in the Ancient Near East, 1600–1100 BC.* London: Palgrave.

For the 'Sea Peoples' and the collapse of the Late Bronze Age:

Drews, Robert, 1993, *The End of the Bronze Age.* Princeton, NJ: Princeton University Press.

7 CONTINUITY WITH METAMORPHOSIS

The main study of Egypt from the end of the New Kingdom to the twenty-sixth dynasty is:

Kitchen, Kenneth A., 1973, *The Third Intermediate Period in Egypt (1100–650 BC).* Warminster: Aris and Phillips (revised 1986, 1995).

There has been considerable revision of the detail of Kitchen's reconstruction, notably:

Aston, David A., 1989, 'Takeloth II – A King of the "Theban Twenty-Third Dynasty"?', *Journal of Egyptian Archaeology* 75: 139–53.

For Libyan Egypt:

Leahy, M. A., 1985, 'The Libyan Period in Egypt: An Essay in Interpretation', *Libyan Studies* 16: 51–65.

Leahy, M. A. (ed.), 1990, *Libya and Egypt, c. 1300–750 BC.* London: SOAS and the Society for Libyan Studies.

For post-New Kingdom Nubia and the twenty-fifth dynasty see:

Morkot, Robert, 2000, *The Black Pharaohs: Egypt's Nubian Rulers.* London: Rubicon Press.

Dynasties 26 to 30 are still inadequately covered. See most recently:

Myśliwiec, Karol (trans. David Lorton), 2000, *The Twilight of Ancient Egypt. First Millennium B.C.E.* Ithaca, NY: Cornell University Press.

For Ptolemaic Egypt:

Hölbl, Günther, 2001, *A History of the Ptolemaic Empire.* London: Routledge.

For Roman and Late Antique (Byzantine) Egypt:

Bagnall, Roger, 1993, *Egypt in Late Antiquity.* Princeton, NJ: Princeton University Press.
Bowman, Alan, 1986, *Egypt After the Pharaohs.* London: Oxford University Press.
Frankfurter, David, 1998, *Religion in Roman Egypt. Assimilation and Resistance.* Princeton, NJ: Princeton University Press.

8 RULERS AND RULED

O'Connor, David and David P. Silverman (eds), 1995, *Ancient Egyptian Kingship.* Leiden: E. J. Brill.

For literacy:

Baines, John, 1983, 'Literacy and Ancient Egyptian Society', *Man* 18: 572–99.

For industries and technologies in general:

Nicholson, Paul and Ian Shaw (eds), 2000, *Ancient Egyptian Materials and Technology.* Cambridge: Cambridge University Press.

Newer approaches to interpreting the archaeological evidence:

Lustig, Judith (ed.), 1997, *Anthropology and Egyptology.* Sheffield: Sheffield Academic Press.
Meskell, Lynn, 1999, *Archaeologies of Social Life.* Oxford: Blackwell Publishers.
Meskell, Lynn, 2002, *Private Life in New Kingdom Egypt.* Princeton, NJ: Princeton University Press.

Women:

Robins, Gay, 1993, *Women in Ancient Egypt.* London: British Museum Press.

9 TOWN AND COUNTRY IN ANCIENT EGYPT

One of the best books for understanding how ancient Egypt worked and for its analysis of the evidence for settlement:

Kemp, Barry J., 1989, *Ancient Egypt: Anatomy of a Civilization.* London: Routledge.

For the Egyptian economy:

Janssen, Jac, 1975, 'Prolegomena to the study of Egypt's economic history during the New Kingdom', *Studien zur Altägyptischen Kultur* 3: 127–85.
Bleiberg, Edward, 1996, *The Official Gift in Ancient Egypt*. Norman, OK: University of Oklahoma Press.

10 THE CULTURE OF ANCIENT EGYPT

Religion

There are many good books on Egyptian religion. Among the best introductions are:

Hart, George, 2004, *A Dictionary of Ancient Egyptian Gods and Goddesses*. London: Routledge.
Pinch, Geraldine, 1994, *Magic in Ancient Egypt*. London: British Museum Press.
Quirke, Stephen, 1992, *Ancient Egyptian Religion*. London: British Museum Press.
Quirke, Stephen, 2001, *The Cult of Ra, Sun-worship in Ancient Egypt*. London: Thames & Hudson.
Shafer, Byron E. (ed.), 1991, *Religion in Ancient Egypt. Gods, Myths and Personal Practice*. Ithaca, NY and London: Cornell University Press.
Taylor, John H., 2001, *Death and the Afterlife in Ancient Egypt*. London: British Museum Press.

Art and architecture

Aldred, Cyril, 1980, *Egyptian Art*. London: Thames & Hudson.
Arnold, Dieter (trans. Sabine Gardiner and Helen Strudwick), 2003, *The Encyclopedia of Ancient Egyptian Architecture*. London: I. B. Tauris.
Malek, Jaromir, 1999, *Egyptian Art*. London: Phaidon.
Robins, Gay, 1997, *The Art of Ancient Egypt*. London: British Museum Press.
Smith, William Stevenson (revised and enlarged by William Kelly Simpson), 1981, *The Art and Architecture of Ancient Egypt*. London: Penguin.

For understanding taxonomy and words see:

Quirke, Stephen, 2001, 'Colour Vocabularies in Ancient Egyptian', in W. V. Davies (ed.), *Colour and Painting in Ancient Egypt*. London: British Museum Press: 186–92.

Weeks, Kent, 1979, 'Egyptology, Language, and Art', in Kent Weeks (ed.), *Egyptology and the Social Sciences*. Cairo: American University in Cairo Press: 57–81.

Literature and music

The most comprehensive collection of all varieties of Egyptian text is:

Lichtheim, Miriam, 1975–80, *Ancient Egyptian Literature*. (3 vols) Berkeley, CA: University of California Press.

Other recommendations:

Foster, John L., 1995, *Hymns, Prayers, and Songs. An Anthology of Egyptian Lyric Poetry*. Atlanta, GA: Scholars Press.
Foster, John L., 2001, *Ancient Egyptian Literature: An Anthology*. Austin, TX: University of Texas Press.
Foster, John L., 1992, *Love Songs of the New Kingdom*. Austin, TX: University of Texas Press.
Wente, E. F., 1990, *Letters from Ancient Egypt*. Atlanta, GA: Scholars Press.

There is remarkably little on ancient Egyptian music. The only book in English is:

Manniche, Lise, 1991, *Music and Musicians in Ancient Egypt*. London: British Museum Press.

The classic text (well illustrated) is:

Hickmann, Hans, 1961, *Ägypten*. Musikgeschichte in Bildern 2,1. Leipzig: Deutscher Verlag für Musik.

The most recent:

Anderson, Robert D., 1995, 'Music and Dance in Pharaonic Egypt', in Jack M. Sasson (ed.), *Civilizations of the Ancient Near East*, New York: Scribner, vol. 4: 2555–68.

INDEX

Numbers in *italic* type indicate illustrations

INDEX

eBooks – at www.eBookstore.tandf.co.uk

A library at your fingertips!

eBooks are electronic versions of printed books. You can store them on your PC/laptop or browse them online.

They have advantages for anyone needing rapid access to a wide variety of published, copyright information.

eBooks can help your research by enabling you to bookmark chapters, annotate text and use instant searches to find specific words or phrases. Several eBook files would fit on even a small laptop or PDA.

NEW: Save money by eSubscribing: cheap, online access to any eBook for as long as you need it.

Annual subscription packages

We now offer special low-cost bulk subscriptions to packages of eBooks in certain subject areas. These are available to libraries or to individuals.

For more information please contact webmaster.ebooks@tandf.co.uk

We're continually developing the eBook concept, so keep up to date by visiting the website.

www.eBookstore.tandf.co.uk